ROUTLEDGE LIBRARY EDITIONS: ETHNOSCAPES

Volume 3

NEW DIRECTIONS IN ENVIRONMENTAL PARTICIPATION

NEW DIRECTIONS IN ENVIRONMENTAL PARTICIPATION

Edited by
**DAVID CANTER,
MARTIN KRAMPEN
AND
DAVID STEA**

R Routledge
Taylor & Francis Group

LONDON AND NEW YORK

First published in 1988 by Avebury (Gower Publishing Co. Ltd)

This edition first published in 2025
by Routledge
4 Park Square, Milton Park, Abingdon, Oxon OX14 4RN

and by Routledge
605 Third Avenue, New York, NY 10158

Routledge is an imprint of the Taylor & Francis Group, an informa business

© 1988 David Canter, Martin Krampen, David Stea

British Library Cataloguing in Publication Data
A catalogue record for this book is available from the British Library

ISBN: 978-1-032-86590-4 (Set)
ISBN: 978-1-032-81646-3 (Volume 3) (hbk)
ISBN: 978-1-032-81653-1 (Volume 3) (pbk)
ISBN: 978-1-003-50073-5 (Volume 3) (ebk)

DOI: 10.4324/9781003500735

Publisher's Note
The publisher has gone to great lengths to ensure the quality of this reprint but points out that some imperfections in the original copies may be apparent.

Disclaimer
The publisher has made every effort to trace copyright holders and would welcome correspondence from those they have been unable to trace.

New Series Introduction to
RLE: Ethnoscapes

The neologism *Ethnoscapes*[1] was created by David Canter and David Stea in 1987 when they happened both to be in Yogjakarta at the same time. They wanted a term to cover the rapidly emerging multidisciplinary field of research into many aspects of how individuals, groups and cultures interact and transact with their surroundings. It was derived as follows:

Ethno (combining form) indicating race, people or culture.

Scape (suffix-forming nouns) indicating a scene or view of something.

Ethnoscapes (plural noun) Scholarly and/or scientific explorations of the relationships people and their activities, have with the places they create and/or inhabit; historical, psychological, anthropological, sociological, and related disciplines that study the experiences of places, attitudes towards them, or the processes of shaping, managing, or designing them. The term was subsequently used to provide an umbrella for a series of books. These cover topics that are so multidisciplinary that they do not sit comfortably in any of the constrained silos of academic and scholarly research. As indicated on the opening page of the first book in the series, many disciplines "have developed marauding sub-groups who move freely across each others' borders, carrying ideas almost like contraband, without declaring that they have crossed any disciplinary boundaries."

They include domains labelled as Behavioural or Perceptual Geography, Environmental/Architectural Psychology, Urban History, Social Ecology, Behavioural Archaeology, Urban Planning, Behavioural Architecture, and Landscape Architecture. There are also many other areas of research and practice that, whilst not being overtly psychological, social, or cultural, do explore and act on the built and natural environment in a way that recognises the importance of the human transactions with those settings. These professions include interior and product design, comparative linguistics, and even aspects of criminology and mental health providers.

Like all such implicit and explicit transactions between different domains, a community of interest and support has emerged in which those who cross the boundaries often find they have more in common with other transgressors than with their mother disciplines. This has given rise to common means and forms of communication, with a shared understanding of the issues and approaches that are of value. Although, of course, these are not always understood in the same way by all those involved,

The *Ethnoscapes* series of books provides a forum for these multifarious, cross-disciplinary, determinedly international, studies and practices. Each of the books takes on board one or more of the environmental challenges that that individuals, societies and cultures are facing. Emphasising a social perspective, rather than the dominant 'hard' science viewpoints embedded in physical, geological and climate changes.

It may now be regarded as rather prescient that it was over three decades ago that the need and importance was recognised of bringing together the many strands of environmental social research and practice. But there is no doubt that there were academics and professionals exploring Ethnoscape topics, going back to the 1960s, often in isolation and with little recognition, that are today front-page, and podcast, news. The challenges in the environmental social sciences that Ethnoscapes explores are just as pertinent now as they were when initially identified.

The series, in essence, deals with four challenges the environmental social sciences embrace.

1. Addressing "the awareness of governments and public alike of the problems of environmental degradation and pollution."

This includes the challenge of providing acceptable housing and related environmental conditions that also encompassed the support for environmental and related cultural heritage. It also requires detailed consideration of the assessment and evaluation of designs and design proposals as well as background research on policy related issues.

2. Developing ways of conceptualising human interactions with the physical surroundings.

This may seem somewhat abstract but has practical implications. The dominant view that people are passively controlled by their surroundings supports a paternalistic, management of what it is assumed people need. That ignores the active way in which people make sense of their environment, drawing on cultural and historical influences. This recognises the importance of user participation in decisions about built and natural settings. That, in turn, requires a much richer understanding of how people interact with where they are or want to be.

3. A much wider range of ways of exploring people's transactions with the environment is needed to contribute to policy and practice as well as developing richer insights into human experiences.

The stock in trade of surveys, or the inevitably artificial laboratory-based experiments, whilst of value for some explorations, need to be augmented by methodologies that enrich an understanding of what the experiences are of being in, acting on, and developing places. They need to connect not just with the endeavours of individuals but also with how cultures and societies express these transactions.

4. Finding ways to enable practitioners and researchers to express their own encounters with the contexts they are influencing or studying.

Much of the research that is carried out in what are curiously called 'Ivory Towers', even when it is studying the big wide world, allows the pretence of distancing from the direct experiences of the issues being studied. Yet the challenges of moving across disciplinary boundaries are as much personal challenges of finding new ways of thinking, communicating, and acting, as an academic demand to develop more effective intellectual systems. The Ethnoscapes series recognises the value of exploring these challenges by hosting a variety of formats. Many of these go beyond the staid and limited formulations that academic discourse assumes to be the norms.

The Ethnoscapes series brings together a vibrant mix of cutting-edge explorations, from all over the world, of human transactions with the built and natural environments. This includes, for example, consideration of vernacular architecture that contrasts with the architecture and urbanism of the colonial enterprise, the meaning of home, aesthetics, well-being and health, and consideration of how environmental psychology has become 'green'. All of these topics, and more, provide an exciting basis for dealing with current challenges in the environmental social sciences.

Note

[1] Not to be confused by the term *Ethnoscape* later concocted by Arun Appadurai in 1990, to refer to **human migration**, the flow of people across boundaries. This includes migrants, refugees, exiles, and tourists, among other moving individuals and groups, all of whom appear to affect the politics of (and between) nations to a considerable degree. Ignorant of the lexicographical origins of the term 'scape' he rather confusingly added it to many ideas of flow, such as the flow of technology – technoscapes and the flow of ideas ideoscapes. Appadurai, A. (1990). "Disjuncture and difference in the global cultural economy." *Theory, Culture and Society* 7(2–3): 295–310.

Routledge Library Editions: Ethnoscapes

1. *Environmental Perspectives* David Canter, Martin Krampen & David Stea (Eds) (1988) ISBN 978-1-032-81616-6

2. *Environmental Policy, Assessment, and Communication* David Canter, Martin Krampen & David Stea (Eds) (1988) ISBN 978-1-032-81635-7

3. *New Directions in Environmental Participation* David Canter, Martin Krampen & David Stea (Eds) (1988) ISBN 978-1-032-81646-3

4. *Vernacular Architecture: Paradigms of Environmental Response* Mete Turan (Ed.) (1990) ISBN 978-1-032-82023-1

5. *Forms of Dominance: On the Architecture and Urbanism of the Colonial Enterprise* Nezar AlSayyad (Ed.) (1992) ISBN 978-1-032-84164-9

6. *The Meaning and Use of Housing: International Perspectives, Approaches and Their Applications* Ernesto G. Arias (Ed.) (1993) ISBN 978-1-032-84781-8

7. *Placemaking: Production of Built Environment in Two Cultures* David Stea & Mete Turan (1993) ISBN 978-1-032-86434-1

8. *Environmental Psychology in Europe: From Architectural Psychology to Green Psychology* Enric Pol (1993) ISBN 978-1-032-83324-8

9. *Housing: Design, Research, Education* Marjorie Bulos & Necdet Teymur (Eds) (1993) ISBN 978-1-032-86388-7

10. *Architecture, Ritual Practice and Co-determination in the Swedish Office* Dennis Doxtater (1994) ISBN 978-1-032-81774-3

11. *On the Aesthetics of Architecture: A Psychological Approach to the Structure and the Order of Perceived Architectural Space* Ralf Weber (1995) ISBN 978-1-032-82034-7

12. *The Home: Words, Interpretations, Meanings and Environments* by David N. Benjamin (Ed.) (1995) ISBN 978-1-032-86411-2

13. *Tradition, Location and Community: Place-making and Development* Adenrele Awotona & Necdet Teymur (Eds) (1997) ISBN 978-1-032-84608-8

14. *Aesthetics, Well-being and Health: Essays within Architecture and Environmental Aesthetics* Birgit Cold (Ed.) (2001) ISBN 978-1-032-86577-5

Other Ethnoscapes series titles also available:

Integrating Programming, Evaluation and Participation in Design: A Theory Z Approach Henry Sanoff (1992) HBK 978-1-138-20338-9; EBK 978-1-315-47173-0; PBK 978-1-138-20339-6

Directions in Person-Environment Research and Practice Jack Nasar & Wolfgang F. E. Preiser (Eds) (1999) HBK 978-1-138-68674-8; EBK 978-1-315-54255-3; PBK 978-1-138-68677-9

Psychological Theories for Environmental Issues Mirilia Bonnes, Terence Lee & Marino Bonaiuto (Eds) (2003) HBK 978-0-75461-888-1; EBK 978-1-315-24572-0; PBK 978-1-138-27742-7

Housing Space and Quality of Life David L. Uzzell, Ricardo Garcia Mira, J. Eulogio Real & Joe Romay (Eds) (2005) HBK 978-0-81538-952-1; EBK 978-1-351-15636-3; PBK 978-1-138-35596-5

Doing Things with Things: The Design and Use of Everyday Objects Alan Costall & Ole Dreier (Eds) (2006) HBK 978-0-75464-656-3; EBK 978-1-315-57792-0; PBK 978-1-138-25314-8

Rethinking the Meaning of Place: Conceiving Place in Architecture-Urbanism Lineu Castello (2010) HBK 978-0-75467-814-4; EBK 978-1-315-60616-3; PBK 978-1-138-25745-0

Ethnoscapes: Volume 3

New Directions in Environmental Participation

Edited by
DAVID CANTER
Department of Psychology
University of Surrey

MARTIN KRAMPEN
Department of Aesthetics
Hochschule der Kunst, Berlin

DAVID STEA
School of Architecture
University of Wisconsin

Avebury

Aldershot · Brookfield USA · Hong Kong · Singapore · Sydney

Published by

Avebury

Gower Publishing Company Limited
Gower House
Croft Road
Aldershot
Hants GU11 3HR
England

Gower Publishing Company
Old Post Road
Brookfield
Vermont 05036
USA

ISBN 0 566 05570 8

Printed and bound in Great Britain by
Athanaeum Press Limited, Newcastle upon Tyne

Contents

SECTION TWO
The Use of Models in Participatory Placemaking

SECTION THREE
Present Challenges for the Future

Editors' introduction

BEYOND PARTICIPATION

Our physical surroundings are shaped by many forces. Even
those aspects that are influenced by human agency derive
that influence from a great variety of sources, clients
and designers, financial backers, local authorities,
government controls and different professional bodies. It
is also now apparent that a multitude of influences
operates whether it is the design of a building that is
being considered or the design of a region. There should,
therefore, be no surprise in learning that within the
plethora of pushes and pulls out of which places are
formed it is not uncommon for the views and experiences
of the people who will eventually live and work in those
places to be ignored.

For a number of years environmental social scientists
have worked together with design professionals in order
to develop tools and procedures that will enable users of
places to influence the shaping of those places. This
work has typically dealt with contexts in which there is
an obvious cultural differentiation between the designers
and the users. Indeed, the origins of environmental
psychology in the United States can be traced to a

concern by designers that they could not fully comprehend the experience of mental patients and therefore would benefit from research guidance on this. In effect, they recognised that the sub-culture in which patients lived was so alien to their own that architects could not draw on thier own direct experience to design for it.

The most obvious differences between the culture of designers and of users is to be found in residential developments in third world countries, where not only is the life style of the professional group likely to be very different from those of the residents, but in many cases the designers may come from quite different countries, supported say by international funding agencies that are staffed by yet other nationalities. Many of the developments in participation procedures have therefore evolved to respond to the demands of these contexts.

Although the contribution of participation procedures to residential development in third world countries is now appreciated, and therefore is reflected in the majority of chapters of the present volume it is increasingly clear that the consideration of environmental participation raises broader issues. It points in one direction to a reconsideration of the design process itself and how professional designers take part in it as emerges in Symes´ chapter [2]. In the other direction it points to the role of citizen involvement in global environmental issues as discussed by Galtung [9] and Von Uexkull [12].

One of the consequences of the broadening of the concept of environmental participation is the opportunity it provides to understand some of the mechanisms that are implicit in all participation procedures. The central mechanism is that of communication. Not only is participation a means by which users can inform environmental decision makers of their own actions and aspirations. It is also a means whereby participants themselves can gain a richer understanding of the environmental shaping processes that are significant to them.

AN ASPECT OF RESEARCH

From the perspective of participation as communication it can be seen that user involvement in environmental design is one aspect of environmental social science research. It is not just an endeavour for the political activist but also a way of enriching our understanding of person/place transactions. Sommer [10] argues this point most directly when he presents the case for the harnessing of social science research procedures to the objectives of consumer groups themselves rather than the organisations that make the products that are consumed. By using social science procedures the consumer groups become better informed and so are more able to participate in decision making.

When research is seen in these ways it becomes a different enterprise from the traditional, neutral, academic activity that is usually presented. Yet it is precisely the developments in the approach to environmental social science that has made these rapprochements possible. We noted in our introduction to the second volume in this series that the desire to contribute to environmental policy formulation, which was the focus of that volume, had changed the style and type of research in which social scientists had engaged. It was clear that this also had implications for the conceptual and theoretical underpinnings of the research.

In the first volume to this series the spectrum of theoretical developments were portrayed and it was argued that they formed the basis for a new emphasis in environmental social science. An emphasis that had been present from the earliest days of the field but was only now at the critical mass where it could be recognised as forming the core of a new domain of professional and research activity.

The characteristics of this domain were summarised as follows:

1. Recognising the collaborative nature of human action, the concerns expressed are firmly based in cultural, social and inter-personal frameworks. The isolated individual acting on a personally defined world is replaced by a person who plays a role in society and whose understanding and aspirations are structured by, and structure, that society and its context.

2. The work reported is overtly cross-disciplinary. Historians draw on social theories, psychologists on philosophy, sociologists on design theory and so on.

3. The ethical dimension of social action leads to the view that all research is, at least implicitly, aimed at bettering the human lot. One consequence is that studies with this perspective are also unashamedly cross-professional. Writers move from design considerations to scientific ones and back again.

4. The recognition of the significance of group processes extends to the view that design is fundamentally a social process, that the furthering of community activity in design is of great significance.

5. It follows from the above that the explanations given of human transactions with their physical surroundings find their roots in cultural and interpersonal processes and that they are also inevitably explanations of systems.

Studies of participation are therefore to be considered as an integrated part of environmental social science. They reflect the movement across professional and academic boundaries as well as the exploration of social and cultural aspects of place significance. Above all, of course,they reflect the desire to conduct studies that will have a direct consequence for the experiences being studied.

The consequences of participation research do relate the ability to represent a physical design in some comprehensible way prior to its existence. Yet, one of the great difficulties in shaping the places in which we live is having a clear understanding of what form a place will take at the end of the process. Given the need for communication and periodic assessment during the process it is not surprising that a distinctly useful set of activities has been identified that incorporates the building of three-dimensional models as part of participatory design. These activities are illustrated in the second section. They are not just special uses of a particular technology. By encouraging and enabling prospective inhabitants to collaborate in the shaping of three-dimensional models of future places, a radically different relationship between them and their placemaking is created. They become an essential ingredient in the processes rather than distant contributors to it.

The _final_ _section_ looks to the future, in terms of
types of research and the challenges that the research
community must face. Within these chapters, it is the
changing nature of our relationships with the world about
us that is emphasised. It is not that the environment is
inherently threatening or that we must be fitter in order
the more ably to survive, but rather that there is now
the prospect of radically upsetting the dynamic balance
between humanity and the rest of the natural world.

Environmental participation is, then, a natural part of
being human. It is only the diversification of roles in
our complex society that has given so much more influence
over our surroundings to some groups rather than others.
These various professional groups have much in the way of
expertise to contribute but it is only by enabling all
those who will suffer the consequences of professional
actions to shape intelligently those actions that the
transactions between people and places will continue to
be productive.

1. Psychological variables in participation: a case study

EUCLIDES SANCHEZ, KAREN CRONICK and
ESTHER WIESENFELD

This research was financed by the Council for Scientific and Humanistic
Development (Consejo de Desarrollo Científico y Humanístico), Central
University of Venezuela, Caracas.

The authors would like to thank the following people: Nancy Hachim,
Miriam Acosta, Armando Salgado, Steida Fernández, Tati y Arenas and
the communities of Casalta 2 and Nazareno.

ABSTRACT:

In a study of psychology variables involved in citizen participation,
two samples of people from two different neighborhoods were
interviewed. One of the neighborhoods (Casalta 2) was a made up of
people who were in the last stages of a project of communal
autoconstruction, and the other was a nearby area in which "squatters"
were residing, and in which there was no internal social organisation
(Nazareno). It was found that in the project, the idea of
participation included solidarity, organisational aspects, the ideas
of achievement, struggle, work and effort. Maintaining horizontal
power structures inside the organisation was also a concern. Of
importance was the active stance of the participators as opposed to
the non participators, and the " wishful thinking " that was found in
the unorganised neighborhood. The people of Nazareno considered
themselves or their personal characteristics as both cause and solution
to their problems, and lacking organisation, were trapped into being
frustrated by petty disputes. This " internal " way of attributing
causes and solutions is contrasted to the findings from the
literature of attributional research.

1

INTRODUCTION

There has been a growing interest in public participation in the last
two decades, particularly in terms of urban planning. Together with the
growing interest, there has been a process of change in the concept
itself. In the sixties, citizens were only given the job of offering
their ideas and suggestions to those who were responsible for planning,
but beginning in the seventies, participation has taken on connotations
of community power in which the public has an increasing influence in
decision making (Murphy,1978). The people themselves have been sensing
an increasing necessity to influence in the formulation and in carrying
out plans that before were made on their behalf, and to do this they
have attempted to intervene in the planning process. The context of this
chapter is Latin America, where participation is a concern in both the
impoverished urban and the middle class populations (Castells,1982). In
general, at least on a popular level, it is considered desireable,
because of the favorable consequences which are attributed to it. In
Caracas, it has even been promoted at an official level by the municipal
council in open town meetings in which information has been solicited
from the citizens and in which there was some attempt to involve them in
implementing policies. On other occasions, attempts by the citizens to
arrange these town meetings, which are in reality elaborate public
audiences where the public is present at meetings of the municipal
council, have been resisted by the council members.

It can be assumed that participation develops favorable attitudes
toward autonomy in people (although it might be argued that those who
participate are, beforehand, the autonomous ones, while the passive
citizens allow themselves to be manipulated by the planners). Thus
participation might be assumed to increase active motivation, the perception of environmental control and the satisfaction which is felt with
onés surroundings. It might be considered, furthermore, a facilitator
of interpersonal, group, and institutional adjustment, and in this way
it may create the necessary conditions for better decision making in
planning (Stringer,1977). This is what Jones (1976) has called an
educative strategy which socializes the person for the practice of
democracy.

There are diffrent definitions that have been given of participation.
Edelston and Kolodner (1968) show that participation is the transmission
of information about users needs through questionnaires, as well as the
choices that they then make concerning the options which the experts
offer them, and the pressures which the group leaders exercise in order
to influence some planning aspect.

More recently, Susskind and Elliot (1983) based on european
experiences, have indicated that there are three types of participation
that coincide with the degree to which the citizen becomes involved in
the process. The first is the pattern of paternalistic participation
which characterises the centralised   state; the second is the
conflictive one in which people struggle against that centralisation,
and the third is coproductive in which the major characteristic is that
of negotiation, or the agreement that people make together to elaborate
and carry out policies and social programs.

Stringer (1977) also identifies three participation styles, which are
similar to those above, and which are related to the theory of personal
constructs. In the first, the role of the user is limited to accepting

2

the idea which the expert has of the design. In the second, the user takes on a more active role and tries to impose his own point of view on the designers. In the third style, the ideas of the user and the designer form an active part of the finished product, both being modified in the process. To Stringer (1982) and Lawrance (1982),however, true participation is characterised by this last "interactive" style.

Other authors emphasise the political implications which are inherent in participation. Schwartz (1978) refers to the process in which people attempt to obtain control in questions which are of vital importance to them. This point of view reflects the traditional nineteenth century ideas of popular movements and cooperativism. Castells mentions that participation is a form by which the state and the citizen are allowed to communicate, and Susskind and Elliot (1983) refer to participation as a democracy, because different social groups join in the decision making process over the issues that concern them.

It can be seen that participation in these conceptions is associated with collective action which takes place in relation to a number of problems such as urban, educational or political issues, and in which citizens can become involved, either actively or passively. In passive involvement, people transmit information about their needs or choose between alternatives which are generated by experts, without decision control. In active involvement, citizen control can be complete, when they initiate and develop the process, or can be partial when the power of decision is shared with a planner.

It can be put forth as possibility that participation is born from a coming into awareness on the part of individuals that the unidirectional model of influence, between themselves and those who have both the power to create public policies,is limited. As a result they suggest their right to influence in the planning process. The authors of this work consider that the powerless user of designs or services is not compatible with the essence of what participation means. Fot this reason, we accept those ideas in which the user is in control,whether this control is shared or not.

Castells (1982) has classified the antecedent conditions for participation in four categories, which are institutional,technical, social and political conditions. These conditions can either inhibit or favor participation. When the process is inhibited the goals or the activities of the people who are affected in some situation are not acceptable to the people or organisms which are in charge of the technical support, or the institutional or political policies of the project in question, either because of power conflicts, because of different perceptions of the problem, or because the competence of the user to plan and carry out actions is questioned. On the other hand,when there is agreement among the factions involved in a project, the set of resources is made maximally beneficial for the project.

Wandersman (1979) offers other pre-conditions, in addition to those given by Castells. Participation,he indicates, also depends on individual characteristics of the participants, although he recognizes that there is little empirical evidence for their role, particularly of those that might be described as psychological aspects of the person, age, educational level, social class, marital status (Stringer and Taylor 1974), and the participatory history of the person (Callero and

Piliavin, 1983). Other variables which either precede or mediate the participation process are the attitudes of the participants toward the promotors of the activity, their perception of the conflict, the importance they give it (Draisen,1983; Wandersman, 1978); achievement anticipation, perception of one's abilities to achieve changes, and locus of control (Giamartino et al 1979; Tucker 1979; Wandersman,1979b) the needs, opportunities, and capabilities of the people involved (Singer,1984).

In fact, evidence has been found that supports the claim that when people attribute the consequences of their actions to their own personal effort (Anderson,1983),when they assume responsibility for their situation (Giamartino et al 1979), when they feel their physical and social surroundings to be important, when they identify with their neighborhoods and with the other residents there (Wandersman,1979),then their involvement in participative actions to improve their surroundings or to resolve problems there is greater, as is their satisfaction with their surroundings. On the other hand, the people who do not value their surroundings and who don't feel in control of them will be apathetic in terms of group or community action.

In this sense we can suppose that attributional variables play an important role in the perception that one has of a problem and it's solutions, as well as the perceptions that one might have of one's actions and achievements regarding the problem.

Some authors have considered it necessary to systematise different aspects of the participation process, and for this they have suggested that models be elaborated (Castells,1982; Davis,1982; Wandersman,1979b, 1981). We will describe briefly Wandersman's model, since it provides the elements to guide research for determining the role of psychological variables participatory processes.

Wandersman has proposed a model which takes into account the antecedent conditions as well as the mediators and the effects of participation (Eandersman, 1978, 1979a,1979b, and 1981). The antecedent conditions include the surroundings and the scale in which participation occurs, the planning stages, the type of participant,and the types of participation, including the techniques which are used.

The surroundings and the scale refer to the type of activity which is to be carried out in a particular environment and the amount of time which it involves. The planning stages include programming,that is,the definition of the problem,its goals and the resources which are available, the design,the construction,the use to which it will be put, and the evaluation of the proposal.

The participants should include an expert (architect,contractor,or engineer),the client or financing body,and the user,and their involvement varies between maximum and minumum control for each one of them. Among the participation techniques which are mentioned are modeling, public assemblies,simulation, and surveys, all of which are used to identify people's attitudes and opinions, and also to clear up doubts and to listen to suggestions and contributions.

Among the mediators of the participation process are such variables of individual differences as personality characteristics which are relevant to participation (locus of control, authoritarianism, need for achievement, the search for stimulation,and environmental preferences), demographic characteristics (age,sex,race,socioeconomic level,and residential mobility), effectiveness factors (perceived expertise and previous experience) and characteristics which are related to how people perceive, codify and value participation and its effects (expectations, subjective values, and codification strategies).

In terms of its effects, participation has an impact at both the individual and group levels. It influences the evaluation that is made of the environment, the attitudes one has toward authority, the user's role in the planning process, one's self respect, the perception that one has of control, the frequency of the use that one makes of environmental possibilities, and conservation behaviors. This model is evidently of great utility because in addition to the antecedent conditions for participation, psychological variables which have proven to be relevant in other research have been included. On the other hand, Wandersman's reference frame permits participation to be considered as a complex process which includes different styles in each one of which psychological, behavioural, economic and organisational variables that are included in addition to the consideration of the architectutal desing.

Other approaches which can be conceived as having theoretical connections with social participation are the studies which were stimulated by Garret Hardin's (1968) article " The Tragedy of the Commons" in which behaviours associated with people's relation to commonly held property or resources, in which individual benefits are in direct contradiction to the common welbeing. A recent example is that of Insko et al (1983) in which economic models are simulated in order to examine competition, exploitation and colaboration, given certain structural limitations for the interchange of "goods". Dawes (1980) reports that cooperative behavior has been found to be related to the degree of involvement on the part of experimental subjects, the degree of communication among them, the size of the group in which interaction takes place, and the expectation that the group members have in terms of the other participants. Messick et al (1983) explored the conditions under which subjects in a simulation would either change their legal right to free access to common resources or would modify the amount of private benefits that they obtain from exploiting a common resource. They found that among other factors, interpersonal trust and beliefs about the under-use of the common resource affected the behavior of the subjects. These studies are pertinent to the understanding of participative social behavior, because although they were carried out in laboratories, the themes of inquiry are clearly situated among those of social relations within the community. They stand between the " individualised " posture of traditional social psychology and the community orientation which is the concern of this paper.

THE PROBLEM

Not too long ago, the participation theme was the domain of sociolo-gists and politicians. In the literature those aspects of the phenomenon that emphasise antecedent conditions and general orga-nisational and recruiting strategies were developed. Neighborhood movements and urban renewal projects were the cases to which attention was given. These descriptions however have not included the psychological aspects of participation. Little information exists about motivational, affective and cognitive factors which stimulate people to commit themselves in the initiation and development of a participative process.

The findings of studies, such as those dealing with locus of control, authoritarianism, self esteem and demographic variables, show the importance of psychological variables in participation; therefore it is necessary to continue carrying out research, particulary the study of psychological variables involved in real cases of participation, which systematise them, to gain more information about the psychosocial nature of the phenomenon.

In the present work psychological variables are explored which differentiate participative from non-participative people. These variables were selected considering Wandersman's (1981) model as well as other studies. Two groups of people from the Caracas area were selected who either have or have not participated in an organised self help project,in this case an autogestionary, self-help housing project dedicated to the production of an apartment complex. This project, Casalta 2, is of special interest for the authors because they have been involved for the last 5 years with the community. The other group of people, individuals who come from a nearby neighborhood called Nazareno, was selected because of its physical nearness to Casalta 2 and because many of the residents of Casalta 2 came originally from Nazareno, in fact some of them were the victims of a landslide that happened in Nazareno and constituted the original imperative motivation for the formation of the self-help housing cooperative.

REASONS FOR THE STUDY

1. To understand the meaning of "participation" in subjects with and without the experience.
2. To analyze certain psychological characteristics in their relation to the experience of participation.
3. To formulate some proposals for stimulating techniques in participation projects.
4. To develop a heuristic basis for future research.

METHOD

The instrument: The information was collected mostly through structured interviews which were administered to the two groups. The information included

   a. Demographic characteristics.
   b. Statements about the meaning of participation.
   c. A description of the experience of participation.
   d. A description of the main problems of the neighborhoods.

These descriptions included

1. Statements about the causes of the most important problems.
2. Appreciations about possible solutions to these problems, including

who, or what entities, are responsible for these solutions.
3. Appreciations of possible alternative actions and the reasons the participants had for not carrying them out.
4. Ideas about the achievements of the residents in trying to solve the problems.
5. Reasons for leaving the participation experience or for continuing to participate.

Procedure: Open ended questions were asked and the responses of the interviewees were recorded just as they were given. The questions were of the type "What is participation for you? " and "What are the three most important problems faced by this community? " The interviews lasted a bit over an hour in general, depending on how much experience with participation the interviewee might have had and the degree to which he or she was cooperative and prolific in responding. In the community of Nazareno, the interviewing was done in some cases by residents of Casalta 2 who collaborated in the study (after having had their own interviews and being trained for the task) because they were known in Nazareno. It was considered that rapport would be gained from soliciting the help of these interviewers. In other cases in Nazareno when the questionnaires were not administered by the Casalta 2 members, the interviewers were introduced to the subjects by the Casalta helpers. In all cases, the responses were written by people other than the subjects of the study to eliminate differences which might have been caused by literacy problems.

The analyses of the responses was done by classifying all of them according to categories that began to become evident because of the frequencies with which they appeared in both communities. The authors recognise the role of their own participation, or perhaps contamination, in the formulation of these categories. It is considered that in this exploratory study, the contamination must be considered heuristic because the authors, while not direct participants in the experience of Casalta 2, are intimately associated with it. In all cases the accumulation of frequencies was respected above the preconceived ideas of the authors, and, in some cases, for example in the differences which emerged between "organisation" and "social interaction" as will be seen later, the categories were totally unexpected.

THE CASES STUDIED.

Casalta: In the communuty of Casalta 2 there area 490 residents, 297 males and 193 females; 58 per cent is above 20 years of age. In relation to their educational level 13 per cent have finished first year of high school and 7 per cent second year; 33 per cent have completed elementary school, whereas 47 per cent have not.

Their occupations are: 31 per cent students, 22 per cent house-wives, 27 per cent workers, 13 per cent unemployed, and the remaining 7 per cent are policemen, office workers and merchants. Families' monthly incomes are: 37 per cent earns 600 Bs. or under (43$); 22 per cent earns between 601 and 1.400 Bs. (100$); 26 per cent make between 1400 and 2600 Bs. (186$); and 15 per cent earns over 2600 Bs.; 29 per cent of the 69 families have been living in Casalta for 6 years, 30 per cent for four years, and 41 per cent less than four years.

The community of Casalta 2 was chosen because a large number of the members of this community have been involved, since 1979 in a participative project in which, through formalised system of self determination, self-help user-designed apartment buildings were conceived and built.The present apartments are of 92 square meters,and are grouped in 23 buildings of 3 floors with a total of 3 apartments per building.This was accomplished with financial help from the Venezuelan goverment and technical help from the architecture and psychology departments of the Central University of Venezuela, help which was solicited and negotiated by residents of Casalta 2. Since the landslide which happened on the Nazareno mountainside in 1979 when the original 32 families were left homeless, the group has grown to include other families, some of which also came from Nazareno and others who were placed in Casalta 2 by the government when the project was underway. The night of the landslide,the victims were left outside in the rain, with their children and the few things that could be saved from their destroyed homes.The government at that time offered to move them into emergency barracks, because the phenomenon of being moved into these "temporary" structures is common for landslide victims in Caracas. Every year there are landslides because the areas into which these people move (or "squat", because the people construct their shacks or "ranchitos" on unused land at night in order to avoid being stopped by the police) are geologically very unstable and the yearly rains are very insistant.The people who move into the barracks end up staying there,in very uncomfortable conditions, and far away from where they might work or have family.

After three days of living outdoors, the members of the community broke into a nearby school, where they installed themselves and began to consider what to do about their situation. The stayed there while they began to look for a piece of land that they might acquire (ask to be donated) and begin to build more adequate housing. The original idea was to rebuild their "ranchitos" but as the project developed, the participants began to realize that they might aspire to something more dignified and creative. The process was conflictive and intense for everyone involved, for the residents, for the participants from the university and, one might suppose, from the political pressure that was brought to bear on the governmental officials also for the government. At the present time there are 69 families living in Casalta, in virtually finished apartments, which only lack the finishing touches.

The community had originally asked for help from the Central University of Venezuela in the development of their project. From the faculty of architecture they had asked for help in designing their homes, and from the psychology department they wanted help with the social aspects of group action. One graduate student from the psychology department worked out a simulation program so that the members of the Casalta 2 project could communicate their wishes to the architects, and a number of designs were developed, using a light weight structure appropriate for the land which the project had been given, and making possible the building of the structure by people with few technological skills and very little equipment. The cooperation between the university and the community became intense and a number of important friendships were established.

However,with the arrival of the "new" participants,the hostilities that were growing in the community began to be expressed in terms of the university's role there. With pressure from the government,the community asked the university to leave, and in several highly emotional encounters in which the residents and the university representatives felt betrayed, the university withdrew from the project.

Nevertheless, the experience of participation had influenced the group profoundly. After more than a year of absence, the authors of this report again approached leaders of the community to suggest their collaboration in the present research. They agreed to do so, and in May, 1985, these leaders arranged for the interviews that were used to obtain most of the information in this study. As a result of the interviews, which required the residents of Casalta 2 to examine their participation experience, they again began to hold their weekly assemblies.

An example of this renewed interest is that very recently, at midnight,a jeep with a family and several members of the police department arrived, together with a moving van, at one of the apartment buildings. One of the residents who was outside saw them and approached to ask what was going on. There are about four or five apartments still uninhabited, but all are assigned. The family had property papers, signed by the government, but were not among the people who were known to the community. A dispute followed,and the resident who had observed their arrival originally, let other members of the group know what was going on. In several minutes there were more than 40 people around the jeep challenging the intruders, even in the face of the armed police who threatened to use their guns. Finally, at about 1:00 AM the police and the unknown family left. The next day the true owner of the apartment arrived to thank the community,emotionally moved for their support, especially since he himself had once been asigned to the community by the government. The answer from one of the community leaders was," We didn't do it for you as a person; we did it for everyone,because here we all work together."

9

At the time the interviews were carried out,the residents were all
in the process of moving to their new apartments, and in fact, the
barracks where they had been living during the construction of the
apartment buildings, had been torn down. Some of the people were
still in the " trailers " where they had been placed when space in the
barracks had proven to be insufficient, but these residents also were
in the process of moving. The apartments consist of areas which
accomodate three bedrooms, a kitchen area, a receiving area and a
bathroom. However, the interior arrangements that each family has given
to the apartments has been the result of the taste and requierements of
each one individually. Thus the room divisions are not, in fact, all
the same. At the time of this writing, three months after the beginning
of the interviews, all of the residents of Casalta 2 have in effect
moved into their new apartments.

This short description of the social atmosphere of the Casalta 2
community is considered necessay, before examining the results of the
interviews, because it is considered important that these results be
viewed in the context of the moment at which they ocurred. Later in
the discussion of the results, this context will be reconsidered.

Nazareno: In the neighborhood of Nazareno there were 2591 residents,
grouped in 500 families. Occupations vary; 36 per cent are students,21
per cent are housewives, 17 per cent are workers, and 9 per cent are
unempoyed. The rest are involved in commerce, are office workers,
building guards, or others. In terms of income, 60 per cent earn less
than 1500 Bolívares ($107) per month and 56 per cent have been living
in the area for less than 8 years. Most of the people own their own
homes, but not the land on which they are built; the wallas of the
houses are either cement blocks or tin sheeting while the floors are
either cement or earth. The roofs are usually tin sheeting. Official
figures state that 93 per cent have sewage water disposal systems
(open cement channels) but this figure may be exaggerated. Most obtain
their drinking water by hooking tubes or hoses to the municipal mains

10

and while half pay for their use of electricity, the other half "rob" current by hooking up secretly to the main power lines.

THE SAMPLES

On hundred and sixty residents from Nazareno and Casalta 2 were·interviewed,68 of them from Casalta 2, and 92 from Nazareno. In Casalta 2 this number made up 24 per cent of the population, while in Nazareno it constituted 6 per cent. There was no attempt at developing a representative sample, because the characteristics of these two particular areas as geographical or social-political entities was not an interest of the researchers. An analysis of the samples showed, nevertheless, that, in terms of income and occupational distribution, the samples were similar to the populations, although in Nazareno 73 per cent of the interviewees were women. Mean age was 33 in Casalta 2 and 30 in Nazareno.

The main difference that can be seen in the two samples is that of the history of participation of the people involved. In Casalta 2, 48 respondants, or 70 per cent of the sample, reported having had some experience with participation, and of these, 58 per cent of them reported having held office, while in Nazareno, 21 people, or 23 per cent of the sample had similar experiences and of these, only four people, or 19 per cent of those who had participated, had ever held office.

A JUSTIFICATION FOR PARTICIPATORY RESEARCH

The experience of having influenced the group process, as happened in the case of the interviews which are the basis of this paper, is an example of how the researcher cannot be separated from the object of his research. The act of enquiry is itself a contamination. In recognition of this, and for ethical reasons, the results of this work will be shared with the community.

At this point, a short justification of the participatory methodology which was used in this research is considered necessary. Quintanilla et al (1980) describe research and intervention as "inseparable". They are described as simultaneous processes in which both are "vehicles" for the maximum development of consciousness". This integration is compared to Freire's "problematization" in which problems which have been perceived as individual become considered to be community problems. At the same time a distinction is made between this integration and the "action research" technique from United States in which research and intervention are considered as sequential steps, both of which can be separated from a more general process. This integrated approach is related to an attitude found in Callelo and Neuhaus (1985) in which research is considered as " disolved " and totally mixed with, both the characteristics of the researcher, and his object of inquiry. The research begingswith his theoretical conception which defines and limits his posibilities of characterising "reality", and each methodological choice he makes implies his committment to his own world view. This "committed" view of science is not a new one, but the researchers cited here are considered representative of a growing tendency in Latin America, one which the present authors share, and as such is considered in this description of our own methodology. This view probalby reflects

11

a tendency in the region to formulate a "science" which is increasingly independant of its positivist roots.

RESULTS AND CONCLUSIONS

A brief statement about what the authors consider to be the important contributions of this study will be offered in this report. This statement will include two short considerations: 1) the more important findings of the study, and 2) some cautious recommendations about encouraging citizen participation.

The first comment that we would like to make concerns the definitions that were given of participation. We would like to contrast these "experiencial" ideas with the more formal ones that can be found in the literature. The ideas that come from Nazareno and Casalta 2 included solidarity, the specific activities involved in participation, the organisational aspects, the ideas of achievement, struggle, work, and effort, ideological statements, and simple value judgments about whether participation is "good" or "bad". Usually in the literature, attention is focused on certain key moments of the experience,which are, in a way, achievements, such as planning or decision making. The literature gives little emphasis to the internal workings of the group, such as their organisational aspects or their experience of "solidarity". The effort involved is never mentioned. Power is considered mostly in terms which are a vague "giving power to the citizens", without considering the nature of this power, whether regarding the internal workings of the organisition or particular aspects of manipulating power when dealing with inter-organisational considerations. The step-wise concepts of partial or complete participation do not appear among the practitioners. That is, everyachievement of participation, (when the government functionary agrees to make an appointment to hear the group's complaints, when the group obtains the use of a tract land,and when a truckload of cement is promised and delivered) is considered by itself a little victory in a larger enterprise, which in the case of Casalta 2 was the construction of their apartments. These different ideas of participation must be understood to be dealing with entirely different experiences. In the case of the formal definitions, they are considerations which might enter into the process of city planning;that is at a certain moment, officials in a city goverment might decide to "give" partial or complete power to the citizens. In the case of Casalta 2, there was never any chance of the people being offered the power. They knew that they simply had to take it for themselves, using the contradictions that found in the political environment around them such as the different attitudes that they might find in the news media and the city councils.

Nevertheless, we consider that one difference in these definitions is important, and reflects an aspect that ought to be included in the ones given in the formal literature. This aspect is the difference between internal power use and external power use. In terms of intra-group references, it was found that "horizontal power" is a concern, together with the control of power. However in terms of the relations between the group and outside interests "anything goes". The group uses all its advantages and group loyalty permits and requires this. Also there is the underlying awareness that the world outside the group is often hostile, and will in turn use any means to stop the group. Thus power is considered very differently inside and outside the organisation.

The need for developing horizontal power structures is crucial. It
has been seen with some frequency in Latin America that organisations
that begin as grass-roots associations of people looking for redress or
achievement, deteriorate into groups with a concentrated internal power
arrangement, and either the original characteristics of the group's
struggle are lost, or the members leave in disillusion. Social
psychology can contribute to finding mechanisms which mark a midpoint
between power pyramids and chaos. Also, we consider that centralised
interest groups are not "participative" in the true sense that allows
all " participants to participate ".

The second comment is about the findings concerning the role of
"solidarity". We found that the term means different things to
different people, that it is generally a positive element in participation and an important one, and that it has both affective and active
connotations. It was the most frequently cited category by all the
people interviewed in this study. It is linked to possessions, to
personal crises, to helping behavior and to the emotion of " together-
ness". It seems to contrast with alienation.

The third point that will be made is about the role of organisation
in participation. It seems to be no small achievement, but one that is
cited more by the participators than the ones who do not participate.
It is given as part of the definition of the concept of participation,
as one of the reasons for having solved problems, and its lack is seen
as one of the reasons for not solving them. Its lack is also given as
a reason for not continuing to collaborate for 20 per cent of the
people who said they had given up. It can be contrasted with " interpersonal friction" as a way of getting along in Nazareno among
neighbours when conmmunity problems are being faced. (In Nazareno the
people felt that they themselves, as individuals, were often the
causes of the problems in that neighborhood because of their negative
characteristics, as well as seeing themselves as the solution to the
same problems. Also, there was a contrast that appeared when comparing
the social solutions in Nazareno and Casalta 2. In the first case, "we
ourselves " were seen as both cause and solution, while in the second
"the community" is given as a solution, while "lack of organisation" is
seen as a cause of problems. In a content analysis of all the " we
ourselves " statements made in Nazareno, 67 per cent of these statements
referred to what "we" could have done but haven't or to reasons for not
having done things. In Casalta 2, 74 per cent of these statements refer
to accomplishments, either in the past or in the present, or to active
obligations on the part of the community toward the community.

The same contrast reappeared when the reason for not having taken
alternative actions were classified. "Organisation" is a way of rising
above interpersonal conflict in order to get something done, and it is
a learned skill, which seems to come from the same process of participating.

The fourth finding that the authors consider to be of importance is
the active stance of the participators, both in their self images and
in their relation to official entities. The wishful thinking one finds
in Nazareno, which accounted for 67 per cent of the statements that
described " we, ourselves " is contrasted to the 74 per cent self
descriptions in Casalta 2 in which accomplishments and active
obligations were mentioned. When those people from both groups who had
participated listed what actions of theirs had contributed to the

13

acievements of the groups of which they were members, 36 per cent of
the answers were made in terms of negotiations with the government.
There were dependency statements that were made in relation to the
government both in Casalta 2 and in Nazareno which must be seen in the
light of the fact that Casalta 2 was, in fact, dependent on the
government for materials for construction. The difference lies in the
fact that in Casalta 2 the people went to the officials and demanded to
be helped as citizens in need, and when there was resistance, they
went to the newspapers and radio to complain about the treatment they
had received.

The next point that will be made concerns the contrasting reasons
for continuing to participate and for giving up. Most of the reasons
for continuing to participate are instrumental, that is they are
related to the continuing desire to solve a particular problem.
However, the second most cited reason was that of personal motivations
such as liking the experience, values, and learning possibilities. In
fact, values, or normative reasons was given in 43 per cent of the
responses in Casalta. Some of these values were highly combative and
verbally developed. It is possible that these values are developed in
the experience of participation, but a brief disgression is in order
here to elaborate our discussion In a related study, interviews were
conducted with community leaders in which it was found that almost
every one of them had begun to worry about problems of social inequality
and the need for self-help from a very young age, sometimes before the
age of 12. One person, also a leader, said that he had noticed, around
the age of 6 that some children had navels that protruded and others
had neat navels. When he asked his mother about this she told him that
some children were born in hospitals with doctors attending while
others were born at home with midwives helping their mothers. He always
remembered this as an unjust mark on the body, a sign of proverty that
was imprinted from birth, as a terrible injustice, and one that secretly
motivated him in many community and political efforts. These people who
seem to be motivated from very young, and who look for ways in which
they can contribute may be very different from those who are pushed into
participation because of an experience like the original one in Casalta
2 of being suddenly left homeless. However, the role of values seems to
be important, perhaps less as an original motivator (except for those
who already strongly hold those values) than as a reason for sustained
participative effort.

The last point which we would like to emphasise in this paper concerns
reasons that people give for both the causes of their problems and the
solutions they offer to them. The work that has been done on such
variables as locus of control, need for achievement, and attribution
research would suggest that an internal motivation is important in
participation. However we have seen that people from Nazareno tended to
see themselves as both a cause of their problems (adding "problems of
interaction" and "personal characteristics", the people themselves in
the neighborhood accounted for 21 per cent of the reasons for their
problems) and the solutions to those problems (62 per cent of the
responses). It is interesting that they see themselves as both cause
and solution, and combined with their wishful self-images, we have a
description of utter helplessness. It is sometimes attractive to think
of internal motivation as being a component of active problem solving,
but unless there is also the perception of viable ways is which internal
motivation can be put to use, it is perhaps not only of little help,
but damaging, because all the blame for failure falls back on the

person. The individual no matter how internally motivated,may be helpless. It is only in combination with organisation, and perhaps solidarity, that community participation has meaning. The authors suggest that internal motivation be considered in its double significance in future research: a) the blameful, helpless attitude of the internally motivated individual who has no alternatives, and b) the powerful possibilities that are affered by realistic, group responses.

A line for future research would be to consider the role of repression in participative efforts. Repression can take a number of forms, from the foot-dragging lack of cooperation by public authorities to the open agression of governments when the police are used to stop some particular activity. It is evident that a number of the problems that are faced by this type of participative activity are related to official inefficiency or desinterest. The people involved in these movements are often only claiming what is legally their right, and the fact that they must organise to achieve their goals is evidence that they face opposition from the outset. Nevertheless, the authors consider that awareness raising, internal motivation, and purely organisational considerations must be enlarged to take into account that official or other resistance can often be of enormous importance, and should be studied both in terms of its own very special characteristics and in terms of the reasons why some people are willing to defy it. We agree with Moscovici (1981) that the studies of conformity are interesting in the social-psychological literature, but more interesting is the study of why some people don't conform.

Some cautions recommendations abouth encouraging citizen participation. The authors feel that their recomendations must be made only in the light of the very heuristic nature of their findings. Nevertheless, the considerations are the following:

1. That organisers of group participation should beware of the self defeating nature of the powerless, internally motivated individual. It is important to point out realizable goals. Perhaps short term goals should always be included in orden to permit achievements along the way.

2. That the contrast between organisation and social friction be made manifest and discussed often in the group so that interpersonal conflict can be subordinated to useful mechanisms for handling it, such as breaking the group into small discussion groups so that everyone can have his say and his chance at influence. The danger represented by personal, vindictive comments should be recognised by everyone for what it is, a devisive, self-defeating tendency. This tendency toward social friction can be contrasted with a corresponding tendency toward centralisation of power. Perhaps the same techniques, that organise and permit individual expression, are useful in preventing the destruction of horizontal power structures. At any rate, this apparent contra - diction between centrality and interpersonal conflict is one that should be examined thoroughly as a devisive mechanism, and taken into considera- ration from the begining in any community participation program.

BIBLIOGRAPHY

Anderson,Craig A. (1983). "Motivational and Performance Deficits in Interpersonal Settings. The Effect of Attributional Style", Journal of Personality and Social Psychology,Vol.45,no. 5 pp. 1136-47

Callelo,Hugo and Neuhaus,Susana (1985), La Investigación en las Ciencias Humanas, Tropykos, Caracas.

Callero,P. Piliavin,J.(1983). Developing a Commitment to Blood Donation. " The impact of One's First Experience ", Journal of Applied Social Psychology. Vol 13,No.1 pp.1-16.

Castells,M. (1982). Urban Politics,Citizen Participation and Neighborhood Movements ". Conference presented in Caracas,Venezuela.

Davis,D. (1982) " Participation in Community Intervention Design" American Journal of Community Psychology. Vol. 10, No. 4 pp.429-446.

Dawes,Robyn M, (1980)." Social Dilemmas " Annual Review of Psychology Vol. 31, pp. 169-93.

Draisen,M. (1983)." Fostering Effective Citizen Participation: Lessons from Three Urban Renewal Neighborhoods in the Hague". In: L. Susskind &M. Elliot (Editors): Paternalism,Conflict and Coproduction. Plenum Press, New York, pp. 239-87.

Edelston, H.& Colodner,F.(W/R) " Are the Poor Capable of Planning for themselves ".

Giamartino,G.M. Ferrell &A. Wandersman (1979) " Who Participates in Block Organizations and Why: Some Demographic Considerations " In A. Seidel &S. Danford (editors). Environmental Design: Research, Theory and Application. EDRA 10,Washington.

Hardin,Garrett (1968). " The Tragedy of the Commons " Science, Vol. 162, pp. 1243-48.

Insko,Chester,A; Gilmore,Robert; Drenan,Sarah, Lipsitz,Angela; Moehle, Debra; and Thibaut John (1983). " Trade Versus Expropiation in open Groups: A comparison of two types of Social Power " Journal of Personality and Social Psychology, Vol. 44,No. 5, pp.977-999.

Jones,R.S. (1976). " Community Participation as Pedagogy: Its Effects on Political Attitudes of Black Students " Journal of Negro Education, Vol. 45, No. 4, pp. 397-407.

Lawrence, R. (1982). " Designer's Dilemma: Participatory Design Methods" In: P. Bart,A. Chen G. Francescato (editors). Knowledge For Design Edra 13, Maryland.

Messick,David M; Wilka,Henk;Brewer,Marilynni Kramer, RM; Zemke,Patricia English; and Lui, Layton (1983).
" Individual Adaptations and Structural change as solutions to Social Dilemmas ". Journal of Personality and Social Psychology,Vol 44, No. 2, pp. 294-309.

Moscovici,S. (1981). Psicología de las Minorías Activas. Madrid: Ediciones Morata.

Murphy,J.B. (1977). " American Planners and CitizensTogether. A case Study ". Community Development Journal, Vol. 12, No. 3, pp.165-76.

Quintanillas Rodríguez, L; Gonzales Izaguirre,I; López Gallegos,A.M. Mejía Hernández,J.Ma. Gpe; Santana ,Ma. del Carmen; and Vázquez Banda,F.J. (1980); " El Método Investigación Acción Aplicada en una comunidad Marginada a Partir del Propio Autodiagnóstico ". Consejo Nacional Para la Enseñanza e Investigación en la Psicología, Vol. 4. No. 2, pp. 226-36.

Schwartz, S. (1978). " User Participation in Environmental Change " In: S. Weidemann &J.R. Anderson (Editors) Priorities for Environmental Design Research. Edra 8. Washington.

Singer,Ch. (1984). " Differential Public Participation in Sia ". Social Impact Assessment 90/92. April-May-June, Vol. 5, No. 1.

Stringer, P. (1982). " Towards a Participatory Psychology " In: P. Stringer (Editor). Confronting Social Issues: Applications of Social Psychology. Vol. 2, Academic Press, London.

Stringer,P. (1977). " Participating in Personal Construct Theory " New Perspectives in Personal Construct Theory. In : Bannester (Editor). Academic Press. London.

Stringer, P. & Taylor, M. (1974). " Attitudes and Information in Public Participation: A case Study " Centre for Environmental Studies, London.

Susskind L.& Elliot, M. (1983). " Paternalism, Conflict and Coproduction: Learning from Citizen Action and Citizen Participation in Western Europe ". In: L. Suskind & M. Elliot (Editors). Paternalism, Conflict and Coproduction.Plenum Press, New York.

Tucker, L. (1978). " The Environmentally Concerned Citizen: Some Correlates ". Environment and Behavior, Vol. 10, No. 3, pp.389-418.

Wandersman, A. (1978). " Research Issues Regarding Citizen Participation ". In : S. Weidemann & J.R. Anderson. (Editors). Priorities for Environmental Desing Research, Edra 8, Washington.

Wandersman, A. (1979) " User Participation: A Study of Types of Participation, Effects, Mediators and Individual Differences ". Environment and Behavior, Vol. 11, No. 2, pp. 185-208.

Wandersman, A. (1979b). " User Participation in Planning Environments: A Conceptual Framework. " Environment and Behavior, Vol. 11, No. 4. pp. 465-82.

Wandersman, A. (1981). " A Framework of Participation in Community Organizations ". The Journal of Applied Behavioral Science, Vol. 17, No. 1, p.27.

2. Designers' involvement in design education

MARTIN SYMES

This chapter begins by discussing the presence of
practitioners in schools of design. Their function seems
to be to help students learn to handle design conflicts,
a skill anyone wishing to join in a design process must
develop. The background to this discussion is that
competing theories of the design process have failed to
clarify either the role of an individual designer's ideas
or the importance of recognising conflicts between those
ideas when seeking the resolution of design problems. A
theory of design education is only slowly emerging and its
development is impeded by our limited understanding of the
human behaviours involved. What seems already accepted
is that design abilities mature slowly. It is also
arguable that the institutional context in which design
teaching takes place affects its progress. The chapter
attempts to make a step forward by reporting an educational programme in which the human interaction between
designers was monitored. It attempts a typology of design
problem solving behaviours, arguing that novel ideas are
more likely to emerge when conflicts are clearly stated
and openly debated. An example design discussion is
described in some detail and thirteen others summarised in
the tables. In conclusion it proposes that our theories
of design and of design education be adapted to take full
account of the emotional context in which design problems
are often faced. This could be a valuable insight for
the practice of community architecture.

INTRODUCTION

One of the more striking features of design education is
the extent to which design practitioners who are not
academics appear in the studio, work with the students
and become responsible for the teaching programme. These
people are neither scholars nor researchers in the normal
sense of these terms. Teachers and students alike are
hard put to specify exactly what information it is that
design practitioners can convey to students which
non-designers cannot, yet the latter are treated with the
utmost suspicion if they attempt to replace the former
and teach design in a studio of their own.

In this Chapter an attempt will be made to throw some
light on the intriguing question of what can be learnt
from practising designers by describing and discussing a
programme of professional development for architects in
which groups of practitioners were asked to try and teach
their peers or, looked at the other way round, to try and
learn from each other. The programme seems to show that
although the designers concerned did pass on traditional
forms of information, they also passed on a more subtle,
"tacit" knowledge not only about finding reliable
solutions, but also about evaluating and choosing between
design concepts or design requirements, and thus about
defining and solving conflicts. Most importantly, they
passed on a sense of the social and emotional climate in
which design procedures can operate effectively - the
culture of designerly behaviour. If the everyday user
of buildings is, as the present volume surely proposes,
ever to participate fully in the design of buildings, he
or she must first obtain some knowledge of the design
process, and it is hoped that this Chapter will help make
this more possible.

CURRENT THEORIES OF DESIGN

An important preliminary to the improvement of all design
education must be the development of a better understanding of how design takes place and of the methods which
may be used to assist in the making of designs. As
Rittel (1982) has shown, design problems vary quite
considerably in their degree of complexity. The more and
the less complex problems need to be approached with
qualitatively different design procedures. Some involve
the resolution of important conflicts and some demand
high levels of personal and emotional involvement.
Others may be treated more rationally and even become
matters of routine

In the literature, design methods have been divided
into a number of categories, only some of which explain

the active role designers sometimes play in prompting
their own interpretations of the problem at hand.
Broadbent (1979), for example, seems only to discuss
design method in terms of three different ways external
constraints have been seen to impinge on design. In his
"first generation" of design methods, those developed by
Alexander (1964), Archer (1963), Gregory (1966) and
Jones (1970), the requirements of a task seem to be
derived empirically and the procedure followed for
resolving conflicts between them seems to be an abstract
system of analysis and synthesis. Alexander's main
thesis at this stage of his career was indeed that the
designer's "forms" emerged directly out of conflicts in
the "context" which he or she had identified. Writers
of Broadbent's "second generation", Alexander again (1977),
Fagence (1977), Habraken (1972), Sanoff et al (1978) and
Turner (1976) are shown in a more humane position with
the emphasis placed on user participation and public
discussion. Even this approach still assumes that the
intellectual initiatives come from outside a designer's
own mind - from the minds of others. A designer is still
seen as a technician of sorts, interpreting other peoples'
suggestions and not necessarily bringing forward any of
his or her own. The cynical might say that architects'
ideas are surpressed by user participation and an
artificial concensus achieved. Broadbent mentions a
"third generation" of design methodologist, those who
stress the importance of making reference to prototypes
and to existing models of architectural form in the
process of design initiation and development. Rossi (1982)
and Tafuri (1976) are two architectural theorists who have
written persuasively about the power of inherited formal
concepts. This approach does, of course, refer to
designers' own ideas as it is these which may be transmitted by the corpus of existing buildings and published
drawings, but it also tends to emphasize the ideas of all
designers taken together and to devalue an individual
designer's intervention. A group concensus is assumed to
override this.

The importance of an individual's own drive to clarify
his own ideas and persuade others to accept them has, it
seems, been consistently undervalued in the discussion of
how designers design. Consideration of ways in which this
might be enhanced has often been ignored. One reason for
this may be that there is very little evidence on which
to base such a discussion. It is not uncommon for
observers to collect background data about the constraints
on a design project, to invite the public's opinion of
them and to search the literature for possible precedents.
But much of this kind of work can be achieved without any
direct observation of the design process itself and without any direct discussion with designers of their
experiences during the design period. A data base cover-
ing the latter would certainly be needed if extensive

20

studies of individual contributions to design problem-
solving were to be mounted and this hardly exists in any
reliable form. Cuff (1981) is one of the few researchers
who has followed design processes "from the inside". She
attended and analysed 100 design meetings, which she
called negotiations. The results of this study suggest
that although designing often follows an ordered and
logical procedure, a point also made by Topalian (1980),
it is also often one in which the designer's interpersonal behaviour has an important part to play. As
designs proceed through stages from the general to the
particular a number of people participate in the
creation and resolution of conflicts over critical issues.
They have to develop strategies defining choices, overcoming dilemmas and finding solutions. Cuff's work seems
to provide the beginning of a new "fourth generation" in
the discussion of design methods which will demonstrate
the important role of conflict – identification and
conflict – resolution in the design process.

RESEARCH IN DESIGN EDUCATION

Design education is thus clearly concerned with trans-
mitting a complex of skills, both technical and social.
Many of the problems to be overcome are psychological
as well and it is useful that Powell (1983) has reported
the growing body of research on the personality factors
which affect information transfer in design, arguing that
one of the main constraints on a designer's use of new
knowledge is his or her motivation to absorb it. The
emphasis of much current research in this field should
thus be on the human side, and most of the questions which
it is hoped to answer should be framed in social and
psychological terms. Is there anything about design
which can be learnt from studying the human context? Is
there a regular learning process which develops when
individuals begin to be able to design? And does the
human context itself in which this type of learning takes
place actually affect its progress? The answers to such
questions about design may also help to render design
method more teachable.

    The content of design education has always been broad
but it has not always been comprehensive. Much of it is
of necessity directed towards the immediate needs of
junior professionals, stressing accepted methods, skills
and techniques rather than abstract, theoretical or
critical knowledge. The dominant model in the 1950s and
1960s was still that developed in the 1920s by Gropius
(1965) for the Bauhaus. The course there had three parts
to it: "preparatory instruction", including training with
different materials, "technical instruction", an apprent-
iceship in the workshop, and "structural instruction" which
often included manual work on building sites, all leading

to a Master Builders' Diploma. Each stage included some
training in artistic expression and form-making but there
seems to have been very little, if any, history taught,
and only the minimum of sociology. This pattern was
frequently replicated. Only in some institutions, and
then only in the last decade or so, has the external
human context of design become a significant component
of the curriculum in higher education for environmental
design. Even now, the development of technical competence
is normally stressed in a period of initial professional
education. The encouragement in students of a sympathy
for the social context of user requirements and of an
understanding of the human reactions to built form or of
the roles a designer can play, is often left until later.
So although one problem for researchers is to show that
the human context is an important component of design
knowledge, another is to show that this can be integrated
with more technical aspects in a comprehensive learning
process. One attempt of this kind can be found in the
present author's (Symes 1984) discussion of case methods
in design education.

Design teachers usually assume the skills of their
students are built up over a period of time yet research
often concentrates on the needs of one age-group at a
time. Adams (1984), working on the education of school
children about design, stresses the development of
creativity. Baynes and Roberts (1984) are concerned with
design studies in higher education and emphasize a knowledge of the language of design. Wise (1984) deals with
the continuing development of professional skills and is
most interested in decision-making procedures. Authors do
attempt to locate their contributions within a development-
al sequence but little of their discussion transcends
the steps in this sequence and no master plan for research
in this area has been produced which would enable the
assumed overall pattern to be tested.

A development sequence is, of course, fundamental to
much thinking on all kinds of education. The Latin
meaning of the word "education" must inform our thinking
in ways we find difficult to criticise. In education
for or about design this underpinning is especially strong.
The model produced by Piaget and Inhelder (1956) of a
child's early development of social-spatial concepts has
been absorbed into the culture of design education so
thoroughly that it has the status of a conventional
wisdom. The theory they propounded of a stepwise growth
of new knowledge through action and reflection has not
only become a normal basis of curriculum organisation in
design education. It has also become an intellectual
framework within which research questions are asked. Thus
when Schon (1983) and his collaborators developed their
concept "reflection-in-action", they also carried out

case studies of tutorial methods in architectural studios
which showed the role played there by the combination of
verbal and visual communication methods. Their work
could usefully be extended to shown the frequency of
"mental blockages" causing conflicts of intention between
teacher and student and of "intuitive leaps" when these
are overcome.

There are still many important questions unanswered by
research into design education. These include the
following. Is design education especially highly
institutionalised? Is it available only to particular
social classes? Can it be transferred between cultural
contexts? In referring to them the fact that the
development of formal instruction systems for design is
comparatively recent must be borne in mind. Apprentice-
ship to a master-craftsman was probably still the
predominant method of learning to design in many parts of
the world before the Second World War. Learning about
design is still a rarity in primary and secondary school
curricula. The management of design by industrial
organisations has still no professional body through
which its skills can be transmitted. Partly because of
this, the subject does not appear on the syllabus of
conventional schools of design. If it did, topics like
the resolution of conflicts between designers and users
would have to be included; but since it does not, they
usually do not either. Institutional changes which might
lead to reform of teaching methods have more often been
of interest to design educators because they would
ensure the continued financial support of design education
than because they would increase the realism of the
curriculum. One rare example of an institutional reorgan-
isation accompanying educational reform was that which
followed Richard Llewellyn-Davies' assumption of the
Bartlett Chair of Architecture at University College
London. Here staffing changes and an increase in the
size of the department faciliated the introduction of
scientific subjects to the curriculum. But while in
reporting this set of changes, Abercrombie and Hunt (1977)
have given valuable insights into the effects an
institutional context can have on the effectiveness of
design education and how the introduction of a scientific
approach could make the subject much more accessible than
it was when surrounded by the mysteries of artistic
interpretation, they also showed that a complete revolution of traditional values could not be achieved within
the ten year time span they reported. To come to terms
also with the knowlege about design drawn from the social
sciences is likely to take even longer.

AN EXPERIMENT IN A CONTINUING EDUCATION

A valuable opportunity to discuss the ways in which
designers actually solve conflicts in their everyday
work arose as an unintended consequence of a continuing
education programme organised by the author of this
Chapter in the months of July and August 1983. Originally
intended as one of a number of teaching experiments which
might contribute to improving the performance of a large
architectural practice, the programme began to reveal
more clearly the types of behaviour which arise during a
design process and thus to offer an opportunity for
increasing our understanding of design methods.

The objective of this continuing education programme
was for architectural designers to act as the teachers of
their colleagues and the educational concept was to
reproduce in a controlled group-discussion some of the
actual behaviour in a design office. After an introduct-
ory "example" case-study seminar run by the tutor,
participants were asked to present to each other the
essential features of a design problem they themselves
had addressed and to take their colleagues through various
solutions, evaluating them as they went along. The method
and philosophy of "learning by doing" has been described
in detail elsewhere (Symes and Marmot 1983). Typically
a syndicate of two designers of different ages who had
not worked together before spent thirty minutes or so
telling each other of "insoluble problems" they had
encountered in their work and selcting one for more detailed study. They then assembled a selection of files
and drawings so that for the next hour and a half they
could summarise the events concerned. After a break they
gave copies of their summaries to their colleagues who,
also in small groups, had thirty minutes to come up with
a solution. The set piece of the day was when the original
syndicate led all of their colleagues through an hour-long
debate over all the "solutions", revealing the "real
outcome" only towards the end of the session. After all
had taken their turn in this procedure, a final meeting
was held at which lessons were drawn for the practice as
a whole. The discussions were held in three workshops,
each workshop taking place in a different branch office
of the practice. Between 9 and 16 different architects
of all levels of responsibility took part in each of the
workshops. The majority of the design problems were
presented by pairs of architects, and so a total of 14
problems were discussed in the programme as a whole. The
workshops were held in conference spaces within or near to
the office accommodation of each of the branches concerned.
The author of this paper was the programme tutor and made
notes on various aspects of the workshops as they progress-
ed, as did one of the senior members of the practice, who
attended all three workshops. Photographs were taken

24

and tape recordings made of some sessions, but no other evaluation of the programme was undertaken to the author's knowledge at the time it took place.

In abstracting for this Chapter some of the notes taken on the case problems discussed, it has been assumed that participants behaved as they would in a "real-life" design meeting. Particular attention has been paid to the form of the discussions themselves and to the frequency with which new design solutions emerged within them. In line with categories suggested by the work of Broadbent and Cuff reported above, the discussions about these design problems have been classified using four dimensions. The first three might be thought of as showing behaviour which implies an underlying concensus about the problem and the fourth might be thought of as showing the need to settle underlying conflicts.

1.   Systematic discussions which centre on an analysis of the requirements imposed on the design, on the constraints which surround it and on the logical procedures for finding a solution.

2.   Humanistic discussions which explore the motivations of participants in the situation, their social context, the process of interaction between them and the implications which taken together, these have for the finding of a solution.

3.   Typological discussions of precedents for the design ideas concerned, of their value as prototypes and of the possibilities for using them, singly or in combination, as solutions.

4.   Critical discussions in which participants take on the role of antagonists, debating opposed design ideas and attempting to find new solutions which overcome the differences.

Tables 1, 2 and 3 summarise the author's perception of the discussions held at the three workshops in this continuing education programme and figures 1, 2 and 3 show the atmosphere created. A more detailed description of the fifth case in workshop 1, "the last Symphony", may help readers grasp the complexity of issues which were unravelled. In this particular case a group of professionals learnt, through a critical discussion, of the political role attached to their work. At first the task appeared to be to make a simple aesthetic judgement. It concerned the elevational treatment of a switchroom attached to the hydroelectric generating station of a new dam in a remote area of the Commonwealth. The project had been delayed because the design of the switchroom had been rejected by the dam's project manager, an electrical engineer. His grounds were that its cladding (glass)

25

might be easily damaged, and that its roof (metal sheeting) was inappropriate for a concrete dam. The designers saw the causes of this rejection as interprofessional rivalry and the engineer's lack of visual awareness. What emerged during discussion of the case was an extremely interesting debate over the briefing process set up for the project. Participants noted the superficial treatment of design in the government's initial environmental impact statement ("human scale" was mentioned but only in very general terms) and explored the distribution of design-responsibilities between engineers and architects in the Ministry of Works (the engineer was seen as a dominant "character" whose preferences could not be predicted). After a stormy group discussion an important new analysis emerged - in their political role the designers had been manipulating both a general public interest in the environment and the personal pre-occupations with imagery of their professional colleagues. In their role as managers they had had to control the dynamics of interprofessional collaboration. Further role conflicts were to be foreseen at the time when a new design would have to be negotiated between the various parties. In practical terms the designers' task of producing design details was blocked until much more was understood about the cultural references upon which each party to the negotiations would draw as the debate proceded. An ultimate resolution of this problem might only be possible if the form of the practice itself with its outdated patterns of roles and responsibilities could be changed. Study of a simple aesthetic design problem on which they all had subjective opinions led these professionals to a deeper understanding of society's changing priorities and of the effect this was having on the roles they should play.

The three workshops took place in different branches of the architectural practice and were clearly influenced in their content and outcome by the differing workload of those offices and by the levels of experience of those who worked within them. There may have been some influences too from the size of the group involved on each occasion and from the behaviour of the programme leader, from the senior architect accompanying him and from the details of timing. In Workshop 1, the final discussion centred on the need for an archive of past projects from which new members of the office could draw information and surrogate experience when future problems arose. In Workshop 2, the final discussion centred on the perceived need for better communication between members of the office and deeper criticism of project proposals in their early stages. In Workshop 3, the final discussion centred on the need for a system of quality control in the office, to ensure that initial intentions were carried through. These perceptions or overviews were no doubt largely the product of local

26

conditions or preoccupations, crystallised perhaps by each
workshop but not only the direct consequence of them.
But although there may have been undercurrents of
concern on these issues latent prior to the workshops
and these may have influenced the way the discussions
developed, the discussions themselves did bring these
issues out into the open and make them amenable to debate.

DISCUSSION

The continuing education programme reported in this
Chapter was not designed in advance as a test of any
particular theory of design method. Its format (the
use of case histories) clearly implied a theory of
design, namely that past experience both of solution
types and of design methods are important factors in
the working of a design office. It also (by the use of
group discussion methods) implied a learning theory, that
design education is a social process in which a critical
exchange of viewpoints is often highly creative. Unfort-
unately, no efforts were made, in advance, to record
happenings in the seminars in such a way that they could
be classified as scientific evidence of the design
methods used or of the educational process which developed.
The theories have been imposed after the event on data
about these events which was collected quite informally.
The categories used have certainly not been rigorously
defined. Suggestions could be made about the design of
future events of this kind which would enable scientific
observation to take place then but what is presented here
must be considered exploratory and speculative.

It is nonetheless of some interest to note the number
of occasions (8 out of 14) on which the seminar discussions did produce some form of critical conflict between
participants and to observe that on a large majority of
these occasions (6 out of 8) new design ideas for solving
the problems concerned did emerge as well. The form of
these discussions (led by the programme participants)
was of course strongly influenced by the form of the
example discussions (led by the programme tutor) at the
beginning of each workshop, but these example discussions
did not themselves result in personal conflict. So one
possible explanation of the emergence of these conflicts
is that they formed a normal part of the bahaviour
participants experienced in their day to day design
practice and that this practice was being explicitly
reproduced in the educational programme.

If this is the case and it is also normal for new
solutions to emerge from such conflicts, then not only
may our ideas about how design actually takes place need
to be revised, but also it is possible that our ideas
about how to arrange educational opportunities in which

professionals (or others) may extend their design skills need to be rethought. In order to encourage active involvement by designers in finding new solutions to apparently intractable conflicts, we may have to arrange for them to expose those conflicts to other designers, then show how a new synthesis can arise out of such emotionally charged situations. The personal motivation which is reported by Powell as a significant factor in the absorption of information relevant to design problem solving may be seen as sometimes generated by inter-personal conflict. An ability to work constructively within such a framework may even be an essential part of what practitioners have to offer to design education. It may be a type of behaviour which promoters of community participation in design should attempt to foster.

Bibliography

Abercrombie, M J and Hunt, S M., 1960-1970 Ten Years
    of Development in a School of Architecture, University
    College School of Environmental Studies, London 1983.
Adams, E., 'Local curriculum development in environmental
    education' in Langdon, R. (Ed) Design Education -
    Proceedings of the Design Education section of the
    Design Policy conference held at the Royal College
    of Arts, The Design Council 1984.
Alexander, C., Notes on the Synthesis of Form, Oxford
    University Press 1964.
Alexander, C., The Oregon Experiment, Oxford University
    Press, 1964.
Archer B L., 'Systematic Method for Designers' in
    Design, April, June, August and November 1963.
Baynes, K and Roberts P., 'Design education - the
    basic issues' in Langdon, R (Ed) ibid.
Broadbent, G., 'The Development of Design Methods - A
    Review', in Design Methods and Theories,Vol 13, No. 1,
    pp 41-45. 1979
Cuff, D., 'Negotiating Architecture', in Design Research
    Interactions, Proceeding of the 12th International
    Conference of the Environmental Design Research
    Association, Ames, Iowa, pp. 160-171, 1981.
Fagence, M., Citizen participation in planning, Oxford
    Pergamon Press, 1977.
Gregory, S A., The Design Method, Butterworth, London,
    1966.
Gropius, W., The New Architecture and the Bauhaus (P Morton
    Shand trans.) Faber and Faber, London 1965.
Habraken, N. Supports: an alternative to mass housing,
    (trans. B. Valkenburg), Architectural Press, London
    1972.

Heath, T., Method in architecture, Wiley, Chichester, 1984.

Jones, J C., Design Methods. Seeds of Human Future, Wiley, London, 1970.

Piaget, J and Inhelder, B., The Child's Conception of Space (Trans F J Langdon and J L Lunzer), Routledge and Kegan Paul, London, 1956.

Powell, J A 'Technology Transfer - The Design Information Drip' in Proceedings of the Conference on People and Physical Environmental Research, Ministry of Works and Development, Wellington, New Zealand, 1983.

Rittel, H., 'Systems Analysis of the "First and Second Generations" in Laconte, P, Gibson, J, and Rapoport, A, 'Human and Energy Factors' in Urban Planning: A Systems Approach, Nijhoff, The Hague, 1982.

Rossi, A., The Architecture of the City (American Edition) M.I.T. Press, Cambridge (Mass.), 1982.

Sanoff, H, Weber, H, Honn, S, Wells, R, Anderson A, 'Participatory Design, Priorities for Environmental Design Research', Proceedings of the 8th Environmental Design Research Association Conference, available from EDRA, Washington D.C.

Schon, D., The Reflective Practitioner, Temple Smith, London 1983.

Symes, M, and Marmot, A 'Introducing the Architectural Case Problem' in Architectural Education 3, RIBA Magazines, London, 1983, pp 99-107.

Symes, M, 'Learning from Design' in Powell, J and Lear, S (Eds.), Designing for Building Utilisation, Spon, London, 1984.

Tafuri, M, Architecture and Utopia: Design and Capitalist Development, M.I.T. Press, Cambridge (Mass.) 1976.

Topalian, A., The Management of Design Projects, Associated Business Press, London, 1980.

Turner, J F C., Housing by People - Towards Autonomy in Building Environments, Marion Boyars, London 1976.

Wise, D., 'Informing Design Decisions', in Brandon P, and Powell, J (Eds)., Quality and Profit in Building Design, Spon, London, 1984.

ACKNOWLEDGEMENTS

An earlier version of this paper was presented to the 8th Conference of the IAPS (International Association for the Study of People and their Physical Surroundings) at the Hochschule fur die Kunste, Berlin in 1984. The author would like to express his gratitude to those who took part in the discussion which followed for their valuable comments.

The author also wishes to thank the Government Architect of New Zealand and his staff for the opportunity to carry out the continuing education programme discussed in this Chapter and for their support and encouragment. Naturally the opinions and conclusions reported here are the author's own and should not be interpreted as an official evaluation of the programme or as a critique of any aspect of government policy.

Table 1

Case Problem Seminars in Workshop 1 (9 Participants)

Problem	Type of Discussion	Solutions Emerging in the Discussion
'Fins on the Beehive'	Systematic/Critical	
Centres on a problem of tolerance on pre-cast elements. Whose responsibility is it to ensure accuracy?	A great amount of detailed information was called for during consideration of key decisions. Debate became quite heated and led to conflicts in the group.	None
'Evaluating the Map Centre'	Systematic/Humanistic	
Conflict between two roles for the architect, one advising client on need for a building, the other designing it.	Straight description of events followed by revelation of new information in response to questions.	New options introduced.
'The Government Building'	Humanistic/Critical	
Rehabilitation project where users of the building have to continue working there.	Lively debate centred on a role-playing exercise.	Proposal to reorganise contracts emerged.
'The Ship's Store'	Humanistic/Typological	
The prediction of building costs and evaluation of benefits stemming from alternative designs.	Lively discussion with some role-play attempted. Led to introspection and self-criticism when alternative designs were displayed.	None
'The Last Symphony'	Humanistic/Critical	
Visual questions on ancillary buildings to a power station.	Good drawings were presented but designs shown were strongly criticised.	Design options suggested.

Table 2

Case Problem Seminars in Workshop 2 (12 Participants)

Problem	Type of Discussions	Solutions Emerging in the Discussions
'Post Office Tower" Assessment of alternative site strategies for a mixed-use development.	Systematic/Typological Multiple issues discussed in random sequence. More information drawn out of presenters during discussion	Some tentative, new thinking emerged.
'Design and Build' Site planning around a historic building.	Systematic/Humanistic Lengthy discussion of background history of the case. Role-play helped to clarify issue.	None.
'A Matter of Degree' A simple issue of roof design, raised questions about role of design research.	Systematic/Critical Primarily technical but leading to heated exchanges as the debate progressed.	Alternative aesthetic approach suggested.
'Scott Base' Construction programme disrupted by combination of economic and political circumstances.	Systematic/Critical Lively session involved search for information and debate over issues.	A number of imaginative suggestions made.

Case Problems Seminar in Workshop 3 (16 Participants)

Table 3

Problem	Type of Discussion	Solutions Emerging in the Discussion
'A Tale of Two Offices'	Humanistic/Critical	
Part of the design work is sub-contracted to a second firm where changes are made to the appearance.	Group divided into two to dramatise the issues. Some heated arguments.	Design suggestions made.
'Campus Development'	Humanistic/Typological	
Site planning problems. Conflict between designers and client over use of resources.	Much consideration of precedents and prototypes.	None.
'The Dairy Laboratory'	Systematic/Humanistic	
Redesign at a lower cost or cancel the project already on site.	Detailed implications of each strategy came out clearly. No conclusions reached.	None
'A New Marai'	Humanistic/Critical	
Working with ethnic minority	Interesting discussion of background to design. It emerges that one of the designers is also a member of this minority group.	Innovative design suggestions made.
'Winding Gear'	Systematic/Critical	
Window opening equipment has to be specified but has not been included in the budget.	Witty and well-informed discussion. Some conflicts but no resolution.	None.

34

Figure 1.   A typical Workshop - Setting the Scene.

Figure 2.   An architect presents a problem from his own work.

Figure 3.   The discussion is underway.

3. Participation and community: transcultural perspectives

JOAN SIMON

Community Design Integrating Social-Cultural Aspects into the Basic
Programme. Work on this project was financed by the University of
Guelph Rural Outreach Development Project funded by the Kellog
Foundation and a Part V Research grant from Canada Mortgage and
Housing Corporation. Joan C. Simon and Forster Ndubisi.

ABSTRACT

Although Socio-cultural aspects of the residential environment are as
significant as the biophysical, they are more difficult for planners to
handle. During the 1970's programming techniques for biophysical
inputs increased in sophistication and were integrated into the standard
practice of community design. At the same time there was considerable
discussion of and research on the cultural, social and psychological
aspects of the environment. Despite the institutionalization of
participatory provisions in Canadian planning, the incorporation of
social-cultural considerations into the development of conceptual plans
has remained outside the realm of normal practice. The paper sketches
the significance of socio-cultural factors to the design of communities,
especially for sub-cultural groups, suggests procedures for collecting
this data and illustrates the application of this approach in the
Burwash Natives People Settlement Project.

THE NEED FOR CULTURALLY BASED DESIGN: PROJECT CONTEXT

The economic and social situation of Native Canadians is in many ways
analogous to those found in third-world countries. Dispersed settlement in rural and remote areas has made delivery of housing and site
services to urban Canadian standards problematic.

Approximately 300,000 Amerindians live in Canada. They include ten different language groups and 58 dialects and represent 573 bands. Except in the far north, Indian bands live on reserve lands set aside by treaty for their exclusive use. In 1979, there were 2,242 separate parcels of land with a total area of 10,021 square miles. Over 30% of the native population lives outside the reserves. (DIAN).

The federal government's responsibilities for Native Canadians are handled by the Ministry of Indian Affairs and Northern Development. (DIAN). With the growth of the welfare state in the 1950's and 1960's, DIAN expanded its involvement in the lives of Native-Canadians. By the early 1960's senior administrators were perceiving Indian problems as poverty problems, and as part of its "war on poverty", the government instigated a number of development programs. Like most development agencies at the time, DIAN was convinced that modernization was inevitable, irreversible and highly beneficial. Modernization included physical improvements in living conditions as well as attempts to provide the same social services which were available to all other Canadians. The culture of the native populations was also seen as a barrier to modernization. Given this context, it is not surprising. that a policy was adopted of relocating bands onto new "town-sites" to improve access to services (Simon et al, 1984).

Euro-Canadian public servants defined native community needs. The findings of Justice Thomas Berger in his seminal inquiry into the Mackenzie Valley pipeline are applicable to the community development program nationwide.

"White society dictated the places and terms of exchange, took care to ensure that its rituals (social as well as religious and political) took precedence in any contact between native and white" (Berger, 1977, p. 86).

"Because so few were able to find out how native people really lived or what they wanted, much less to heed what they said, many government programs were conceived and implemented in error" (Berger, 1977, p. 88).

A 1980 survey of Native Conditions found that Indian living conditions had improved in terms of the quality and availability of housing and the number of dwellings with water and sewage. Also more Amerindians had gained access to health care, welfare and social services. However, during the same period of time there had been an alarming increase in alcohol abuse, welfare dependency, juvenile delinquency and violent death rates on reserves (DIAN).

Many factors have contributed to the tragic conditions of Canada's Native Peoples. There is some evidence that the design of new Native communities which were based on Euro-Canadian attitudes and values has played a significant role in the increasing social pathology (Shkilnyk, 1981; Simon et al, 1984). High on the list of Native Canadian's complaints is the lack of respect given in government programs to their traditions, their definition of their needs and to supporting their way of life.

In 1981 DIAN attempted to increase band control over the planning process by introducing comprehensive community planning and allocating funds for the hiring of planning consultants. Guidelines issued to consultants state that: "Special consideration must be given to cultural, social and traditional characteristics which differentiate the community requirements from those of non-Indians." (Rogers, 1981)

The guidelines contain detailed outlines in explaining how to collect and address a broad range of physical and economic planning inputs but similar instructions pertaining to socio-cultural data was conspicuously absent. The problem is compounded by the dirth of professional planners who have any understanding of reserve life or the intricacies of Indian culture (Wolfe and Lindley, 1983).

The theory regarding socio-cultural dimensions of the physical environment needs to be clarified for planners and appropriate methodologies and techniques developed to facilitate the collection and use of appropriate data.

TEST CASE: THE BURWASH SETTLEMENT PROJECT

The opportunity to test a socio-cultural planning approach in an applied situation arose when the University of Guelph was asked by the Burwash Native Peoples Project to assist them in planning a new settlement. The Burwash Native Peoples Project was created by natives and non-natives from Sudbury, Ontario, Canada, who were convinced that ways must be found to deal with the appalling level of social breakdown in native communities. Burwash was conceived of as a community where those who have had troubles with alcohol, drugs or the penal system could be healed by a program that stresses their cultural traditions.

They had obtained a lease on 9,000 acres of land and had rejected a conceptual plan prepared by a professional planning consultant. (Fig. 1). The plan demonstrated the imposition of middle-class North American cultural values and institutional standards. For example, houses were arranged on regular lots along the sort of street layout common to small Ontario subdivisions without regard to native concepts of privacy and territoriality. Recreation is an integral part of Indian living patterns, not a discrete activity carried out in a specific recreational time-place setting. Yet the plan designates "Beaching Activities" with cottages and recreational trailer sites.

The Burwash Project members believe that their traditional environmental values are central to the growth and development of the individual native person and to the maintenance of the culture of the group. Their value system is deeply concerned with how man dwells and his rootedness in the earth. They were seeking a community design which respected their socio-cultural values.

THE THEORETICAL UNDERPINNINGS OF THE SOCIO-CULTURAL PLANNING APPROACH

Environment behavior literature was scoured for theoretical under-pinnings for a socio-cultural planning approach. Kevin Lynch's "good settlement concept" expressed the characteristics the Burwash Group were seeking. A good settlement, according to Lynch is one which is "meaningful to its inhabitants. Meaning derives from elements linked to events and places in a coherent mental representation of time and space." Such a representation "can be connected with the non-spatial

concepts and values. This is the join between the form of the environment and human processes of perception and cognition" (Lynch, 1982
p. 131).

Canter's visualization of placedness forming when actions, conceptions
and physical attributes are inter-related gave form to the concept and
proved helpful in establishing linkages with planning practice.

Fig. 1

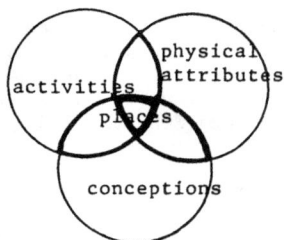

A visual metaphor for the Nature of Places. (Canter, 1977 p. 158.)

Canter's model also married well with the literature addressing
cross-cultural environmental research. Without entering into the
perplexing web of definitions of culture which are apt to ensnare
the researcher, the often used Kroeber and Kluckhorn definition was
selected as being the most helpful.

> Culture consists of patterns, explicit and implicit, of and for
> behavior acquired and transmitted by symbols, constituting the
> distinctive achievements of human groups, including their embodi-
> ments in artifacts; the essential core of culture consists of
> traditional (i.e. historically derived and selected ideas and
> especially their attached values; culture systems may on one hand,
> be considered as products of action, on the other as conditioning
> elements of further action." (Kroeber & Kluckhorn, 1952 p. 180).

The anthropoligists "actions" correspond well with Canters'
"activities" and reinforces the need not to impose the designers'
activity framework on the clients' actions.

Canters' discussion of the physical attributes component is given
solely in terms of man-made elements. This assumption that meaning is
imposed upon the natural landscape through the acts of human designers
is such a fundamental part of the practice of planning, architecture
and landscape architecture that it is usually not noticed. Amerindians
attach values to elements in the natural environment which most North
American/European designers do not recognize as being important.

Canters' "conceptions", which is similar to Relph's "meaning" was
expanded to include the mythical aspects of human experience to bring
into the designers' consciousness the need to attune to "essential core
of the culture." This is the most problematic aspect of the rotation
of theory into practice. It is recognized that today architects and
planners often have cultural backgrounds different from that of their
clients. If the designer is working with a client who speaks a
different language, the need for translation is not questioned.
Cultural "translation" of conceptions and meanings is also necessary.

39

Placedness was limited to the core of the visual metaphor.

Individuals within a subculture possess both private (Jalonde, 1968) and public knowledge which collectively form their image of reality (including the environment). This image influences the way a subculture satisfies its needs, and the satisfaction of needs are reflected in the nature of their activity (Boulding, 1956).

Cultural knowledge is ordered into experiential categories (Rapoport, 1969; Spradley, 1972; Goodenough, 1961). "Place" occurs when there is a clear and consistent fit between the physical and experiential realms. When there is congruence between the experiential categories and the physical environment, the environment is meaningful to the members of the subculture (Norberg-Schultz, 1968).

THE PARTICIPATORY/PHENOMENOLOGICAL APPROACH

Although participatory planning is recommended by DINA, frequently this amounts to little more than contemporary professional rituals with the consultants dictating "the places and terms of exchange".

Because most planners attempt to maintain the myth that planning is politically neutral, they have been reluctant to acknowledge the fundamental divisions in society arising from differences in values and life experiences (Brownstone, 1984). Socio-cultural planning requires that these divisions be acknowledged and that the client becomes the cultural consultant.

The central values are of prime importance in relating the way of life to the environment. The knowledge of those values unique to a subculture must be made explicit in a form useful for environmental decision-making. However, the issues that are inherent in these values are abstract and do not readily lend themselves to rational, functional, planning methodology. Therefore, a phenomenological approach was devised in which the process (techniques) are linked to the product (design values).

The approach involves structuring the information into three typological categories. Questions of placedness and environmental quality are explored from, in category one, the cultural groups historic conception and activities, as well as the physical attributes of the spaces they lived in and incorporated into their myths; moving to current perceptions of the ideal environment and then relating those perceptions to a specific site. Continual referencing between information categories needs to occur. The process helps to make explicit, to both the consultant and client, the spatial behaviors which distinguish the culture.

Category one provides background information concerning the evaluation and cultural development of the group focusing on information about their way of life and especially those aspects of their historic lifestyles which were physically manifested in their past environments. Motify in myths and folklore should be included because they provide a symbolic expression of historical values. Environmental values may be discerned within myths which should be perpetuated in environmental form.

40

The success and effectiveness of the documentation in this category
is a function of the homogeneity of the specific sub-cultural group
(Lynch, 1972). Information should be gathered from both primary and
secondary sources. Secondary sources include written histories, records
and archival material. Primary source interviews with group members are
best undertaken after at least a partial review of secondary sources.

University of Toronto and Royal Ontario Museum anthropologists also
specialize in the study of historical and contemporary Amerindians
were contacted. They directed us to the most appropriate and useful
secondary data sources including books, articles, early travelers
descriptions, maps, drawings and photographs. We were the first people
involved with contemporary planning issues to have asked for their
assistance and they were intrigued by the project.

The following brief example illustrates the use of a piece of Category
one information. One sub-theme emerging from both the historical and
mythological information was that settlements were located on land
"where food grows on water". Discussion with elders confirmed that this
is a theme which persists today. It is an environmental manifestation
of the Ojibway symbolism of water as the "giver of life". The design
response was to recognize that settlements should be near water,
preferably accessible to stands of wild rice. The water's edge must be
accessible to all community members.

Category two structures information pertaining to the cultural definition of environmental quality as expressed through the spatial images
of the "ideal" environment of the members of the group (Jung, 1964;
Lynch, 1972, 1981; Dubos, 1961). Concepts of environmental quality
provide the contemporary linkage between central values and environmental form.

This information category deals with cognitive images, and the
mapping techniques developed by Kevin Lynch (1960) are useful in
gathering data. Images of both actual and imagined ideal environments
were recorded. A series of cognitive maps were drawn by members of the
client group.

Seven men and five women volunteered to meet individually with a
member of the planning team. All of them were familiar with the general
site and the rejected masterplan and they had participated in the
groups' discussions concerning their aspirations for the new community.
The two part interview began with an exploration of their ideas
pertaining to an ideal community and then moved to considering the site
of the proposed community.

Initially each subject was given a large piece of paper with a choice
of pens and pencils and asked to draw their ideal community, identifying
all the activities and land uses they considered to be important. The
reasons for the selection of each feature were explored and then they
were asked to arrange them into a hierarchy that reflected the features'
importance to them. If the volunteers were not comfortable with paper
and pencil, coloured plasticine and a board were substituted and
features and hierarchy lists recorded by the planner. The plasticine
maps were photographed. The second stage of the interview was less

abstract and explored their ideas regarding an ideal community on the intended site. A site model showing the basic landforms was provided and this information was supplemented by photographs of a larger number of locations on the site. Photograph locations were keyed site model positions. The volunteers were asked to use plasticine of different colours to represent features they wanted to see in the new community and to position these features in the best possible location on the actual site. They were asked to explain the reasons for the choices and reference was made back to their ideal community plans. The models were photographically recorded.

Each set of maps was then abstracted to compare the similarities and differences into the features selected by the subjects and between their ideal and site specific plans. The reasons for the relationships between activities and landforms were used to tap their concepts of environmental quality.

The maps provided us with the list of activities and land uses which were essential in the development of an Ojibway community, as well as insight into the organization of space and infrastructure. The activities and land uses identified by this means varied considerably from those used in the consultants' master plan.

Three levels of activities and land uses were identified based on the frequency of their occurance and their significance in both sets of plans. The most important level included individual dwelling for the member families; a community centre with associated open space for cultural gatherings; a school as a place for learning for both children and interested adults; ceremonial lodges for spiritual enrichment; workshop areas for agriculture including wild rice cultivation, animal husbandry and aquaculture; bush areas for hunting and trapping; fishing areas; dancing areas; pedestrian trails.

The second most important group of features included communal and private gardens for vegetable production; an emergency health care station; the summer camp where town children could learn traditional; fish hatcheries; tree nurseries; greenhouses; and space for traditional social activities such as archery, hoop and stick, now snake and snow shoeing.

Small business developments, such as sawmill, woodlot reserves, smoke and icehouses, root cellars and area for skiing, skating, swimming and picnicing were third level activities.

Comparing the features with the master plan by the consultant one can identify some features which appear similar: houses, a school, nurses' station, community hall and band office. However when the analysis is extended to the relationship between elements and the basic organization of land uses fundamental disparities become more evident.

Important similarities in the patterns of activities and land uses could be seen in all the maps except those done by a volunteer who we learned had spent most of his life in a large metropolitan area and had only a fragmentary understanding of the Ojibway traditions.

In analyzing the cognitive maps for relationship we used a concept of "solids" and "voids" to help us understand that the spaces between functional areas were highly significant. Voids could be land, water or air. Air denoted viewing right of ways and acoustic separations. Thus voids had characteristics which had to be respected in the same way as those associated with "solids". For example, the consultants plan showed houses, eg. "solids" on lots. The "void" we identified was a minimum spacing between houses which had to be great enough to ensure acoustic privacy from loud voices.

Category three information relates concepts of environmental quality to the particular site and planning project. Information is collected from the client regarding their experiences of the site; features that are beautiful, best places to live, significant features etc. People and place were examined together because the components of a site: the land, water, plants, and animals have significant traditional, symbolic and psychological meanings specific to the cultural group. One purpose of this category of information is to heighten the professional's awareness about how others value, perceive and use their environment. It gives the professional/researcher the capacity to recognize and incorporate into the design potential "places" on the site that may evoke different types of reactions, "places" which induce or inhibit different behavioral tendencies.

Collecting this data involved documenting the peoples' experience of place on site. Volunteers were taken to the site for "environmental walks". Since they had some knowledge of the site, they determined where they entered the area and the direction moved through it. Because the tape recorder proved to inhibit comments, the planner/ researcher recorded notes. Comments about specific features were keyed to small scale site plans and significant physical attributes were photographed. Volunteers were asked to express their feelings and preferences for sites for the activities previously identified. Probing questions were used to clarify the physical attributes of the site which would support or inhibit these activities.

Significant issues identified were land ethics, location of core settlement, scenic beauty, high places and ecosystem relationships between man and nature. Considerations for the location of the core settlement included traditional concerns such as proximity to water as well as contemporary access to highways. Scenic beauty was related to the individual state of mind but also involved an index of the "naturalness" of the environment. High places were natural focal points affording different types of views and providing orientation. Settlements were perceived as a part of an ecological system. Man is only a small part of a larger system.

The structure of the information collection reflects a circular flow of time. Category one deals with the lived experiences and values gathered through time, and their implication for the changing present and future. Category two deals with the present values and images projecting into the future by relating to an ideal environment. Category three links the past and future images in a lived experience of the present.

This documentation procedure established a participatory design process. The client group were actively involved in the data collection, interpretation and analysis. An important role reversal occurred: the clients were the experts, their "terms of exchange" took precedence. As a result, when the planner offered technical advice about their planning issues, his views were more readily incorporated into the group's deliberations.

MASTER PLAN DEVELOPMENT: INTEGRATION OF SOCIO-CULTURAL FACTORS

Design values were arrived at by a synthesizing of the responses from all categories of information. The design values were organized into five subjects.

1. Philosophical basis.

The land ethics of the Ojibways are based on a relationship with the environment and they lie at the core of their central values. In planning and design terms, this implies an ecological approach in which man-made elements and the natural environment are mutually supportive.

2. Choices for settlement location.

The following factors guided the site selection: spiritual and cultural beliefs surrounding the areas and geography; the presence of bodies of water that can support aquatic life (i.e. not polluted); lands with a diversity of landscape forms including marshes; variety of vegetation and diversity of wildlife for hunting and trapping. Availability of pine, birch and cedar trees; availability of berries; access to adjacent settlements and major highways.

3. Organization of settlement in terms of space and infrastructure.

The circular relationship of elements in the primary structure was a dominant design theme. Four levels of territorial organizations emerged: dwelling units, groups of dwelling units, development islands, the settlement.

The need for small sized settlements (140-250 dwellings, 575-1,000 people) was documented. This related to historic size of community and system of government. A low density was imperative. Somewhat "higher" densities at the middle, near the symbolic centre, were tolerable. A primary centre containing major communal facilities emerged, supported by small centres at strategic points to create a network type of organization. The centre included the common land shared by members. The main center required visual and physical proximity to water. Edges of spaces should be strongly defined by natural elements, not buildings.

4. Function elements.

The functional elements identified were: residential, agricultural, commercial, industrial, communal and quasi-recreational. Only the quasi-recreational will be touched upon in this paper to highlight the difference between the phenomenological solution and the traditional approach.

Recreation within the Ojibway society is an integral part of everyday life. Based on the reciprocal relationship between people and their environment, it closely mirrors the true definition: the refreshment of mind and body. Hence, "recreational" activities express the connection of "mother earth". No areas within the phenomenological plan are designated as "parks", "beaches", "cottages", etc. Specific landforms, rock configurations, groups of trees, parts of a stream embodying "meanings" for the members of the settlement will be protected because these places help to reinforce the connection with "mother earth".

Parks are not a satisfactory way of preserving open space for this cultural group because they are distinguished from natural areas by such human manipulation of the environment as grading, planting, grass cutting, pruning, paths, special equipment and clearly defined boundaries. The client wanted life surrounded by nature, not to confine it to reservations and to respect the land by not manipulating it.

5. Ecological character.

All the living and non-living substances within the settlement interact to produce a cyclical exchange, a concept central to the Ojibway world view. This creates an ecological balance. Traditional values have been modified by technology to a certain degree, but chemicals for pest control will be kept to a minimum and sewage systems will be designed to create compost.

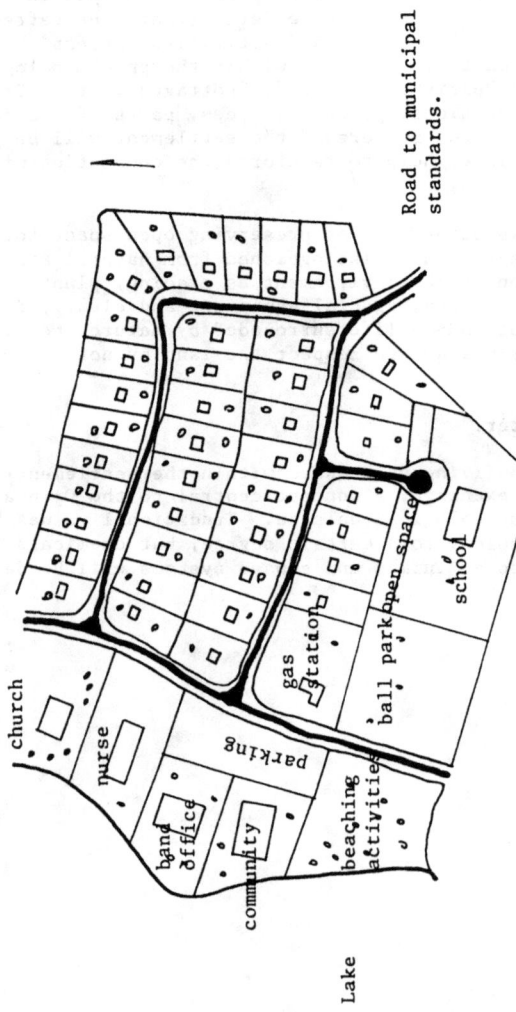

Fig. 2 Consultants Plan showing residential layout with piped water and sewage.

church

nurse

band office

community

Lake

beaching activities

parking

gas station

ball park open space

school

Road to municipal standards.

houses

central open space

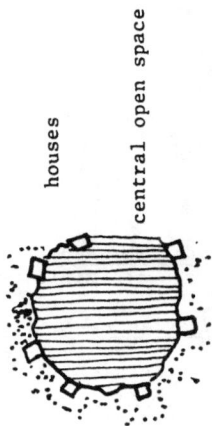

Fig. 3A Residential Cluster

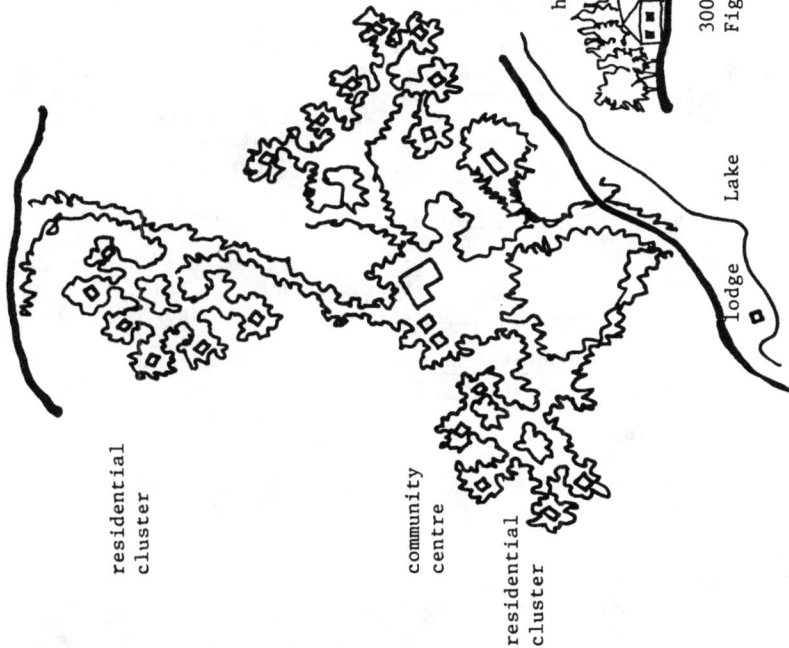

residential
cluster

house

house

house

300 metres minimum natural area
Fig. 3B Siting Principles, Houses

lodge

Lake

residential
cluster

community
centre

residential
cluster

Fig. 3 Culturally based plan without conventional site servicing.

47

Bibliography

Bechiel, R. (1977). Enclosing Behavior. Stroudsberg, PA: Dowden,
Hutchinson and Ross.

Berger, Mr. Justice Thomas R. (1977). Northern Homeland: The Report
of the MacKenzie Valley Pipeline Inquiry Volume 1. Ottawa: Ministry
of Supply and Services.

Boulding, K. (1956). The Image: Knowledge in Life and Science. Ann
Arbor: University of Michigan Press.

Brownstone, Meyer. (1984). "The Political Economy of Participation"
p. 255-274 in Citizen Participation in Library Decision Making: The
Toronto Experience edited by John Marshall. Halifax: School of
Library Science, Dalhousie.

Canter, David. (1977). The Psychology of Place. London: The
Architectural Press Ltd.

Department of Indian Affairs and Northern Development. (1980). Indian
On Reserve Housing Program: Discussion Paper. Ottawa: Department
of Indian Affairs and Northern Development.

Dubos, R. (1961). So Human an Animal. New York: Scribner.

Goodenough, W. (1972). "An Exploration in Cultural Anthropology" in
Spradley, J. (ed.). Culture and Cognition. San Francisco: Chandler
Publishing Co.

Jolande, J. (1942). The Psychology of C.C. Jung. London: Routledge
Kegan Paul Ltd.

Lynch, K. (1960). The Image of the City. Cambridge, MA: MIT Press.

Lynch, K. (1972). Site Planning. Cambridge, MA: MIT Press.

Lynch, K. (1981). A Theory of Good City Form. Cambridge, MA: MIT
Press.

Ndubisi, F. (1982). Community Planning for North Amerindian
Subcultures: A Phenomenological Approach. University of Guelph,
Master's Thesis (unpublished).

Norberg-Schultz (1965). Intentions in Architecture. Cambridge, MA:
MIT Press.

Roger, E. (1981). Physical Planning Guidelines for the Native
Community: Report. Ottawa: Department of Indian and Northern
Affairs.

Rapoport, Amos (1969). House, Form and Culture. New Jersey:
Foundations of Cultural Geography Series, Prentice Hall Inc.

Shkilnyk, Anastasia Maria (1981). Government Indian Policy and Its
Impact on Community Life: A Case Study of the Relocation of the
Grassy Narrows Band. Ottawa: For Mr. K. Goodwin, Assistant Deputy
Minister of the Indian Program, Department of Indian Affairs and
Northern Development.

Simon, J., R.R. Forster, T. Alcose, E.A. Brabec, F. Ndubisi (1984).
Culturally Sensitive Approach to Planning and Design With Native
Canadians. Ottawa: Canada Mortgage and Housing Corporation.
Spradley, J. (1972). "Foundations of Cultural Knowledge" in Culture
and Cognition. San Francisco: Chandler Publishing Co.
Wolfe, J. and Stephen Lindley. (1983). "Comprehensive Community
Planning with Canada's First Nation's: Observations on Theory,
Policy and Practice." Paper presented at the 6th Annual Applied
Geography Conference. Toronto.

4. Participatory planning and design in intercultural and international practice

DAVID STEA

ABSTRACT

When clients and users are separate individuals - which is typically
the case in much foreign work as well as in many domestic projects -
participation of the users in early stages of design decision-making is
particularly important. This chapter contends that participation,
which was so popular during the early 1970's, has fallen out of favor
not because participation itself is "wrong", but because it was pursued
in the wrong ways.

Designers trained in the Western tradition are not well-equipped to
understand the needs of client/user groups in cultures markedly
different from their own. Different ways of understanding the nature
of community, distinct patterns of decision-making, and differing
values concerning the built environment, when combined with language
barriers, make communication very difficult.

A framework for a theory of participation is proposed, which suggests
that both communication and the representation of design ideas are
interlocked, and that both must be altered to make the participation
process useful and rewarding to both designers/planners and the
potential users of the built environment. Examples are presented of
the applications of "environmental modelling" to both building design
and site planning with diverse cultural groups in several countries,
indicating that alternative participation processes must invoke mutual
learning and cultural synthesis as rewarding experiences for both
parties involved.

FOREWORDS

Bruce Goff had designed a residence for a wealthy Texan, and invited the late Ludwig Mies Van der Rohe to view the product. Mies admired it immensely. "What wonderful space," he said and, turning to the Texan, "do you know what wonderful space you have here?"

"Sure," replied the Texan, "we got lots of room." (Callister, 1963)

* * * * *

An Eskimo villager once told me that he did not attend an important public hearing being held in his area because he " .. didn't know enough to ask a good question." Citizens are not going to voluntarily go out of their way to appear stupid, ignorant, or weak. Under these circumstances, non-attendance becomes a rational, even honorable act. It is not a manifestation of apathy or lethargy. (Kennedy, 1980, pp. 8-9)

The first of the above quotations is about communication, the second about participation. In a very real sense these are interrelated, especially in designing with Third World people, who share neither language, nor culture, nor socio-economic status with Western elites. The process of communication between members of the underdeveloped and overdeveloped parts of the world involves bridging all of the above gaps. Obtaining participation requires simulation as well.

PARTICIPATION THROUGH SIMULATION

All design communication involves simulation of one sort or another: verbal or visual, static or dynamic, in real time or condensed time. Architectural lectures and physical models are as much simulations as computer models and games. Both Appleyard (1977) and McKechnie (1977) have provided typologies of simulations. The two are amalgamated in Table 1A, which presents illustrations of the four types of simulations represented.

Table 1B divides dynamic simulations still further, into "participatory" and "non-participatory," and introduces the approach to participatory design called "environmental modelling," discussed later in this chapter, as a technique of dynamic/perceptual simulation. Certain simulations are intended primarily to communicate between people of like professional backgrounds and similar training, leading to identical systems of cognitive representation (in a psychological sense). Architectural "boards", along with elegantly executed drawings (plans and elevations for example) facilitate communication in a very particular symbolic language, shared primarily by architects.

In designing residences for the elite, there may be problems of communication, but not of participation: the client is the same person as the user, and face-to-face discussions, negotiations, dinners, and other activities between architect and client proceed over months, and even over years. Participation is only an issue when the client and users are different people, as in governmentally-sponsored public housing (where the government, or its housing agency, is the client, and the user, prior to building occupancy, is unknown). In this case, the client is usually represented in direct negotiations with the designer(s), and the users not at all. How to "involve" the latter is the fundamental issue we have come to call participation; whether to involve the user is a fundamental architectural dilemma of our time. Some argue that the architect, as a well-trained expert, in fact knows best what the users need, that they (the users) lack sufficient

TABLE 1A

A TYPOLOGY OF ENVIRONMENTAL SIMULATIONS
(MODIFIED FROM McKECHNIE, (1977)

CLASS OF SIMULATION

	PERCEPTUAL (Experiential, Concrete)	CONCEPTUAL (Abstract)
STATIC	Sketches Photographs Drawings (Perspectives, Axonometrics	Maps Floor Plans Some Mathematical Models
INFORMATION PROVIDED		
DYNAMIC	"Berkeley Simulator" 3	On-line Computer Simulation

TABLE 1B

PARTICIPATORY AND NON-PARTICIPATORY SIMULATION

	PERCEPTUAL	CONCEPTUAL
NON-PARTICIPATORY	"Berkeley Simulator" 3 Public Hearing	On-line Digital Computer Simulation
PARTICIPATORY DYNAMIC	Environmental Modelling	Interactive Graphic Computer Simulation

52

imagination to comprehend the bold leaps that constitute truly
innovative design: in this view, users participate best by just
appreciating what they get. Others argue that it is necessary to ask
the users what they want, and that the answers will tell them - the
architects - what to provide.

In international practice, both may be wrong.

BABIES AND BATHWATER

A group of us landscape architects were to work with a small
community on a playground project. So we went to them and said
"what do you want?" and they said, "well, what have you got? So we
went back and worked up some drawings of what we thought they
should do. When we showed them the drawings, they said, "Oh, no,
that's not it at all." So we said "Well what do you want?" and
they said "well, what have you got?" (Kaplan, 1977, p. 221)

The two approaches caricatured at the end of the last section,
according to Kaplan, cast the public " ... in one or more of the
following roles: the 'What do you want' role and the 'isn't it
beautiful' role ... the public is unlikely to provide fruitful answers
to the 'What do you want' question ... the acknowledgement that it is
beautiful is of ourse the consequence of seeing only the final
solution." (Kaplan, 1977, p. 230)

But designers understand solution-oriented approaches better, and
these seem more in line with intuition and the mystique of creativity.
Moreover, participation, as practiced in the late 60's and early 70's,
didn't seem to work very well - or at all, in some cases. So the baby
was thrown out with the bathwater: few questioned whether it was
participation itself, or the specific methods of inducing
participation, that had failed. Thus, exit participation - until the
dawn of the 80's, when the entire question was re-opened:

... if participatory design methods have shortcomings these should
not automatically be leveled at the tenets of public participation,
but primarily at the means currently employed to involve building
users in the architectural design process. (Lawrence, 1981, p.
261)

THE RETURN OF THE REPRESSED

It may be that the need to reconsider participation arose because
designers began to work in situations where not only were the client
and user separated individuals, but where the user was from a very
different group than either client or designer: foreign practice
reintroduced user needs to practitioners who thought that they had that
problem solved. Post-occupancy evaluations (which are attempts to
assess the degree to which buildings, once occupied, "work" as intended
and satisfy relevant user needs - and thus require criteria of
satisfactory function) could not have supplied the answers because the
projects were often without precedent - new developments in newly-
developing areas - so designers turned to pre-occupancy assessment,

which raised the old issues of simulation, communication, and participation. However, the participation models which had worked none-too-well with Anglo-American groups were often even less effective with Third Worlders, and occasionally disastrous when applied to tribal (Fourth World) societies.

PARTICIPATION : AN ALTERNATIVE MODEL AND ALTERNATIVE APPROACHES

An Alternative Model: Cognition and Communication

Kaplan (1977) has attempted to provide a basis for participation by identifying what people, universally, can be expected to be able to do. These are the "intellectual assets of ordinary people":

(1) People have great facility in nonverbal cognition. Many of the tasks and circumstances in which humans appear to be incompetent depend heavily upon verbal facility. Differences in school learning are probably particularly important here; cultural factors too may play a central role ...

(2) People have highly developed and efficient internal models of the environment ... They have compact representations for houses and buildings, streets and sidewalks, grass and trees ...

(3) People have a capacity for involvement, for putting themselves into a hypothetical situation. This "as if" stance is central to the capacity to try something out in the head before trying it out in the world. (Kaplan, 1977, p. 226)

An Alternative Model: Culturally - Sensitive Procedures

The foregoing are "universals." But many aspects of the participation process may be expected to vary with culture. "Westerners", as we have come to be called, are used to certain ways of doing things, and of interacting with each other. We follow instructions, become "test-wise," learn to ask only the right questions and to answer other peoples' questionnaires. We act individually and competitively, accept majority rule (as a normative definition), and think before acting. There are "right ways" and "wrong ways" of doing things; wrong ways are not just errors from which learning takes place, but genuine failures (and often moral failings as well). Words are our dominant symbol system and so skilled are we at manipulating them that they even enable us to avoid learning. Other people have "culture," (in the anthropological sense); we are rational. Whatever the temporary setbacks, things do not just change; they progress. And progress is defined in material terms.

We function in a system dominated by white middle-class modes and all the characteristics and values that such a system nurtures, and have difficulty conceiving of other "realities" (Schaef, 1981). Thus, we tend to accept all of the above not just as assumptions but as givens. In reality they are simply our myths. However - because they fit within these myths - we have accepted certain methods of participation, such as the public hearing and the survey (questionnaire), as "natural". The public hearing, with experts seated on a raised

54

platform, presenting design and planning solutions, and the community seated as audience, prepared to ask the "right" questions, seems a rational form of participation to most of us.

But many Third-World people, and especially tribal (Fourth World) societies, are fundamentally different in their relationship to each other and to the outside world. The opening story about an Eskimo village is indicative of this. Illustrative of these differences, which are differences not just in behavior, but in values, are the following:

(1) material acquistion may not be as important as other aspects of life, e.g. hospitality (Polynesia), proper observance of kinship relations (rural Latin America), religious ties to land (Native American) or geographical knowledge (Australian Aborigine);

(2) maintenance of a sense of community may be more significant than individual achievement;

(3) decision-making may take place in different ways in some societies:

(a) decisions may be reached in a communitarian fashion rather than individually;

(b) decisions may be made in ways other than by majority rule, such as consensus;

(c) egalitarian rather than hierarchical relations may prevail;

(4) ideals of relations to land and land tenure may be decidedly different;

(5) roles and aspects of architecture may be differently conceived (e.g. Rapoport, 1969)

(a) the significant elements of house and settlement may be categorized in ways other than ours;

(b) the dimensions along which things vary may be distinct from ours;

(c) ideas of "what goes with what" are unlikely to be the same;

(d) in summary, the architectural patterns (Alexander et al. 1977) indicative of environment-culture/behavior relations are likely to be different.

(6) finally, the nature of communication, and the understanding of communication about house, settlement, and other aspects of environmental design is likely to be different, as illustrated by the following little tale (Van Oudenallen, 1982):

Some villagers in Latin America were shown examples of houses designed for them, in the traditional architectural mode of plans and elevations. "Que bonito! (how beautiful!)" they all said - so the houses were built and the responsible government officials were astonished to find that, once erected, the people didn't like them at all. Their "Que bonito!" was a response to the drawings alone, and not to what the drawing represented. They liked the paper, felt that the lines were nice and straight, and that it was, in all, quite well drawn.

What we are seeking for international and intercultural design participation, therefore, is both a method of communication and a technique of representation. In Anglo-American-style participation, for example, we try to communicate through the community meeting: experts represent environmental design through graphic and verbal means, and the community through verbal means alone.

With renewed interest in participation in the late 1970's, several alternatives to the "standard" modes were considered and, with some success, applied (e.g. Cashdan et al, 1979; Patricios, 1979; Sanoff, 1979; Smith, 1978; Witzling, 1980). A few (e.g. Baldassari et al. 1980) incorporated input from unconventional user groups, such as children. An emerging emphasis has been new ways of applying an old form of simulation - environmental models (Bentz, 1981; Kaplan, 1977; Lawrence, 1982; Stea, 1980, 1982; Turan, 1980). While Bentz, Kaplan and Stea have used small-scale models, Lawrence has been experimenting with full-scale representations. An examination of these and other experiments in participation suggests that there are three major aspects to the process:

(1) Transduction. "Architects are visual, not verbal," goes the old cliche. But most non-architects are educated to be verbal, not visual. The conventional participation process involves the transduction of visual images in the head of a citizen into verbal form, and the reception of this verbal form by a professional who must transduce this into his/her own mental images, then present a design presumably based on citizen input. Diagrammatically, it looks like this:

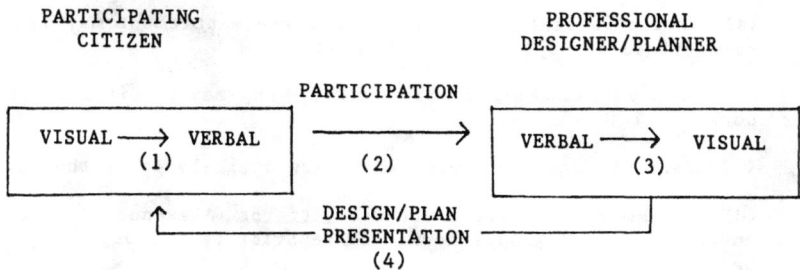

```
    PARTICIPATING                              PROFESSIONAL
      CITIZEN                                 DESIGNER/PLANNER

                          PARTICIPATION

  +---------------------+      ------->    +---------------------+
  | VISUAL ---> VERBAL  |                  | VERBAL ---> VISUAL   |
  |       (1)           |       (2)        |        (3)           |
  +---------------------+                  +---------------------+
              ^                                         |
              +--------------- DESIGN/PLAN -------------+
                            PRESENTATION
                                (4)
```

Figure 1: Simplified flow of transduced information, conventional participation process.

The numbers (1) - (4) represent opportunities for distortion - small wonder, perhaps, that the designer/planner's presentation rarely matches what was originally in the head of the participant: the participant's cognition of his or her environment.

One goal of the participation process should be reduction of the number of steps, the number of opportunities for distortions and misunderstandings, in the process. This is especially true where linguistic, cognitive, and other cultural differences exist between participants and professionals.

(2) Communication. Because it is assumed that environmental designers are visual and the public verbal, it is also assumed that the public should present its ideas, its desires, in verbal form and that the designer should interpret this information visually. There are at least two problems in this. The first is transduction, already introduced. The second is the "what do you want?" "what have you got?" dialogue described earlier. This is not simply a problem of "education." Even a well-respected scientist, asked by an architect what he or she wants in a laboratory, is as likely to reply simply "more space" as to come up with a detailed list of recommendations. "As if" thinking is difficult to do in a vacuum: some "prods" to the imagination are needed early on. "As if" thinking in other words, must be facilitated.

The solution may be to stand the conventional participation process, as it were, "on its head". Instead of having participants respond verbally to graphic design, verbally explained, have designers respond both verbally and graphically to something graphically produced by participants. The result can be mutually educational.

Diagrammically, again:

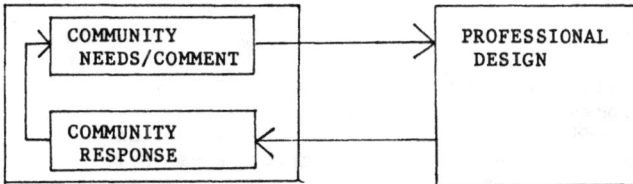

Figure 2A. Communication in Conventional Participation

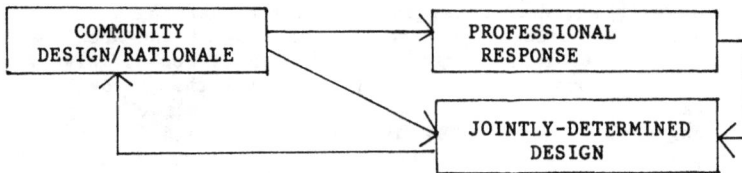

Figure 2B. Communication in an Alternative Mode of Participation: Environmental Modelling.

There are other ways of representing the process, of course. But the central questions remains:

How can the ordinary human achieve the compactness, the access, the capacity for manipulation that are such an asset to the expert in thinking about environmental design? A possible solution follows

rather directly from this abbreviated overview of intellectual
assets. What is required must (1) be in a visual/spatial form, (2)
by composed of familiar elements, and (3) permit an "as if" stance.
(Kaplan, 1977, p. 226)

Kaplan suggests that what is needed is "a highly simplified physical
model of the environment in question (containing) a minimum of
extraneous information." Architectural models are much too detailed to
fit this, and their beauty, their perfection, discourages manipulation
or other direct interaction with the model. In the experimental (but,
alas, not experiental) presentation, for example, of "the Green
Machine", a radical housing concept (Small, 1980), not one of the
hundreds of adults who viewed the models ever touched them, even though
encouraged to do so. It is easy to understand why Patricios (1979)
found architectural models not very useful as aids to participation.

(3) Interaction. An earlier section described some fundamental
cultural differences in ways of doing things between "First Worlders"
and Third Worlders. Evidence indicates that Western, "First World"
formats of participation - ways is which participation happens, or
means used to induce participation - often work badly with Third
Worlders. In some instances, these formats do more harm than good,
exacerbating existing suspicions and distrust. There is a single
caveat here: work within the framework already established by the
culture for conducting meetings and/or exchanging information. It is
bound to be more trusted, and better understood.

ENVIRONMENTAL MODELLING

"Environmental modelling" has its roots in much earlier work on the
development of environmental cognition (Blaut and Stea, 1971, 1974).
But the idea of using models to induce participation in design is not
new. What is new about environmental modelling is the way in which it
has employed models, embedding the process in the traditional contexts
of decision-making in societies of the developing world. Environmental
modelling also emphasizes the use of non-precious, "throw-away"
materials. In planning workshops, people are given a wide variety of
such materials with which to work, including, for planning workshops,
generalized house and building models, outline maps of the area to be
planned, pens, pencils, labels, clay, balsa and bass woods, knives, and
the all-important removable adhesive (which permits the "revokable
decision" detailed later). In housing workshops, cardstock is provided
for walls along with schematized furniture models to aid in established
both personal identification with the model and a sense of scale.

In this process, people are encouraged to work in whatever they feel
are normal decision-making units, to model collectively before
discussing (the opposite of the Western norm). Each subgroup is asked
to present its product, along with the reasons why each "revokable
decision" was made, to the entire group for discussion. Professionals
can be included in the working groups as equal partners - and children,
as well.

In the following sections, five examples of environmental modelling
with Third and Fourth Communities are presented. These are divided

into two environmental scales: "community scale" and "housing scale".
The first deals with physical planning of a substantial area, stressing
the siting of places, the second with buildings and building interiors.

Environmental modelling at the community scale.

1. A project involving a Maori community called Waahi was the
earliest application of the environmental modelling procedure described
in the foregoing to participatory design (Stea, 1981). Our purpose was
to elicit design suggestions for the entire marae (meeting ground) in
the context of a hui (meeting) in which people worked (or, rather,
played - they were asked to enjoy themselves) and reached decisions,
after model manipulation, by consensus.

But our study incorporated an element of "control" (in the research
sense), as well. At a meeting conducted at the University of Waikato,
Pakeha (European) academics and professional planners prepared site
proposals for Waahi Marae, using the same environmental modelling
"toys" and procedures as did the Waahi community. These enabled
comparisons between the two culturally-distinct groups. An outstanding
example of a finding which had never emerged in either traditional
academic research or traditional participatory planning is the
following:

While the professionals were considerate of the physical issues
involved, their divergence from the Waahi Community in the plans they
produced reflected an incomplete understanding of the spatial
attributes of Maori cultural organization. Waahi people referred to
the meeting house as "Taane" and the dining hall as "Miria" (both
ancestral names), and even a meter change in location of either of
these buildings was a matter of serious discussion. The "peopleness"
of such ceremonially important buildings was recognized in these ways
by the Maori -- but not by the Pakeha planners.

The program called for the provision of "pensioner flats" for
retires, and planners tended to place these close to the store, while
Maoris placed the pensioner flats next to the meeting house.
Pensioners will have a grandchild or two living with them, argued the
Waahi residents, who can do whatever shopping is required; but they
must be near the Marae so as to "keep it warm", to more easily attend
to their duties as representatives of the tangata whenua (hosts) in
preparing for the welcoming, feedings, and housing of guests.

Waahi is also the "Queen's Marae", and many Maori participants
desired to see the Maori Queen's house moved to higher ground, to avoid
flood hazard, and effected this change in such a way as to shorten the
already small separation (by Pakeha standards) between the Queen's
house and that of her son. Small separations apparently do matter in
Waahi, but Pakeha professionals, understandably, failed to perceive
this.

Maori are capable of describing their needs most eloquently in verbal
terms; it is a skill encouraged from childhood and well-practiced in
huis, tangis, etc. Pakeha (European) environmental designers, by

contrast, are graphically eloquent. Both groups now have English as a common language, but environmental images expressed verbally by one and graphically by the other do not mesh. Our intent was to bridge this gap by using all possible avenues of communication.

2. Upon our departure from each Maori community we visited, the elders would bid farewell with the statement "Give our love to our American Indian brothers." With this perceived similarity of circumstances in mind, we began to think of applying a similar participation technique to planning problems of Native American communities. The opportuniry was presented in Autumn, 1980, when the Confederated Tribes of the Umatilla, in Northeastern Oregon, asked us to assist in assessing part of the General Plan for the Reservation. Specifically, they were concerned with the future of Mission Valley, adjacent to the City of Pendleton, and had formed a citizens group, made up of tribal members and "Anglo" (white) residents, to deal with the problem. The tribal planners were interesed in the environmental modelling approach, and a workshop was scheduled for December, 1980. In the interim, several environmental modelling workshops had been held with members of the Aprovecho Institute, an appropriate technology/Third World development organization based in Western Oregon. One of these workshops, concerning land-use determination for a rural area of Kings Valley, Oregon, formed the basis of the Umatilla Project.

At Umatilla two predictions (hypotheses) were made. The first was that people would prefer the new, the modern, the progressive, those things most characteristic of "Anglo" society. The second was that participants would express traditional cultural values and a desire to return to the old ways.

What was not predicted but what actually emerged as a result, was a balanced combination of the two. In Umatilla, on the one hand, participants located models representing light industry in the Mission Valley, an expression of the desire for more employment through industrial development. On the other hand, their modelling also indicated strong concern for protection of such culturally-significant landmarks as sweat houses and ceremonial grounds. Finally they amalgamated zoning (a "modern" concept) with "traditional" activities. One important economic activity traditonal to the Umatilla, for example, is root gathering. The continuation of this activity was threatened by possibilities of building development on root-producing lands. In order to protect their traditional activity, then, the Umatilla proposed that a zoning ordinance be enacted to establish "root-gathering zones".

Environmental modelling at the building scale.

3. An environmental modelling workshop was held in Bishop, California, in 1981, with the Paiute-Shoshone people of the Bishop, Big Pine, Independence, and Lone Pine Reservations. Unlike Umatilla, where the area of concern spanned two square miles, the Owens Valley communities were most concerned with house design, and an environmental modelling "kit" was developed accordingly. As at Umatilla, it was predicted that people would prefer either the "modern" or the traditional. The modelling exercise again allowed both to emerge. In

Owens Valley, people expressed a desire for a house that was externally "modern", then, in "traditional" fashion, questioned the need for internal divisions (Ebele, 1981).

4. In late 1981, the Texas Farm Workers requested assistance with the design of housing for elderly members of the community, from graduate architecture and planning students at UCLA. The clients were the Union members, the users a group of retired people without pensions. The site was to be Rangerville, Texas near the Rio Grande and only a few miles from the Mexican border. The community had little money, but building skills in plenty. The challenge was to design structurally-adequate, energy-conserving, culturally-appropriate housing at a material cost of under $5,000/unit.

Environmental modelling, conducted in the context of a *fiesta*, revealed the very different role played by senior citizens in this Mexican border community than in conventional "Anglo" communities. Part of the program involved the design of a community center. The participants in the modelling session sited the community center in the middle of the elderly housing indicating the central role played by older people in the community. "Anglo" students who had not been involved in the participation exercise invariably designed housing for the Rangerville elderly with very small kitchens and a single bedroom: their concept of elderly was of a couple or a single person living alone. The Rangerville workshop, however, produced housing concepts with substantial kitchens and two bedrooms: the elderly, as revealed, were the hubs not just of extended families, but of social and occupational networks spanning the entire community: they are the repository of the community's accumulated wisdom.

5. Yet another workshop, in mid 1982, involved the Lake Tyres aboriginal community in a rural area of Victoria State, Australia. Four years of attempts to get community input in housing decisions had exhaused both the Commonwealth Department of Transportation and Communication and the community in a "what do you want? - what do you have?" exchange. Environmental modelling engaged the community members in developing their own house plans in two days, some of which ingeniously incorporated "socially deviate" (e.g. alcoholic) family members into the home while maintaining their separation from the rest of the household.

There was conventional participation going on at the same time, and the extraordinary contrast in effectiveness between discussion and modelling was thereby revealed. A representative of the Department of Aboriginal Affairs asked the members of the community "steering committee" to "sit down to a meeting". All did so and all but two remained silent. But, when the question of siting arose, an aerial photo and a set of tiny house models were produced. Suddenly, there was a frenzy of activity, as community group members enthusiastically debated the siting of the house models. Ten minutes later, they were asked to sit down to a resumption of the meeting. All sat down, and dutifully fell silent, once again.

Environmental modelling: essential elements

Analyzing what has made environmental modelling "work" as a participatory planning tool reveals certain striking points.

(1) the research technique is also a participatory design/planning tool and the tool also a research technique. Carl Werthman (1980) has pointed out that environmental modelling, as applied to participatory planning/design problems, is potentially a powerful research tool for understanding the cognitive systems of intact communities: it is part of the tradition of "action research" established by Lewin (Marrow, 1969). As a research technique it utilizes a learning tool by which people "naturally" come to know the geographical contexts they inhabit.

(2) The need to liberate participants and the participation process from reliance upon largely verbal techniques is indicated.

(3) Emphasis is placed upon the manipulatability of non-precious objects. Architects, for example, often communicate with each other using very elegantly-executed models of buildings and their immediate surrounds. As indicated earlier, the result of attempting to use the same techniques for communicating with lay people is often failure (Patricios, 1979).

(4) Environmental modelling emphasizes and facilitates the concept of the "revokable decision". In conventional forms of community participation, people are often faced with what they perceive as two alternative courses of action - or, rather, action versus inaction. On the one hand, purely verbal discussin lends itself beautifully to no decisions at all (inaction); alternatively, there is the possibility of reaching a decision, usually by majority vote, which is often ill-understood and to which participants frequently feel (prematurely) committed. Environmental modelling, on the other hand, requires decisions, but decisions which can be changed ("revoked"). Participants must decide upon the form of a model, but this form, in participatory planning, is primarily a vehicle for conveying values. In earlier research, children had been observed to alter their models a number of times during standardized testing periods, as recorded by time-lapse motion-picture photography (Blaut and Stea, 1974). Similarly, even relatively minor impediments to "revocation" can hinder the participation process:

> ... the participants did not want to commit themselves to a design enough to use glue or tape. Because of this they often did not stay together long enough to finish a discussion. The method could be improved by using components that held their form when placed (without adhesive). (Ebele, 1981, p.4)

(5) Environmental modelling is "natural", and fun. "Playing with toys" is natural, as Spencer and Darvizeh (1981) indicate. Adults, for the most part, have forgotten how to play; they have accepted that "play" is what children do and that the closest they can come is "constructive use of leisure time." Many of them must re-learn "fun", because it is through fun, rather than intensely serious focussing upon the solution to a problem, that the most creative and useful results emerge from the environmental modelling process.

SUMMARY AND CONCLUSIONS

The utility of environmental modelling as an _overall process_ for internation and intercultural participatory design has been indicated. It would be useful to summarize, for the sake of argument some of the theoretical and procedural distinctions between the most conventional and most radically different alternatives in participatory design, as done in Table II:

TABLE II
THE EXTREMES OF PARTICIPATION
PARTICIPATON FRAMEWORK

ELEMENT PARTICIPATION	MOST CONVENTIONAL	DESIRED ALTERNATIVE
Information exchange	Verbal (discussion led by ¨experts¨)	Graphic/verbal (discussion led by community)
Development of ideas	Linear	Non-Linear
Communication	Primarily monologic	Primarily dialogic
Direction of exchange	People express needs/ desires; experts plan/design	People plan/design, then indicate what cultural values, needs, and desires underly their plans/designs
Verbal/graphic interface	Translational	Non-Translational
Mode of community input	Primarily isolated individual	Small ¨working groups¨
Overall atmosphere	Competitive and normative (¨Am I doing it _right?_¨)	Cooperative
Decision-making	Primarily amenable to majority rule	Amendable to any form of decision-making (consensus, majority rule, etc.)
Effect on community	Sometimes devisive	Usually uniting
Assessment	Largely passive	Largely active
Facilitators' strategy	Meet with homogeneous groups separately. Anticipate conflict and mediate accordingly.	Bring all groups to a common forum. Open agenda and public posturing increase understanding of complexity.

Genuine participation can give Third World peoples a sense of real power over their destinies: graphicacy (Balchin and Coleman, 1965) can combine with literacy to produce liberation. Ironically, it can in other ways contribute to the liberation of hide-bound professionals, as well. One lacks power to the extent that one is slave to a system, be it an educational system or a planning syste; one has power to the extent that one can participate in understanding, influencing, and changing such systems. The concern is with a type of action referred to by Freire as cultural synthesis:

> In cultural synthesis, the actors who come from "another world" to the world of the people do so not as invader. They do not come to teach or to transmit or to give anything, but rather to learn, with the people, about the people's world (Freire, 1970, p. 181).

NOTES

(1) This chapter is a modified version of a paper presented at the Annual Meeting of the Association of Collegiate Schools of Architecture in Santa Fe, New Mexico, U.S.A., in 1983.

(2) Many of the ideas contained in this paper were developed while the author was a Nell Norris Fellow at the University of Melbourne. The field work was supported in part by grants and other forms of funding from the American Indian Studies Center, the School of Architecture and Urban Planning, and the Committee on International and Comparative Studies at UCLA; the Aprovecho Institute; the Texas Farm Workers Union; and the governments of Australia and New Zealand. Thanks are extended to Harry Van Oudenallen for his helpful suggestions and enthusiastic encouragement.

(3) The "Berkeley Simulator" is a remarkable device constructed at the University of California-Berkeley, which uses "real time" films of models of entire regions to enable potential user to "experience", beforehand, the visual consequences of projected changes to those regions (Appleyard, 1977; McKechnie, 1977).

Bibliography

Alexander, C., Ishikwa, S., and Silverstein, M. (1977) A Pattern Language. Oxford, New York.

Appleyard, D. (1977) "Understanding Professional Media: Issues, Theory, and a Research Agenda" in Altman, A., and Wohlwill, J.F. eds. Human Behavior and Environment: Advances in Theory and Research. Plenum, New York.

Balchin, W.G., and Coleman, A.M. (1965) Graphicacy Should be the Fourth Ace in the Pack. The Times Education Supplement. Nov. 5.

Baldassari, C., Hart, R., and Lockett, M. (1980) "Participation" Special Issue of Childhood City Newsletter. Dec. No. 22.

Bentz, B. (1981) Transition: User Participation in the Design of Housing. Open House. 6(2).

Blaut, J.M., and Stea, D. (1971) Studies of Geographic Learning. Annuls of the Association of American Geographers. June, 61 (2), 387-393.

Blaut, J.M. and Stea, D. (1974) Mapping at the Age of Three. Journal of Geography. 73, 5-9.

Callister, W. (1963) Personal Communication.

Cashdan, L., Fahle, B., Francis, M., Schwartz, S., and Stein, P. (1979) "A Critical Framework for Participatory Approaches to Environmental Change". in Francis, M. (ed.) Participatory Planning and Neighborhood Control. Center for Human Environment, New York.

Darche, B. (1978) "The Social Determinants of Local Participation in Rural Development: A Guatemalan Case Study". Unpublished MS., University of California.

Ebele, C. (1981) Unpublished Report on Owens Valley Participation Workshop, UCLA.

Freire, P. (19/0) Pedagogy of the Oppressed. The Seabury Press, New York.

Kaplan, S. (1977) "Participation in the Design Process: A Cognitive Approach" in Stokols, D. (ed.) Perspectives on Environment and Behavior. Plenum, New York.

Kennedy, T.W. (1980) "Skyriver Process of Communication: An Alternative to the Traditional Public Hearing Process". Unpublished paper presented at conference on "The Social Impacts of Rapid Resource Development on Indigenous Peoples" at Cornell University, Ithaca, New York, August.

Lawrence, R.J. (1982) "Designers Dilema: Participatory Design Methods" in Francescato, G. ed. Knowledge for Design (EDRA 13). EDRA, College Park, MD.

McKechnie, G.E. (1977) "Simulation Techniques in Environmental Psychology" in Stokols, D. ed. Perspectives on Environment and Behavior: Theory, Research, and Applications. Plenum, New York.

Marrow, A.J. (1969) The Practical Theorist: The Life and Work of Kurt Lewin. Basic Books, New York.

Patricios, N.N. (1979) "Users Comprehension and Perceptions of Design Solution Representation". Unpublished paper presented at N.E. Regional Meeting, Association of Collegiate Schools of Architecture, Carnegie-Mellon University.

Rapoport, A. (1969) House Form and Culture. Prentice-Hall, Englewood Cliffs, N.J.

Sanoff, H. (1979) Design Games. Wm. Kaufmann, Los Altos, California.

Schaef, A.W. (1981) Women's Reality. Winston Press, Minneapolis.

Small, G. (1980) Green Machine Feasibility Study. National Endowment of the Arts, Washington, D.C.

Smith, R.W. (1978) "Public participation in Planning and Design: Implications From Theory and Practice for the Design of Participatory Processes". Unpublished Ph.D. dissertation, University of California, Berkeley.

Spencer, C. and Darvizeh, Z. (1981) The Case for Developing a Cognitive Environmental Psychology that does not Underestimate the Abilities of Young Children. Journal of Environmental Psychology, 1, 21-31.

Stea, D. (1980) "Environmental Modelling as Participatory Planning". Fourth World Studies in Planning No 5. UCLA School of Architecture and Urban Planning, Los Angeles.

Stea, D. (1981) "Participatory Planning and Design: The Waahi Marae, in Erickson, Neil (ed.) Environmental Perception and Planning in New Zealand. University of Waikato, Hamilton, N.Z.

Stea, D. (1982) "Cross-Cultural Environmental Modelling" in Baird, J., and Lutkus, A.D. eds. Mind, Child, Architecture. University Press of New England, Hanover, NH.

Stern, J. (ed.) (1974) _Citizen Participation in the Planning Process: A Methodology._ UCLA School of Architecture and Urban Planning, Los Angeles.

Turan, M. (1980) An Interview with David Stea on 3-P's of Environmental Cognition: Perception, Positivism, Participation. _M.E.T.U. Journal of the Faculty of Architecture._ (Fall) _6_(2), 101-128.

Van Oudenallen, H. (1982) _Personal Communication._

Werthman, C. (1980) _Personal Communication._

Witzling, L.P. (1980) "Developing a Vocabulary of Images for Pluralistic Design Processes." _Language in Architecture: Proceedings of the ACSA 68th Annual Meeting._ ACA, Washington, D.C.

5. Active user participation in the housing process

BRUCE BENTZ

SUMMARY

Active user participation in the housing process, for those who choose it, is seen as an opportunity for more user control leading to more desirable housing and more user satisfaction.

User participation in the design process has been achieved through the use of a modelling kit with which inexperienced users have verified chosen house designs or have generated their own designs. Both approaches have been satisfactorily tested. The modelling kit corresponds with a factory produced building system which can be used by people with only modest building experience to construct a house. User involvement in housing construction is directly related to the extent to which manufactured components are used in the design.

This research is progressing in two directions. Internationally, a simplified modelling kit has been tested in Mexico where it served as a common language between users and professionals of two different cultures. Locally, the potential of the building system is being expanded to better realize the characteristics of desirable housing. Both directions are efforts to increase user satisfaction in housing through participation in the housing process.

BACKGROUND

Introduction

Many factors tend to exclude the user from the housing process. Traditional approaches to the provision of housing may discourage involvement. Availability of building sites, local building regulations and other controls may rule out active participation in this process. And, many people who, because of age, economic or social circumstances, or attitude, may choose not to become actively involved in housing decisions which effect them. If, apart from these considerations, a choice is made in favour of participation it is commonly discovered that the prevailing obstacle is a lack of knowledge and skill. User involvement, I believe, can be increased by providing more knowledge and skill and by simplifying both housing design and construction. Self help programs, both locally and abroad, are addressing the first of these areas of concern. This research recommends an approach to user participation in housing through simplifying the design and construction process.

What is the value of user participation in the housing process? Two closely related benefits are more desirable housing and greater user satisfaction. A number of international researchers agree on the importance of these benefits and have come to similar conclusions about them. This group includes Alexander, Boudon, Habraken, Hardie, Lawrence, Olivergren, Rabeneck, Terner, Turner, Warshaw and Wilkinson (see Bibiliography), to name a few. Desirable housing, John Turner (1967) summarises, is comprised of those designs "that can cope with both social obsolescence and technical obsolescence." For many users, satisfaction with housing is directly related to greater user control of the housing product through participation in the housing process. The following discussion of research in user participation provides a rationale for the users' involvement in the housing process to realise more desirable and satisfying housing.

User satisfaction and the architecture

Boudon (1972) emphasizes the importance of user satisfaction in relationship to housing design as discovered by Le Corbusier upon the completion of is 1926 villa settlement at Pessac in France. Despite Corbusier's design and technical innovations, the people for whom the housing was intended refused to live in it. Corbusier's failure to take into account regional attitudes, user needs and expectations generated almost insurmountable resistance to his futuristic design.

Over a fifty year period the inhabitants of Le Corbusier's project have become their own "architects". They have made changes both internally and externally by altering roofs, walls, windows and doors, adding annexes and arches; and repeatedly redesigning interiors. The users have effectively taken possession of their housing by making it their own through ad hoc participation in the housing process.

Contemporary housing only moderately reflects the lessons of Pessac's postfacto participation. The architectural profession and the building industry have been slow to respond to the obvious need for user involvement in the housing process articulated by N. J. Habraken in the early 60's.

An alternative to mass housing

Habraken (1972) condemned mass housing as an inadequate, insensitive solution to the housing problem and proposed what has come to be regarded by many as a viable alternative. As the professionals continue thier search for the perfect design, Habraken says, they make assumptions about human requirements. These assumptions or generalizations inevitably contribute to the failure of thier design.

His proposal attempts to embody what he feels architects have never understood about housing in relationship to human need. According to Habraken:

> ... [housing] is about personal considerations and decisions, the formulation of one's own desires... It concerns the assessing and choosing of innumerable small details, the manifestation of preferences and whims. It concerns the freedo to know better than others, or to do the same as others. It has to do with the care to maintain, or the carelessness about private possessions, with the sudden urge to change as well as the stubborn desire to conserve and keep. The need to give one's personal stamp is as important as the inclination to be unobtrusive... It all has to do with the need for a personal environment where one' can do as one likes; indeed it concerns one of the strongest urges of mandkind: the desire of possession (Habraken 1972).

Habraken criticizes mass housing as rigid and unchanging; unable to respond to renovation, amenities, new technology, new concepts of living or changes in appearance. Mass housing, he insists, has not made use of the potential of industry and technology to achieve the variety in housing capable of meeting the user's needs. Habraken's alternative is based on satisfying individual requirements through participatioin in interior design with infill panels, partitions, fixtures, etc., manufactured by industry and readily available as consumer products in supply centers. The most significant and self-determination. Flexibility, for Habraken, plays a large part in achieving these goals.

> ... when considering housing of the future, we should not try to forecast what will happen, but try to make provision for what cannot be foreseen (Habraken 1972).

Options In Housing

Writing on the subject of Canadian housing, Warshaw (1974) contends that traditional Canadian housing types are similar housing options because of the similarity in their plans and only subtle differences are effected by cost related variables: location, size, finish quality, equipment quality, and the quality and quantity of services. These cost related choices are the only opportunities for participation in a restrictive system. The products produced by the housing industry limit the user in changing his environment to meet his need and increase his cost by imposing standards that are greater than those required. The amount of interaction the occupant may have with his dwelling is only somewhat modified by the type of dwelling occupied (Warshaw, 1974).

Warshaw's Option In Housing includes a number of imperatives which echo Habraken's alternative to mass housing.

Housing must be versitile and must "be considered as a process rather than as a product."

The house can only be relevant to the users' needs if the householder is active in the housing process.

The householder must discard the role of consumer and become a creative and/or labor resource.

The housing process should encourage human (imagination and skills) and social (neighborhood interaction) development.

A new approach to housing will unify and rationalize housing technology, which is inadequate and fragmented.

Through the simplification and dissemination of housing technology information, the user could take a more active part in the construction and maintenance of his own home (Warshaw 1974).

Warshaw expresses an ideal which, if realised, would optimize the quality and potential of the housing process and product for those who choose this alternative.

Internal design of preconstructed shells

The PSSHAK (primary support system and housing assembly kits) project, designed by Hamdi and Wilkinson and built in London in 1972, is virtually a textbook example of Habraken's philosophy and begins to realize some of Warshaw's imperatives. PSSHAK attempted to satisfy an impressive list of objectives:

Increasing the range and quality of choice, satisfying individual user needs, encouraging phased renewal and adaptation, catering with late stage modifications to the design brief, maintaining the benefits of standardization for building and increasing the efficiency of design, production and building operations (PSSHAK brochure).

The primary support system and the housing assembly kits comprise two independent but related systems with which it is possible to vary the size and mix of dwellings and achieve user participation in the design process.

The factory-produced components that make up the assembly kit and determine the internal layout and finishings are independent of the basic structure. This facilitates user design of each dwelling, allows for future change and layout, and modernization independent of other dwellings in the structure. After the shell was completed, the future tenants made design decisions about room functions, size, shape, and relationship with the help of simple instructions, scaled plan views in graphic form, and models.

The project is judged a success by the tenants, the architects and the housing authorities. It stands as an example of the viability of this approach to user design of preconstructed shell interiors.

Brukarplanering (user planning)

Swedish architect Johannes Olivegren (1975) and a group of twelve families have taken the housing design participation process a significant step further. In the short period of two months (also the length of the PSSHAK process), in 1974, decisions on land use, house form and materials, costs, and interior design and finishing resulted in a "small village" at Klostermuren, just outside of Gothenburg. Unlike the participant decisions of PSSHAK, the Klostermuren participants acted both individually and collaboratively. The group decisions were facilitated by employing "procedures for decision making... [and] ...techniques for working toghether co-operatively" (Olivergren 1975).

The design process included: site planning with patterns (after Alexander); choice of site; block model unit design; interrelationship of units; floor plan models; architectural drawings of plans and final details; professional model of development; choice of interior materials and colours; and costing, financing and contrast.

The process of individual and group decision making has produced a neighbourhood of economically built, handsome, single-family dwellings. The houses, in four groups of three, are individual in their design. The construction of the houses (beams and columns) is such that the users are free to change the arrangement of rooms to some extent on both floors to allow for changing needs.

The architect feels the result is a successful "social process which brings people together to new relationships and patterns of living." Interviews with residents indicate the users are well satisfied with the houses they have designed and agree with the architect's appraisal.

Full scale modelling

One of the most convincing committments to the user participation process can be found at the Ecole Polytechnique Federale de Lausanne, Switzerland. In the Laboratory for Architectural Experimentation, Roderick Lawrence and a team of researchers have demonstrated the value of full scale modelling to facilitate housing design decisions. Lawrence (1980) has found the facility provides an understanding of 'real' house space in a way that two dimensional representations and models cannot. In this way user satisfaction with the housing product can be more 'readily' and completely assured. This approach to user modelling approximates 'reality' most closely. Its disadvantages are its cost and its immobility as a modelling tool.

The housing industry's response

Rabeneck, Sheppard and Town's comprehensive review in Architectural Design (11/73 and 2/74) indicates that a number of contemporary building systems in Europe and Britain reflect the philosophical directions of Habraken, Warshaw, and Hamdi and Wilkinson because of their design, flexibility, adaptability and, by extension, opportunity for user participation. Nearly a decade later, our review of 'traditional' housing manufacturers in Japan, Sweden and Canada indicated that housing products generally fall into two categories: those which accommodate some form of participation and those that do not.

The largest companies (two from Japan, two from Sweden and one from Canada), as manufacturers of housing 'packages', made no provision for user participation. Five smaller companies (three from Sweden and two from Canada) did provide opportunities for user imput in the design process by allowing clients to discuss individual requirements with a designer or draughtsman. In this process, standard company designs are used as a starting point to develop designs that reflect user needs.

The early 80's was a time of uncertainty and failure in the housing industry, however, manufacturers who provided for user involvement in the housing process were less affected by the irregularities of the market than were the inflexible companies. Whether through a conscious change or through evolution, the necessity of accommodating the user in the housing process is becoming more apparent. What is also apparent is the industry's inability to understand the value of (or want to provide) flexible/adaptable housing.

Design requirements

Architects, developers and the housing industry are less successful in their attempts to increase user satisfaction when they design and build for the user rather than with the user. User satisfaction encompasses user participation and the application of technical innovation, while complying with building codes and regulations. Both of these concerns correspond directly to a house's ability to cope with social and technical obsolescence.

Social obsolescence is very difficult to predict: social, political, and economic change will create a situation in which an object is no longer valued as most appropriate for its particular function.

Technological obsolescence, as well as relating to the inability of individual objects or subsystems to provide the desired performance, relates to the degree or interdependence between subsystems (Rabeneck 1974).

"The physical changes people might wish to make to their homes are, for practical purposes, finite". But it is a house's ability to facilitate change that makes it a desirable well designed house. There are five identifiable occasions that require changes in the design of a home: 1) to accommodate or to signify a change in family make-up or family activities; 2) to improve the quality of the home with respect to social or market criteria; 3) to alter relationships between rooms; 4) to reallocate functions within existing spaces; and 5) to be different, to conform, to keep up with the Joneses (Rabeneck 1974).

Flexibility, adaptability, add-on and add-in potential, and flexible furnishings and equipment are the five related, often overlapping,

73

characteristics a well designed house should have to make it resistant to social and technological obsolescence and resilient for change.

Flexibility: Flexibility in house design is the "... method of avoiding or delaying obsolescence ..." based on principles of construction and service distribution, rather than on planning and layout. The basic components of flexible schemes are: non-loadbearing internal subdivisions; central heating; "long"- span structure of shell; pre-planned relationship between basic space and services, wet and electrical; choice ...of internal wall infill.

Adaptability: The adaptable approach, in contrast to the flexible, emphasizes planning and layout rather than constructional techniques and services distribution. It is based on carefully considered room sizes, relationship between rooms, slightly generous openings between spaces and the design of spaces which are not function specific.

Add-on: If a house is designed with add-on potential, the cost of land, infrastructure, kitchens, bathrooms, and basic services are borne in the initial cost and the add-on is moderate in price. If adding on is intended it must be pre-planned for though "limited constructional over-provision."

Add-in: "Add-in means the gain of usable floor space without actually increasing the ground area occupied by the house. The most usual form of add-in is lost conversion." Roof pitches and various truss systems are determinants in the feasibility/practicality of conversion.

Furniture, Equipment and Decorations: Flexible, easily movable furniture (including storate systems), equipment, and decorations contribute to and accommodate change.

These items in themselves do not provide a directive for desirable house design, ...yet they are important. Their incorporation into the home environment is made easier by a house design that does not resist them (Rabeneck 1974).

Technology in aid of user involvement

Ian Donald Terner's (1972) proposal for partially industrial intermediate technology indicates the possibility for the industry to "unify and rationalize housing technology" as Warshaw recommends and to achieve Rabeneck's five characteristics for resilient housing. Whereas Habraken's "Alternative" and Warshaw's "Options" are related to mass housing, Terner's approach can be seen as relating to single and multiple family dwellings.

[In] that housing is most clearly seen as a dynamic process rather than a static process - the provision of incrementally additive components is crucial if the intermediate technology is to reflect this process properly. Where change is desired, indeed where it must become a way of life, a construction system must provide for alterations with minimal waste. This implies not only a componentized system, but a system in which

74

components, once joined, remained individually discrete and replaceable. One thing is clear, technology can significantly reduce the skill and experience requirements for participation in the building process. Technology can increase the individual's self-reliance by making construction easier. It can liberate the individual dweller from his present reliance in masons, carpenters, plumbers, and electricians in the same way that it has liberated him from the painter (Terner 1972).

Terner offers three factors in support of small unassembled components: 1) they are considerably less expensive; 2) the building process can occur without substantial credit and accrued savings; and 3) a relatively small number of standardized buiding elements can be combined in a large number of ways to suit a great diversity of individual needs. Terner predicts, that in the near future, industry will significantly help us in our pursuit of autonomy in building through the development of "structural-envelope systems, water-waste systems, power-energy systems, and foundation-footing systems." Until these developments occur, we must actively search for ways to circumvent the prevailing technological and professional mystique, building codes and other obstacles to design, construction and user involvement in the housing process.

Self help in Alberta

The Cooperative Housing Action Program (CHAP) in Alberta is an example of users becoming actively involved in the housing process. A committment to this program means the family unit chooses a house design and manages construction by acting as a general contractor co-ordinating the sub-trades. This economical approach is sometimes enhanced by cooperative buying and by "sweat equity" - contributions of labor by the participants toward framing-in, interior finishing, exterior finishing, exterior finishing, etc. Housing design in CHAP is restricted to modest choices, usually bungalows or bi-levels but despite this limitation, later changes and additions to home can be accommodated through planning. During their general education in the housing process, the participants choose an appropriate design and frequently modify it so that it better meets their needs. Although this approach has worked satisfactorily, it is somewhat remedial in that existing plans must be redesigned. A definite improve would be a design initiated by the user with a modelling kit representing a manufacturer's building system.

Summary

With a view to realizing some of the above stated objectives through developing an approach to the user design and construction of housing, Lisa Peattie, professor of Urban Anthropology at MIT, summarises our intentions:

...because of the desire of people to identify with, to manipulate, to control, to make something their own, they resent having things designed for them, however suitably the product may be designed... What designers ought to be spending their time on is trying to design a product which can be decentralized, which can be marketed, which is some set of components among which people can pick and choose, manipulate,

reassort, do things to, with, or on top of, and all at a price
which they can afford. ...Designing in such a decentralized
manner is the only way we'll be able to allow for decisions
which are relevant to people (Peattie 1973).

USER DESIGN OF HOUSING

Introduction

The modelling kit we have designed is intended to represent an
industrially produced building system. The kit and the building system
are based on the regional vernacular (and internationally accepted)
"shed roof" design. Standard materials, fenestration dimensions and
locally produced long-span floor joists have conditioned the modelling
kit design. The kit makes it possible for the user to design a house
that meets personal requirements, to understnad the implications of
house form, and to perceive "real" house space through a three
dimensional scale representation.

The modelling kit/building system, despite its apparent simplicity,
can generate a substantial repertoire of house designs but our
immediate concern was its viability for the design and construction of
small single family houses. For this reason, the modelling kit was
tested in the Cooperative Housing Action Program (CHAP). This context
also assured the level of user involvement for which the kit had been
deigned.

Modelling kit design

A modelling kit is comprised of three sets of components: blocks,
panelss and furnishing. The blocks (photo 1) are used for modelling
house form and volume, for determining relationships to site and
adjacent buildings, and for making preliminary decisions about the
location of doors and windows. The panels (photo 2) are used for
modelling interior spaces, room/area relationships, movement patterns,
and locating doors and window. The furnishings (photo 3) are used for
modelling spatial relationships and determining room/area sizes. An
extensie repertoire of house forms can be generated by using blocks
from the modelling kit, but only one storey, bi-level, split-level and
two storey houses are shown (photos 4,5,6, and 7).

Because the modelling kits are used in different locations,
portability is essential. This consideration effects the size (or
scale), weight, and number of components. An early decision was made
in favour of "table top" scale models. The block elements in a scale
of 1:48 include smaller increments of the basic module which makes
possible a substantial variety of house forms. The panels and
furnishings in a scale of 1:16 was found to be optimum.

The panel model base comes in two halves, one of which can be
elevated for modelling split level houses. Clear plexiglas sheets are
used for "second floors" and provide an unobstructed view of the "first
floor". The floors are gridded in "two foot" squares to provide a
dimensional reference. There are enough block elements in the kit to
model several designs for comparison. The range of panel and
furnishing elements in the kit is extensive enough to model virtually
any good sized single-family dwelling.

Modelling methods

Those who have used the kits are in low and middle income groups and their ages average in the mid to late twenties. None of the participants had any previous design education or formal design experience. Approximately ten minutes of orientation is required to acquaint users with a modelling kit. In-person instruction, the only method tested to date, could probably be replaced with printed illustrated instructions. Few questions arise that require consultation, indicating the likely success of modelling without supervision.

The assembly of a panel model with furnishings, to verify an existing design from house plans, can take as little as one hour; whereas, the generation of a house design, the exploration of alternatives, and redesign can take from five to ten hours contingent on the number of alternatives modelled (photo 8)

There are few special requirements for the successful use of the modelling kit. The presence of other housing references, unless they represent designs also generated with the kit, tend to confuse the users and to keep them from appreciating the constraints and realizing the potential of the kit. Several modelling periods of several hours each over a number of days provide continuity, objectivity and time for reflection on perceived needs.

Modelling kit applications

The kit has been used to verify existing house plans chosen by participants. In testing, it was found that the space indicated on drawings was perceived to be larger than it really was. Constructing models corrected these misperceptions and provided a better understanding of "real" house space and, as a result, people changed plans otherwise thought to be acceptable.

When the modelling kit it used to generate a house design, a number of house forms can be explored very quickly with the block elements. An acceptable form is then modelled with the panel elements. Decisions about interior spaces are made by locating the interior walls and by the placement of furnishings.

The kit can also be used to explore possibilities for add-ons and add-ins and for designing multiple family dwellings and planning neighbourhoods. Ideally, the kit should represent a manufactured building system which would allow the user to order building components from the factory as indicated in the completed model.

USER CONSTRUCTION OF HOUSING

Introduction

An Alberta company is now producing a complete building system, including: basement walls, exterior walls and roofing panels. The panels' wood frame construction and expanded polystyrene insulation infill make this system energy efficient, light wieght, cost effective and easy to assemble (photo 9). The system can be combined with locally produced long-span floor joists (photo 10) to create housing that is flexible, adaptable and that can accommodate add-ons and add-ins. A modelling kit/building system combination would make it possible for a user to design and construct his own house.

The building system

The system is comprised of fenestrated and unfenestrated panels of wood frame construction with expanded polystyrene infill. There are a number of advantages to building with this system. In traditional buildings, up to ten percent of the wood delivered by suppliers for framing is unusable because it is badly warped or is checking. This is not a problem with pre-built panels in which kiln dried lumber is used and quality is controlled. Theft is virtually eliminated because the building panels can not be integrated into a conventional house without being conspicuous. The panels are quick to build with and obviate the use of less satisfactory insulation (e.g. fibreglas) while the cost is comparable.

Design flexibility

The building system facilitates the construction of standard house forms and, according to the company's brochure, can also be used for "school, garages, walk-in freezers, warehouses, hospitals, cottages, and saunas." This versatility is made possible by the product's simplicity. Elements are joined together in the factory and are then combined on site to construct entire walls. This makes it possible to locate doors and windows almost anywhere and provides virtually unlimited design flexibility.

Delivery

All the panels for the construction of a single family house can be delivered to the site in one truck load. The panels' size and light weight make unloading an easy task of approximately thirty minutes for two men. The panels, in varying lengths of eight to twelve feet, are numbered for easy identification.

On site construction procedures

With an assembly drawing for reference, the grooved panels are "locked" together with a connecting spline of styrene insulation. There are three different ways to erect a continuous wall: 1) the panels can be assembled on the floor and manually lifted into place, 2) wall jacks can be used, or 3) the panels are stood up one at a tme and nailed to the second top plate. When the walls are in place, they are toenailed to the floor, braced and squared in the traditional manner and nailed to the adjoining wall at the corner. Only standard tools and a modest level of skill are required for assembly.

Construction of houses with this system

The house documented in this case study (photo 9) was a split leel single family design with an attached garage. The two carpenters, who had never before worked with the system, assembled and erected the walls in six hours. They felt this time could be cut in half in the construction of subsequent houses of the same size. It is reasonable

to suggest that a moderately skilled user would similarily have little
or no problem building with this system and participation could be
increased if the building system included prebuilt interior walls and
roof panels. Long-span floor joists, a readily available building
component, would make the use of interior movable partitioning walls
and roof panels possible. Together with obviating the need for
internal load bearing walls, long span floor joists have the ability to
internally carry heating ducts, plumbing and wiring. Their use would
increase user participation and provide more desirable housing.

User participation in housing construction will increase autonomy in
the housing process.

USE OF THE MODELLING KIT IN THE THIRD WORLD

Introduction

Problems of communication have always existed between architects and
clients who share the same cultural background; however, the problem is
more serious when cultural backgrounds differ. If professional who
plan and build in cultures different from their own are unfamiliar with
or insensitive to the client's cultural context, their efforts may be
frustrated and their results may be either totally or partially
inappropriate to user needs and a violation of culture. This problem
can be substantially reduced if the professionals and the users share a
common language.

Developing nations unquestionably need our help; but, equally
important, this help must be responsible. From past experience we have
learned that, rather than helping foreign clients, we have often added
to existing problems or created new ones by trying to impose solutions
appropriate to our culture but inappropriate to theirs.

This concern is being addressed by Professor David Stea of the
Department of Architecture, University of Wisconsin, Milwaukee, who is
proposing a Domestic/International Field Center for Cross-Cultural
Architecture and Planning. He claims that the center, if realised,
"will train architects and planners to work in culturally different
areas and with people who may not share their views of the world. This
training involes recognition of common dimensions which characterise
most developing societies and enable a streamlining of the cultural
learning process, and indigenous approaches to planning and the built
environment" (Stea 1984). The lack of this kind of professional
education is one part of the problem being faced in third world
settings.

Rudofsky (1977) cites another problem as "the tendency to ascribe to
architects - or, for that matter, to all specialists - exceptional
insight into problems of living." Rudofsky's concern reflects the
sometimes one-sided, non-participatory approach taken by some
professionals, which is also not always culturally responsible. It
should be noted that popular solutions are possibly less culturally
problematic when they result in a hospital, an athletic facility or a
university building. The more serious problems of cultural violation
are likely to occur in the area of housing.

The "problem of living", which are best known by the user and can not always be verbalised, could be communicated through the use of a modelling kit. A modelling kit stimulates the innate perceptions and skills common to the people of all cultures. It facilitates an active involvement in the representation of form and space and brings to life the substance of dreams and the imagination. A modelling kit as a common language can bridge the gap between the planner or architect/designer and the client to provide the user participation in the design and planning process necessary to assure user satisfaction.

Third world applications

Graham Hardie (1983) has developed "a house modelling apparatus... as a research tool to enable people to model their desired house and thus discover their preferences. This apparatus is now widely used in South Africa, particularly in self help projects, as a means by which participants can design their own homes." He reports that "three dimensional simulations can be an extremely effective means when working with a semi-illiterate population. The simulations provide information about physical form, and the organisation of space, for they enable participants to describe their preferences... (physically)...rather than in the abstract" (Hardie 1983).

The results of our Alberta testing compare with those of Hardie. The representation of form and space are easily understood; users can relate to scale without any problem; they are gratified by having the opportunity to design their own house; they make decisions relating to space/cost trade offs; and they can easily communicate their housing needs through the use of the modelling kit.

In 1984, I collaborated with David Stea and Harry Van Oudenallen of the University of Wisconsin to design a modelling kit which was used by the natives of northern Mexico to help them organize, plan and design their housing. We felt a simple kit would make this task more participatory and easier. The kit is comprised of pieces made of card panels representing walls, doors and windows of several sizes. The panels are held in place by lengths of extruded plastic. Scale model furnishings are provided so that the model's interior space could be better understood.

The kits were used by the natives with mixed results. They had little difficulty with perception of scale or understanding what the elements represented. There was some difficulty, however, fitting the pieces into the retaining strips, which required some dexerity. The consultants felt that the pieces may have represented a "machine esthetic" and may have been perrrceived as somewhat "precious". This observation suggests the future use of indigenous materials and introduces the possibility that the modelling kit could be made by the people that use it. These concern must be accounted for in a future kit design for use in this kind of setting.

This sampling provides an indication of the usefulness of modelling kits as a means of communication in third world settings. They make use of a natural ability for three dimensional modelling common to all culture and they obviate problems of the perception of two dimensional form and space. Modelling kits break down language barriers thus

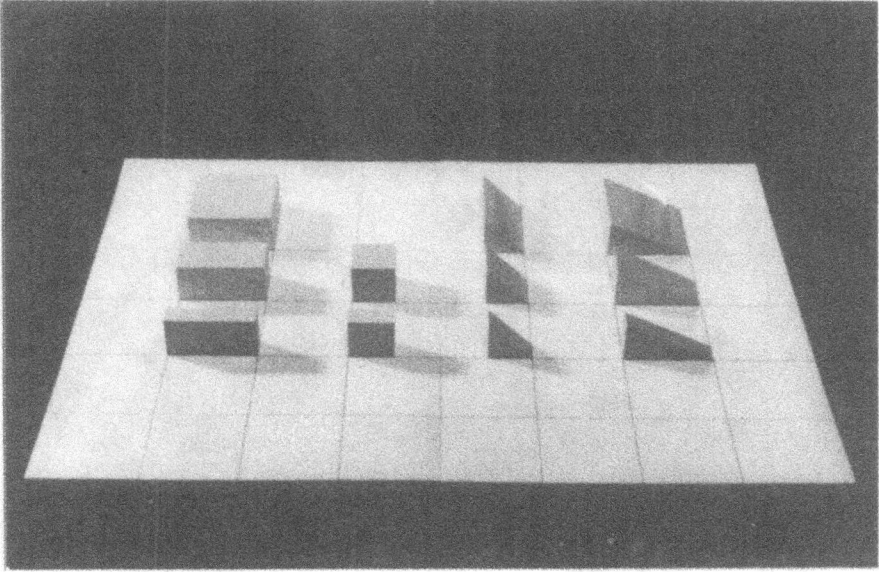

1. blocks for generating house forms

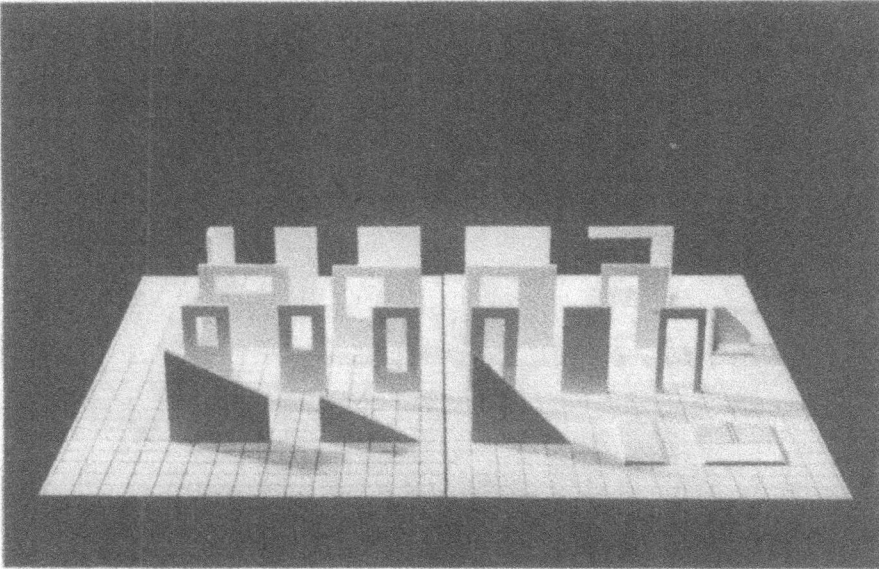

2. panels for establishing spacial relationships

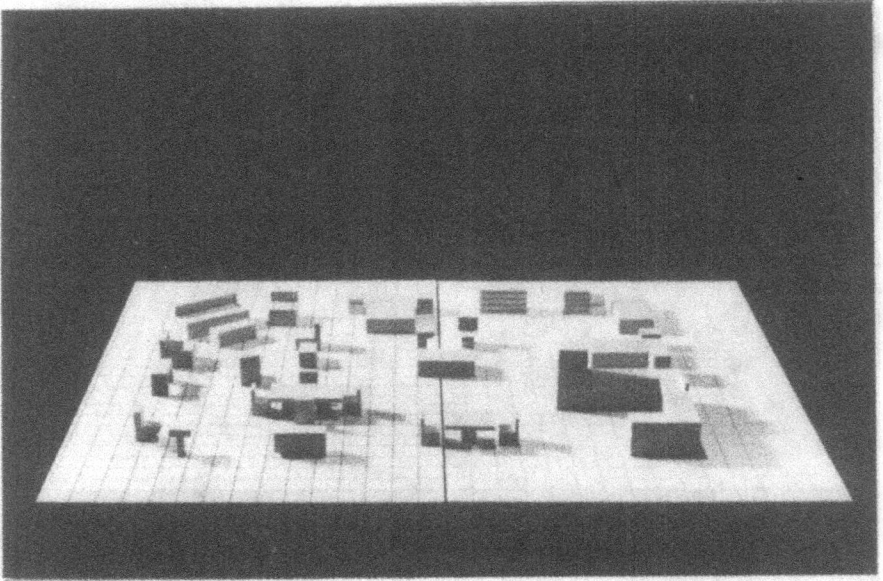

3. furnishings for determining spatial relationships

4. single storey design

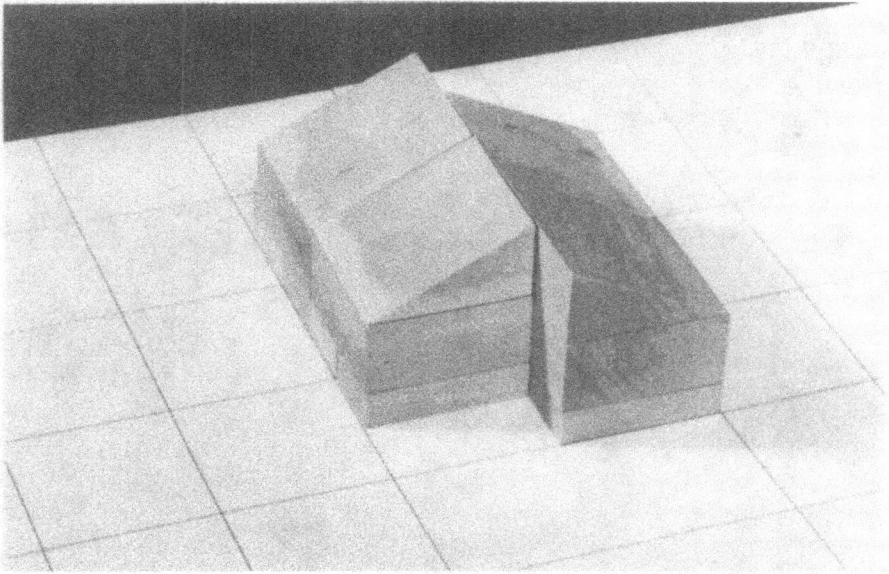

5. bi-level design

6. split level design

7. two storey design

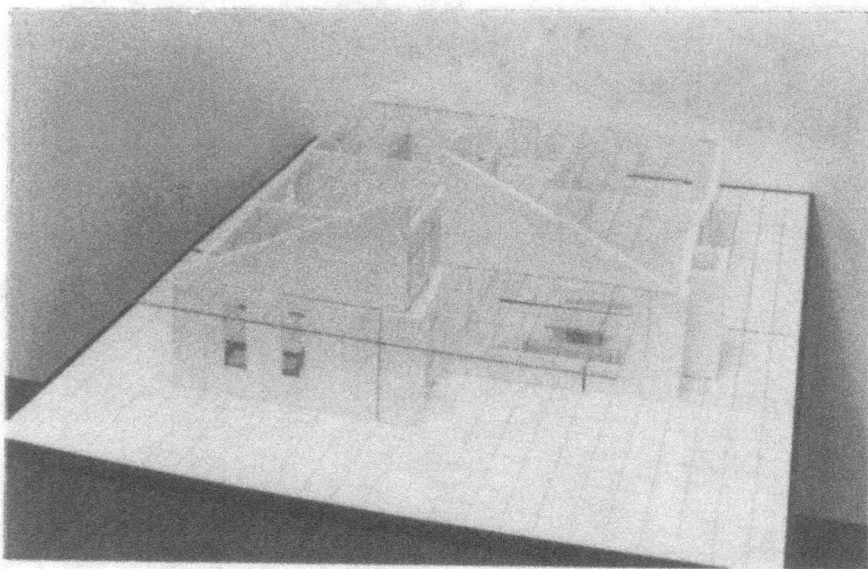

8. user designed model

9. building system with conventional roof trusses

10. house with long span floor joists

allowing the user to express a personal insight into housing need. The kit makes the relationship between the planner/architect/designer and the client a more wholesme non-threatening interaction through the use of a common language. Modelling kits can assure a higher degree of user participation and satisfaction and can begin to provide the level of cultural responsiveness the professional should find desirable.

FUTURE DIRECTIONS

Although the modelling kits have been satisfactorily tested in western Canada and northern Mexico, this testing admittedly represents only two user groups. Likewise, the building system has also been limitedly tested, however, the results suggest continued success for this approach. User participation in the housing process has promise and my research, I feel, demonstrates a way to realize this promise. While this approach is not universally applicable or desirable, I strongly believe it is a viable alternative for those who choose it.

There are a number of directions in which to develop this research; two are: the further development of modelling kits for use in third world settings and the expansion of the building system to increase user involvement in the building process. Cross-culturally, professionals who are planning and building in third world countries must be helped to bridge the culture/communications gap with their clients. Locally, the next step is to test all the characteristics of "desirable" housing. This would mean the design of a house or a housing project in which the use of long-span floor joists (for flexibililty), the use of insulated roof panels (for add-in potential), the design and use of a movable internal partitioning system (for adaptability), and the implementation of post construction add-ons could be tested. A unique working prototype embodying these characteristics could demonstrate the viability of a genuinely "flexible" alternative to conventional housing.

Further research can demonstrate to government agencies, the housing industry and the public an approach in which the benefits of "desirable" housing and user participation in the housing process can be realized.

BIBLIOGRAPHY

Bentz, B. "An Approach to User Design and Construction of Housing". International Housing Conference at Amsterdam, The Netherlands, 1985.

Bentz, B. "Model Making: A Common Language". EDRA Conference at New York, 1985.

Bentz, B. "Transition - User Participation in the Design of Housing" in Open House. Stichting Architecten Research, Vo. 6 no. 2 1981.

Bentz, B. "User Design and Construction of Housing" in PAPER Conference Proceedings, New Zealand Ministry of Works and Development, Wellington, New Zealand, 1983.

Bentz, B. "User Design of Housing With Scale Model Kits". EDRA Conference at San Luis Obispo, California, 1984.

Boudon, P. Lived-in Architecture London, Lund Humphries Publisher Ltd., 1972.

CHAP Training Course Manual Edmonton, Alberta, Co-operative Housing Action Program, 1983.

Habraken, N. Supports: An Alternative to Mass Housing New York, Praeger Publishers, 1972.

Hardie, G. "The Use of Simulations as a Means of Informing Design From a People Perspective". National Institute for Personnel Research, Johannesburg, 1983.

Lawrence, R. "Simulation Models As A Medium For Participatory Design". in R. Jacques and J. Powell (Eds) Proceedings of the DRS Conference at Portsmouth, England, December 1980.

Lawrence, R. "The Optimization of Habitat: The User's Approach to Design". Open House, 1981 Vol. 6 No. 3. p. 35-43.

Olivegren, J. Brukarplanering - Ett Litet Samhalle Fods Goteborg, Olivgren's Arkitektkontor AB, FFNS Gruppen, 1975

Peattie, L. "Design and Planning: Abstract Methods or Political Process?" in Moore, G. (ed) Emerging Methods in Environmental Design and Planning Cambridge, Mass., MIT Press, August 1973.

PSSHAK - Primary Support System Home Assembly Kits London, Greater London Council.

Rabeneck, A. et al "Housing - flexibility/adaptability" in Architectural Design, 2/74, pp. 76-90.

Rudofsky, B. Architecture Without Architects Bath, The Pitman Press, 1977.

Stea, D. "A Domestic/International Field Centre for Cross-Cultural Architecture and Planning" (proposal), Department of Architecture, University of Wisconsin, Milwaukee, 1984.

Terner, I. "Technology and Autonomy" in Turner, J. et al (eds) Freedom to Build New York, The MacMillan Company, 1972.

Terner, J. "Planning for Obsolescence" in Architects Journal, October 18, 1967.

Warshaw, L. et al Options in Housing Ottowa, National Design Council, 1974.

6. Environmental modelling for house planning

ROD LAWRENCE

Although it has become increasingly common to involve laypeople in the
architectural design process, this approach has not always proved
successful owing to inherent problems with the simulation, communication and evaluation of design proposals. These problems are discussed
with respect to two-dimensional (graphic) and three-dimensional representations of domestic space. In view of these shortcomings, small-
scale and full-scale models of dwellings have been assembled during the
design process to elicit the participation of laypeople in the elaboration of house plans. It is apparent that this approach enables the
residents to adopt a more active role, that the role of the researcher
and professional designer ought to be considered in view of the redefi-
ned role of laypeople and that new insights can be gained about the
impact of behavioural factors in the planning of houses.

INTRODUCTION

During the last two decades some architects and town planners have been involved in a complex debate on design methodology. Many professional designers studied how information was used in the design process, specifically how design schemes were generated by the analysis, syn-thesis and evaluation of design parameters. Many hypotheses were developed and varied models of the design process were proposed (Broadbent 1981a; Jones and Thornley 1963; Heath 1984). Generally, the intention was to make the design process overt, explicit and syste-matic rather than to rely upon intuition. There are diverse ways of doing this, as Heath (1984) has noted. The opportunity to design a building offers two different contexts for behavioural research. Firstly, the observation of a building in use over a long period of time enables the design team to test assumptions about the interaction between people and their physical surroundings. Second, by incorporat-ing the role of the building user into the design process, the designer can elicit information that is pertinent to the layout and fabric of buildings. Whereas the first option is relatively slow, the second is more rapid and, in this latter context, there has been a significant trend towards the direct involvement of laypeople in the definition of new buildings.

Participatory design is an important means of generating communication between public and professional groups in any community. Inevitably, such communication requires a shared language to analyse and evaluate current environment settings and to conceptualise proposals for the future. As Pyatok and Weber 1978, p. 203 have observed:

> To ensure that making the physical environment achieves its full cultural and political potential, the language for dia-logue "what could be" must stimulate the same physical and visual images that will exist in reality. In order for these images to have meaning and significance they must emerge from those who will eventually use them when they become physical realities.

Nonetheless, in the current design and construction of the built envi-ronment, the authors note that architects, town planners, and social administrators 'employ a language that is detached from the reality of the dwellers but attached to the reality of those who presently own and produce shelter as a commodity.'

Drawings have traditionally been the medium for communicating design proposals. They have been criticised and defended as an appropriate way to convey intentions and ideas. There would appear to be merit in Cuff's (1980) defence of drawings, because her argument is based on their misuse as a medium for communication. Cuff has envisaged drawings as an integral part of the design process rather than the end product of that process. In this respect they acquire the purpose of tools for design during the architectural design process. The criticism of the traditional use of architectural drawings can also be levelled at archi-tectural models. Indeed, the criticism is even more warranted, because design models have generally been considered like the showpiece in a shop window, and rarely as working instruments during the design pro-cess. In contrast to this custom, there has been a steady growth in the

study and application of the simulation of architectural design proposals during the last decade (Bonta 1979). This trend has accepted the
principle that architectural design involves a transaction between different groups of people with different goals and values, including the
building users, the owners, the government planners and legislators,
and the architects. There has been a reason for the acceptance of this
principle: it was one thing to admit that people should be involved in
decisions about the design and management of future environments, but
quite another thing to find an expedient way of involving the public in
the decision-making process. Underlying this problem is the medium of
communicating between professional designers and others.

On the one hand, some authors endeavoured to overcome the dilemma of
traditional intuitive and creative approaches to architectural design
by establishing design programmes that structure decision making during
the architecture design process (Heath 1984; Moore 1970). On the other
hand, it became increasingly recognised that the medium of representing
and communicating design proposals was the essence of the strengths and
weaknesses of participatory design methods (Lawrence 1979, 1982).
Consequently, a number of architectural modelling techniques that enable
either small-scale or full-scale simulations of buildings have been developed and applied (Bentz 1981; Eisemon 1975; Hardie 1983; Lawrence
1979, 1982). The application of this approach for architectural design
will now be given consideration.

DESIGN BY SIMULATION

The practice of simulation as a simplified rendition of a proposed or
naturally occurring environment, or event, is not new to the behavioural
sciences or the design professions. It has been an integral part of the
decision making apparatus of diverse disciplines for many decades (Raser
1969). Communication of design projects involves some kind of simulation, be it a verbal, an iconic, or an analogue model of a static or a
dynamic kind. Traditionally, small-scale models have been used to
translate graphic representations of buildings into three-dimensional
form.

The mode of simulating environmental settings has been the subject of
considerable discussion and experimentation in environment - behaviour
research (Seaton and Collins 1972; Danford and Willems 1975). A wide
range of simulation techniques including drawings, photographs, films
and scale models involving a variety of scale representations and detail
have been used to elicit responses and preference ratings of subjects
under experimental conditions. It is clear that the degree of abstraction of these simulations and their pertinence for studying behaviour
in real life settings is often treated in a cursory fashion or ignored
(Lauf 1970; Sadalla and Oxley 1984). Yet, several studies show that the
mode of environmental simulation can yield distinctly different results,
particularly with respect to the perception and judgement of the third
dimension (Lawrence 1979; Seaton and Collins 1972). These findings
bear important implications for the design professions. First,
designers communicate their ideas visually, so that modes of simulations which enhance communication between designers and their clients
are advantageous. Second, some professional designers are increasingly
aware of the need for the predictability of the behavioural effects of
diverse kinds of environments so that research and real-life settings

which are congruent can help anticipate future environmental settings. Third, simulation techniques can enhance the predictive skill of the behavioural impact of design projects and also provide a context for the analysis of the pertinence of behavioural parameters in architectural design. Finally, when simulation models are used during the design process to represent incremental changes to the projected environment, then the social scientist and the architectural researcher have a context enabling the analysis of the design process and the building form as it evolves.

In an important text on this subject McKechnie (1977, p. 172) has provided a useful typology of simulations which he classifies as perceptual (concrete) or conceptual (abstract) and either static or dynamic:

> Building plans, for example, provide much conceptual information - dimensions, angles, abstract shapes; when perceptual information is given, it usually involves construction details that subsequently will be hidden from view in the finished building. Little is provided in a set of blueprints to show the observer how the building will look. In contrast, the scale model at its best provides abundant perceptual information: colors and actual three-dimensional shapes of building, textures of vegetation, variations in terrain and ground cover, etc.

Static simulations exist for both conceptual and perceptual modes of representations. Photographs and scale drawings are static perceptual simulations, providing a specific, unchanging rendition of the represented space, and the interrelationships amongst the components of the setting cannot be manipulated. The dynamic capacity of perceptual simulations is illustrated by the Laboratory for Architectural Experimentation in Lausanne, Switzerland (to be discussed later in this chapter) and the Berkeley Simulation Laboratory at the University of California. Both these instruments provide an interactive capacity, the former in the context of full-scale models of interior spaces (Lawrence 1979, 1982), and the latter with respect to small-scale models of urban quarters (McKechnie, 1977).

According to Raser (1969) the principal reasons for making simulations are the economy of experimenting with a facsimile rather than the real object, the observation and measureability of a visible model and the reproducibility and safety of simulations. The purpose of the simulation model ought to be addressed with respect to these parameters and, above all, with respect to the inherent capacity of its simulation technique. The task can be descriptive or evaluative, and it can focus on some variables at the expense of others at a specific point in time, or through the passage of time. In general, the purpose of the simulation model determines the degree of approximation to reality. A simulation is not a replica of a real-life situation but a representation of it. In most instances, the degree of abstraction from reality impinges on the kinds of purpose simulations can serve in any situation. In architecture, where the representation of contextual contingencies is fundamental to the definition and resolution of design problems this principle must be born in mind. From this viewpoint, a limited number of full-scale modelling kits will now be presented and discussed.

SIMULATION MODELS

In recent years, there have been several attempts to include the simulation of design proposals at full-scale in order to assess ergonomic and functional criteria, and to encourage decision making during the architectural design process. Four simulation facilities of this kind include:

(1) The Environmental Simulation Laboratory at the University of California at Irvine.

(2) The Spatial Development Laboratory for Housing of the Municipality of Amsterdam.

(3) The Spatial Experimentation Laboratory at the Swedish Institute of Technology at Lund.

(4) The Laboratory for Architectural Experimentation at the Federal Institute of Technology, Lausanne, Switzerland.

On the one hand, three of these four simulation facilities are located at institutions devoted to tertiary education and they are used for teaching and research in architectural and social science disciplines. On the other hand, the simulation facilities in Amsterdam and Lausanne have been used in the context of professional practice. In fact, since 1975, no housing unit can be approved for construction by the Municipality of Amsterdam unless it has been simulated and evaluated in the Housing Laboratory operated by this Local Authority. As the mockup is simulated at full scale, the appraisal of the design of the house includes the layout of furniture and household equipment, as illustrated in the fourth number of the review Bauen und Wohnen published in 1979. When the house design has been evaluated, modified and approved by the Municipal architects it can be constructed. As the Laboratory for Architectural Experimentation in Lausanne has been observed in use by the author, for both academic and professional reasons, over a period of six years, the design and use of this facility will be the focus of the remainder of this chapter.

The Laboratory for Architectural Experimentation

The Laboratory for Architectural Experimentation (L.E.A.) is a recently developed instrument enabling the simulation of architectural space at full scale. With the aid of a system of building blocks and movable platforms, one can build a facsimile of a given project or of its parts, e.g. apartments, classrooms, seminar rooms, a library, offices, patient rooms, exhibition space, and so on. In contrast to conventional building research facilities, the purpose of the L.E.A. is not to test the performance of building components, materials or prototypes, but primarily to explore and experiment with spatial form and dimensions.

The Laboratory was constructed at the new campus site of the Ecole Polytechnique Fédérale at Lausanne, Switzerland during the 1970s. It is a building with a 300 square metre floor area and a 7 metre floor to ceiling height which has been designed to accommodate full-scale models of man-made space. The simulation of space is achieved with the use of lightweight modular building blocks. These blocks can be easily manipulated, and the modification of a wall or room which has already been

built is a simple and quick process. A series of modular door and
window frames, as well as other architectural elements, supplement
these blocks. The Laboratory is also equipped with two platforms which
permit the construction to be simulated at more than one floor level if
required. In addition, the series of perforated intermediate girders
can be shifted longitudinally along the platforms in increments of 10
centimetres. The shifting of these girders permits the creation of
openings in the platforms to allow for two-storey spaces and assemblies
on two levels. The intermediate girders support mobile floor and
ceiling slabs. A series of electric power rails permit the connection of lighting fixtures at any desired point on the ceiling. A
system of lightweight plastic blocks has been developed for the construction of walls and enclosures. A system was sought which would
provide lightweight and manageable elements which could be assembled
quickly, yet provide stability. The building blocks chosen for this
task are made of expanded polystyrene that has been injected into steel
moulds, either 10cm x 10cm x 10cm, or 20cm x 10cm x 10cm, or an angular
block 20cm x 10cm x 10cm with a rounded end. The blocks permit walls
of varying height and thickness to be simulated according to a 10 centimetre module, which corresponds to the requirements of an international
modular coordination system. With only three different types of blocks,
any vertical dimension is possible as well as any angular or curved
surface. Furthermore, a system of prefabricated door and window frames
has been designed and built. A design solution was sought which permitted the use of the same timber section for the jambs, sills, and
heads of all openings. This universal profile has been made in varying
lengths, making possible any size of opening according to 10 centimetre
increments. Doors and windows can be installed in the frames as required. Finally, a series of small, preassembled podiums have been
made to enable the simulation of small changes in floor level. There
are three sizes, having a plan dimension of 60cm x 60cm, 60cm x 90cm,
and 90cm x 90cm, with each 15cm high.

Whereas the Laboratory has commonly been the venue for design studies
by architectural students, it has recently also been used for the simulation of houses which are part of a cooperative housing scheme. The
context for this study provides a small group of people who have decided
independently of this research project to simulate their future house
during the architectural design process. These people are members of a
housing cooperative, who have used their resources collectively, aided
by government housing subsidies, to design and build their own homes.
The cooperative has elected six of its members to administer its affairs
including the appointment of an architectural practice to develop a site
plan and assist with the design of each dwelling and all communal
spaces. The architects have developed a process of participatory design which is applicable to each family joining the cooperative. After
defining specific requirements which are noted by extensive design
checklist, the owner family and the architects have developed preliminary sketch plans. These sketch plans are the basis for the simulation
of the three-dimensional characteristics of the future houses in the
Laboratory by the user family, with the aid of the architects, as shown
in Figure 1. In this respect the Laboratory has been the vehicle for
direct participation by laypeople in the architectural design process.
Concurrently, it has also provided the opportunity to undertake research
by observational studies of the simulation process. Specific attention
has been given to how people integrate their ideas about houses and

Figure 1 Successive stages of the design-by-simulation process for
a full-scale model of a house

family life with the evolving spatial form of their future houses. [1]

The population included in this study is not a controlled group. The
context for this research is not equivalent to those traditional experimental situations unrelated to the daily life of the residents. This
problem has rarely been addressed with respect to simulation techniques,
as noted earlier. Here it is acknowledged that the artificial setting
of the L.E.A. cannot correspond to the domestic realm of household life,
yet it has one important advantage over small-scale simulations of
houses. The primary advantage of the L.E.A. is that people fabricate,
then experience and perhaps modify the space. This experiential component of the full-scale models is a rare feature in architectural
design and planning practice.

Research Method

The focus of the research which has been undertaken during the process
of participatory design has included the collection of data from the
activities of the users and the architects as the activities have occurred. Thus, the first phase of the research has been nonparticipant
observational studies of the simulation of the full-scale models of the
future houses. These activities were recorded by photographs, sketches,
notes, and tape-recordings as the built form evolved and as specific
decisions were made. A measured drawing of the design of the houses
was made. The second phase included an interview with each family at

their present apartments, about one month after they had simulated their
future houses in the Laboratory. The interview was structured so that
the residents discussed the design of their future and present dwellings, rather than administrative or technical matters about the cooperative. Each of the interviews was recorded and then transcribed.
The third phase followed the interview and involved the completion of
measured drawings of each of the resident's present apartments. These
drawings were supplemented by numerous photographs which documented the
placement and style of furnishings and fittings.

In the first instance, the information obtained from these diverse
research procedures was used to examine those personal and shared ideas
and values attributed to the future houses by the residents. This study
was complemented by a comparative analysis of the layout and use of the
past, present and future houses of the residents. Particular attention
was given to the following themes:

(1) the relationship between external, communal and public spaces and
    internal private spaces, notably the transitions between personal,
    communal and public domains and how they are regulated by archi-
    tectural elements, human behaviour patterns, and social rules and
    conventions (Lawrence 1983);

(2) the relationship between interior spaces and the size and position
    of fixed construction elements (i.e. walls, doors and windows),
    mobile furnishing elements, such as specific pieces of furniture
    with a significant value for at least one member of the household
    (Lawrence 1983);

(3) the association between the design of the house and daily household
    activities, routines and rituals, in particular how spaces and
    objects are classified, positioned and used according to social
    classifications and personal values (Lawrence 1983).

As these themes have been discussed elsewhere they will not be repeated
here. The purpose of the next section of this chapter is to examine
the findings of this research with respect to the function of simulation techniques as a medium for the representation and communication of
ideas during the architectural design process.

Results

The principal findings of this research project can be tabled as
follows.

Reference elements and indices as design tools. During the observation
of the design-by-simulation process it was noted that the residents
made use of diverse elements to assess the layout, shape and size of
rooms, to locate the position of doors and windows, and the intended
position of known items of furniture. These elements can be classified
into three categories:
(1) construction elements, that are fixed, such as doors, windows, roof
    or structural columns;
(2) furnishing elements, that are mobile, such as the dining room table,
    a desk or any large family heirloom that has a special significance
    for at least one member of the household; and
(3) socio-cultural indices, such as the entrance hall which is of
    special importance in regulating the liaison between public and

private domains, or the fireplace, which has been included in all
the houses despite the presence of central heating.
These findings suggest that even if the architect does not consider
these three classes of elements during the elaboration and verification
of house plans, nonetheless, the resident will use these elements to
assess a proposal that was formulated with respect to other criteria.

Graphic/static and spatial/dynamic simulations. Although the research
did not include a systematic comparison of the dialogue between architects and their clients during the design process, the observation of
the design process in the L.E.A. suggests that three-dimensional representations enable the resident to participate in house planning in
his own terms, without being restricted by the graphical language of
design professionals. Those laymen who have used the L.E.A. have spon-
taneously mentioned how much easier it is to visualise their future
house with the facsimile compared with a sketch plan of it, and how the
appraisal of room shapes and sizes is made simpler by the simulation of
reference elements and indices. Moreover, although the resident does
not live in the house for a short period of time the great advantage of
full-scale simulation models compared with small-scale models is that
laypeople not only fabricate rooms but experience them, furnish them,
appraise them and, perhaps, modify them. This experiential component
is a rare feature of other kinds of architectural simulations.

The role of the professional designer. The participatory design process
studied during this programme of research can be contrasted with the
traditional role of the architect and his client during the design process. Traditionally, the architect assumes the role of an expert and
the client responds to one or more design proposals elaborated from a
list of requirements. There is generally no interaction between parties
during the genesis of the house design as it occurs in the L.E.A. The
design-by-simulation process in the L.E.A. is a more interactive
approach that acts as a catalyst for the resident to mould the future
house according to his requirements and the professional expertise of
the architect. In this sense, it is incorrect to suggest that the professional role of the architect is weakened as Broadbent (1981b) has
suggested. On the contrary, this research suggests that his role increases owing to the fact that the multiple requirements of the client
cannot be overlooked. In sum, environmental simulations as used in the
design of the housing cooperative discussed here incorporate the criteria of the resident in the design process in a dynamic way. Moreover,
it encourages all persons to express their personal viewpoint at successive stages of the elaboration of the design. This suggests that
full-scale models of domestic space provide a unique means of engendering a meaningful dialogue between architects and their clients.

Questioning validations of simulations. This limitation of the context
of the L.E.A. ought to be recognised. Although the study is not equivalent to those experimental situations unrelated to the housing aspirations and priorities of the residents, it must be admitted that the
setting of a facsimile of a house in the L.E.A. cannot correspond to
the everyday residential environment of domestic life. First, there is
an abstraction from the site of the future house. A post-occupancy
evaluation of the houses simulated in the L.E.A. confirmed that the

simulation models <u>do not</u> represent the day lighting levels to be found on site (Lawrence 1985). Moreover, there is no way of allowing for contextual factors such as sun penetration or views from windows. In one house, the culmination of these factors led one household to add an extra window in their living room which they judged to be too dull. On the other hand, the lack of colours or textures on walls, ceilings and floors did not present problems for the residents. This may be attributed to the fact that the size and shape of rooms were usually assessed with respect to known items of furniture rather than finishes (Lawrence 1983).

In sum the findings of this research indicate that the pertinence of full-scale simulation models must be restricted to certain aspects of the interior of the dwelling, to test dimensional and ergonomic parameters in the first instance, and then to act as a catalyst for the generation of socio-psychological parameters, implicated in the design of residential environments. This latter subject now requires further attention.

Catalysts for design

When people have the opportunity to participate in the design of their future house some features of present and previous dwellings which have left either a positive or a negative impression on the resident are commonly used as 'tools for design'. For those persons who participate in the design of their new home, there is a strong preoccupation to eliminate the faults of present and previous dwellings. One of the most common defects of contemporary flats is the lack of acoustic insulation from adjoining dwellings. In some cases this defect has been an important catalyst for building a home. Beyond functional criteria, at a psychological level, a house which emancipates the residents from the defects of previous dwellings and synthesises the positive features of these and other homes becomes and important vehicle for the expression of symbolic meaning.

In essence this research shows that the materialisation of the design of a dwelling embodies a psychological project or goal that may be strictly personal, or shared by members of the household. Thus, dwelling space and domestic objects are endowed with polyvalent meanings owing to the divergent viewpoints different people in the same household attribute to them at the same point in time. It is very important to consider the relationship between an individual and his home not just in terms of personal values and preferences (as much research on residential satisfaction has done in the past) but also in terms of compromises and conflicts people have about shared domains. Throughout the design-by-simulation process numerous consensus decisions were made by the residents to illustrate this principle.

Other parameters which impinge upon the values and preferences of the residents can be briefly summarised here. For example, this research has illustrated how people are ordered by implicit non-physical factors including explicit norms and rules (such as building regulations), and implicit codes and controls, which relate to the use of space in customary ways including routines and rituals (Lawrence 1982). Having established the complex nature of those parameters implicated in residential environments, it is important that any dialogue between members

of a household, or between architect and client, ought to explicitly
include these parameters in order to allow each individual to express
his values and priorities with respect to them.

Although this approach implies that the architect will need to conse-
crate more time for the elaboration of a project compared with the
traditional design process, undoubtedly the result is more likely to
conform to the requirements of the client, rather than other criteria.
Moreover, if simulation models are excepted as a viable approach for
the planning of dwellings then it is necessary for both architect and
client to acknowledge that there is not an ideal or optimum design
solution. In this respect, the notion of optimisation, as used in the
field of environmental psychology, ought to be reexamined. According
to Stokols (1977), the notion of optimisation emphasises the active role
of people in the built environment. It assumes that people can evaluate
different physical settings, relate their evaluation to their own requirements and, if necessary, act to improve specific settings. The
study discussed in this chapter supports, at least in part, this interpretation of optimisation, because it illustrates how laypeople use
their resources during the architectural design process. However, this
study also illustrates that designed environments are commonly the
result of conflicts and, therefore, reflect consensus decisions, which
inhibit the development of alternative designs. As yet, this fact has
not been discussed with respect to the notion of optimisation.

In essence, this long-term project of research illustrates that the
values and preferences people develop with respect to residential environments are not static but change during the course of time, either
with respect to successive stages of the life-cycle, or as a result of
personal experiences in the home. It is important to recall this principle during the architectural design process. Moreover, if this interpretation of a temporal perspective is enlarged, there is an interesting
junction between the relevance of time for the architect as well as the
client. In the same way that an architect ought to elaborate a design
proposal without ignoring the history of the site, its present and
future conditions, each resident ought to elaborate and assess house
designs with respect to his or her own concept of time, stage in the
life-cycle and anticipation of the future.

CONCLUSION

This chapter has examined a range of subjects that have been evoked by
the use of small-scale and full-scale three-dimensional models as tools
for design during the genesis of a housing project. The practice of
using three-dimensional models instead of two-dimensional representations of houses raises issues which can be discussed in terms of the
role of environmental simulations as:
(1) an effective context for research in the field of environmental
    psychology;
(2) an effective context for research in design methodology; and
(3) an effective context for architectural design practice, including
    architectural education and public participation in the design of
    the built environment.

The research and design practice reported in this chapter has indicated how three-dimensional representations of domestic space can be used

to serve each of these three roles and why they are a more effective
medium for the elaboration, representation and communication of design
proposals than more traditional approaches used for the planning of
residential environments. The proposed role for full-scale models is
to represent diverse possibilities, to give laypeople and professional
designers a medium to think and communicate with, and to appraise and
modify alternative design solutions. These models are not meant to be
replicas of future buildings because:
(1) they cannot be detailed during the initial phases of the design
    process, when many decisions about fittings and furnishings have
    not been made;
(2) they ought to be simply renditions of buildings that do not
    inhibit the development of alternative designs and enable design
    proposals to be simulated and evaluated as simply and quickly as
    possible;
(3) they ought to focus on the size and shape of rooms, and the
    interrelationships between the interior and the exterior.
In each of these respects, the role of models as tools for design is
quite different from the traditional use of architectural graphics and
small-scale models of buildings.

NOTES

[1] The study reported herein was funded by research grants from the
    Swiss National Science Foundation. These grants were accorded to
    Professor Peter von Meiss and Professor Rémy Droz between 1979 and
    1984. The author undertook the research assisted by Claire Charton,
    Kaj Noschis, the Groupe Y Architects and the residents, whose co-
    operation is gratefully acknowledged.

REFERENCES

Bentz, B., 'Transition: user participation in the design of housing',
    Open House, vol.6, 1981, pp.11-18.
Bentz, B., 'User design and construction of housing', in Joiner, D.,
    Brimilcombe, G., Daish, J., Gray, J., and Kernohan, D. (eds)
    Conference on people and physical environment research, P.D.Hasselberg
    Government Printer, Wellington, 1983.
Bonta, J., (ed.) 'Gaming', Journal of Architectural Education,
    vol.33, 1979.
Broadbent, G., 'Design methods - 13 years after - a review', in
    Jacques, R. and Powell, J. (eds) Design:Science:Method, IPC Science
    and Technology Press, Guildford, 1981(a).
Broadbent, G., 'The morality of designing', in Jacques, R., and Powell,
    J., (eds) Design:Science:Method, IPC Science and Technology Press,
    Guildford, 1981(b).
Cuff, D., 'Design by drawing: a process of image creation and
    negtiation', in Stough, R., and Wandersman, A.(eds) Optimizing
    environments: research, practice and policy,
Danford, S., and Willems, E., 'Subjective responses to architectural
    displays: a question of validity', Environment and Behavior, vol.7,
    1975, pp.486-516.
Eisemon, T., 'Simulations and requirements for citizen participation
    in public housing', Environment and Behavior, vol.7, 1975,
    pp.99-123.

Hardie, G., "The use of simulations as a means of informing design from a 'people' perspective", in Joiner, D., Brimilcombe, G., Daish, J., Gray, J., and Kernohan, D., (eds) Conference on people and physical environment research, P.D. Hasselberg Government Printer, Wellington, 1983.

Heath, T., Method in Architecture, John Wiley, London, 1984.

Jones, C., and Thornley, D., (eds) Conference on design methods, Macmillan, New York, 1963.

Lawrence, R., 'Dual representations of domestic space', in Seidel, A., and Danford, S.,(eds) Environmental Design: research, theory and application, EDRA, Washington, 1979.

Lawrence, R., "Trends in architectural design methods: the 'liability' of public participation", Design Studies, vol.3, 1982, pp.97-103.

Lawrence, R., 'Laypeople as architectural designers', Leonardo, vol.16, 1983, pp.232-7.

Lawrence, R., 'User participation in house design: subtle undertones in the dialogue', Building Research and Practice, vol.13, 1985, pp.25-30.

McKechnie, G., 'Simulation techniques in environmental psychology', in Stokols, D., (ed.) Perspectives on environment and behavior: theory, research and applications, Plenum, New York, 1977.

Moore, G., (ed.) Emerging methods in environmental design and planning, MIT Press, Cambridge, 1970.

Pytok, M., and Weber, H., 'Participation in residential design', in Sanoff, H., (ed.) Designing with community participation, Dowden Hutchinson and Ross, Stroudsberg, 1978.

Raser, J., Simulation and society, Allyn and Bacon, Boston, 1969.

Sadalla, E., and Oxley, D., 'The perception of room size: the rectangularity illusion', Environment and Behavior, vol.16, pp.394-405.

Seaton, R., and Collins, J., 'Validity and reliability of ratings of simulated buildings', in Mitchell, W. (ed.) Environmental Design: Research and Practice, University of California Press, Los Angeles, 1972.

Stokols, D., Perspectives on environment and behavior: theory, research and applications, Plenum, New York, 1977.

7. Modelling as participation in a Botswana village

JOHN MASON

SUMMARY

The use of modeling as a mode of participation in human settlements
research and planning in a Botswana village has proved effective.
Employing traditional community groupings for the purpose of testing
physical planning issues, both prepared and self directed modeling
approaches were evolved. The choice of modeling as an approach to
participatory planning was based on its practical utility in eliciting
information, as well as its sociocultural appropriateness to Botswana.

Four prepared models were designed which incorporated physical
planning factors based on past and present settlement patterns and
derived from formal and informal discussions with the villagers.
Advantages and disadvantages were elicited for each of the models in
ward council meetings. Clearcut preferences emerged from the
experiment concerning: plot size, shape and access; residential
plan; road system; and utilities and services.

The residents' preparation of the self directed models provided
corroboration of both the earlier research and the prepared models
experiment. It also evoked a highly participatory mode of bottom up
planning. While the planning research described here has not yet had
a direct impact on the policy and planning process in Botswana, since
insufficient time has elapsed since it was carried out, there is
evidence that local, regional and national officials view it rather
favorably.

A. INTRODUCTION [1]

The Botswana village settlement pattern has altered significantly over the past several decades in response to general socioeconomic conditions, as well as to specific user needs. Participatory sociospatial planning research carried out in a Botswana village during a four year period, 1981 to 1984, has provided useful indicators for village planning purposes in Botswana. The research included the use of physical modeling techniques employed with villagers during their traditional council meeting.

This chapter focuses on the physical environmental aspects and planning process of human settlements research. More specifically, it focuses on the use of modeling techniques as an effective participatory mode in village planning. Finally the paper addresses the question of the application of the findings to the village where the research was carried out.

B. GENERAL PROBLEM

Working experience in developing countries suggests that bottom up planning and decision making are sine qua non to success. Descriptions of participation on the part of the poor in assisted development projects are abundant and often useful in depicting the opportunities and constraints of such participation. (e.g., Bryant 1980; Cohen 1977; UN 1978) Botswana is an almost perfect example of the effective use of the bottom up, participatory approach in the planning of human settlements.

The participatory mode is an integral part of the social and culture history of the Batswana, people of the Tswana Tribe who inhabit present day Botswana. The tribal council meeting or kgotla, earlier as well as presently, serves as an important occasion for Batswana to communicate with the authorities and with one another in airing their views about their needs and desires. (Shapiro 1943, p.69) In the research described here, the kgotla served the very important role of providing the context for village participation.

C. BACKGROUND

The following brief discussion of Botswana's policy and planning of human settlements serves as a backdrop to the topic of modeling as a mode of participatory planning.

1. Botswana's national settlement policy and the role of major village centres

The approach to integrated town and village planning had only become of some urgency to Botswana in the late 1970's. The country had not undergone the classic problems of greatly imbalanced rural-urban development characteristic of many developing nations. Botswana is traditionally a cattle based village society with few towns as such. Since some of the villages reach a population of 40,000, the inhabitants of this large but underpopulated country are quite familiar with the phenomenon of sizeable human settlements. What they have

not been familiar with until recently is the flocking of unexpectedly
large numbers of individuals to the few towns.

A country of about one million people, Botswana has fortunately
been in a strategic position to positively influence its national
growth and development pattern. This has meant the purposeful and
effective management of villagers who have migrated to the cities and
settled as squatters, mostly in self help housing and upgraded urban
communities. (Mason 1980) Furthermore, efforts are underway presently
to improve rural areas, including key villages, the topic of this
chapter.

Historically in Botswana, village planning originated with the
tribally based district headquarters. The planning process revolved
around a sector focus, schools, health facilities, water, security,
post, etc., rather than on an integrated, regional basis. That
sectoral focus consciously changed in the late 1970's to the early
1980's.

With the recent development of a National Settlement Policy, Botswana
was ready in early 1980 to deal with investment, growth, and migration
through a hierarchically defined classification of its human settlements. The Policy's goals are to reduce an ever increasing rural to
urban movement through developing economic and other opportunities in
the primary rural centres. (DTRP 1979) As part of this process,
those primary centres (the six most important villages) classified as
'major traditional villages,' including the village of our concern,
were to be upgraded both so as to impede migration to the towns and
to attract government and private investment. The increased level
of servicing provided to major village inhabitants was expected to
positively influence those desired results. In this light special
funds in the national budget were designated for improving major
village infrastructure so as to attempt to reduce the disparity in
service standards available respectively in the towns and major
villages.

2. Uniqueness of the Botswana case study.

Botswana represents close to the ideal in terms of its national
development orientation and as a country in which international
development agencies are able to make a difference. Several factors
account for the relative success of development in Botswana: briefly,
the country is endowed with certain sustaining resources, namely
minerals and cattle; its development policies are enlightened, particularly those pertaining to human settlement and the balance of rural
to urban activities; furthermore, because Botswana is traditionally
an open society, which has been able to transform to a modern republic
while maintaining its democratically based values, its people are not
only used to participating in planning which affects them, they
expect to be involved.

D. RESEARCH FOCUS: THE VILLAGE OF MAHALAPYE

The research which informs this chapter was carried out in the village
of Mahalapye, located about 200 kilometres north of the capital city,
Gaborone. Mahalapye transformed from a cattle post settlement to a

Tswana tribal village in the early 1900's when then-Rhodesia Railways decided to place a major crewing station/repair shop there on its line to South Africa. Over the years, migration to Mahalapye for work, transportation, government services and other amenities, has generated a permanent village community of almost 25,000 residents. Growing at about six per cent per year, Mahalapye is expected to reach a population of over 50,000 by the year 2,000.

1. Land tenure and allocation

Land tenure is critical to an understanding of participation in the village planning process, given the fact that Mahalapye residents have cost-free access to land and its use through tribal communal structures and not private ownership. Until recently, residential land in the village was allocated to patrikin residential groups or wards, creating a landholding pattern based substantially on common descent. Now, such land is distributed to individuals, such that at the peripheries of the traditional village, residents of different origin are living side by side.

Present attitudes about residential land distribution reflect a diminishing emphasis on the need to live in the same neighbourhood as a kinsman. The exception to this is the non Tswana tribal groups resident in Mahalapye, namely the South African Xhosa and Namibian Herero. Because of their minority status in the village, they tend to desire to stay together to the extent possible. In any case, wards tend to evolve physically only to the point where the ward headman can reasonably administer the residents, up to 500 family plots, or where ecological boundaries such as farmlands or grazing lands become impediments to expansion.

2. The evolution of Mahalapye's settlement patterns

Before moving to the modeling research itself it is useful to briefly examine the evolution of Mahalapye's settlement pattern over the last half century. Since today's perceptions are at least partly rooted in historical patterns it is helpful to review the latter. A diagram expresses the four major patterns rather succinctly (see Figure 1). The traditional pattern (Figure 1 A), called Bamangwato after the Tswana tribe of that name, is a horseshoe shape which served to protect the kraal in which the highly valued cattle were secured. In time this pattern became infilled (Figure 1 B), reflecting less need for the security of cattle. Recently, in the late 1960's, an allocation pattern developed (Figure 1 C) that followed a grid pattern, which residents recall fondly since it is closer to what they desire today. Presently, an unplanned allocation of plots is made by the Land Board Office in Mahalapye (Figure 1 D) which is less satisfying to residents than the grid layout. Reasons for this derived from the modeling exercise, to which we now turn.

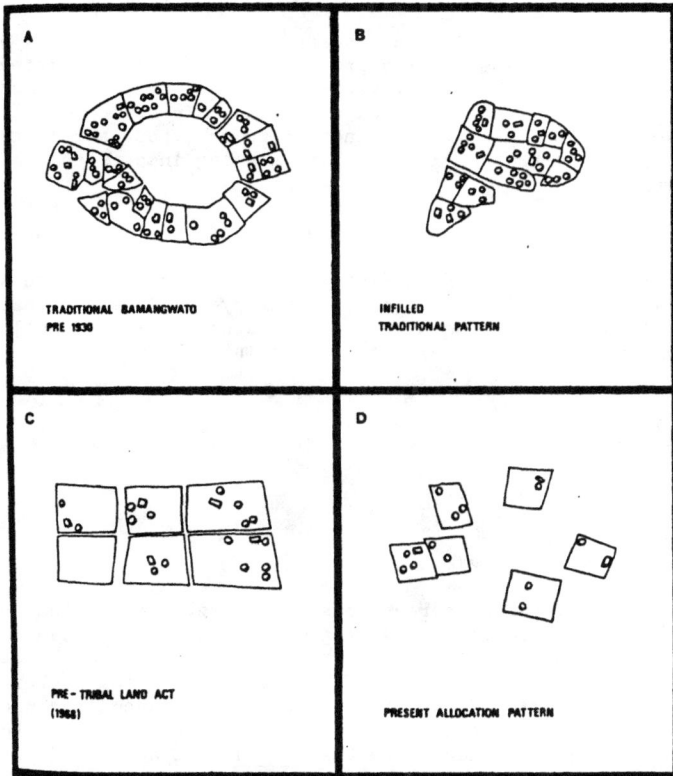

Figure 1 Mahalapye Settlement Patterns, 1930 to Present

E. THE RESEARCH: TESTING OF PHYSICAL PLANNING ISSUES

The Mahalapye village upgrading study was designated by the Botswana
Government to become a model for national village planning. The
policy which informed the study had as some of its tenets the
increased and equitable distribution of resources between urban
centres and rural regions, the expansion of rural services for
Botswana's villages, and the participation of villagers in the planning process.

1. Selection of the modeling approach

Based on earlier work in Botswana which used physical models to test
sociospatial theory as well as assist in village planning (Hardie
1980, pp. 134-158), it was decided to employ modeling in the
Mahalapye study. More specifically, the decision was due to the
joint consultancy on the study of an anthropologist/social planner
and an architect/planner. These specialists felt the study provided

a unique opportunity to test the integration of social and physical factors in the planning and design of a large Botswana village.

The choice of modeling as an approach to participatory planning was made in part because of its practical utility in eliciting information about sociophysical factors. Physical attributes can pose problems of systematizing and analyzing information. Modeling, on the other hand, permits respondents to see those attributes in their material form and to discuss their meaning in personal and social terms.

2. Physical planning factors and the modeling approach

Several physical planning factors deemed critical to the study were derived from earlier studies of Mahalapye villagers   (Mason 1981; DTRP 1980) as well as a more recent study   (Team Consultants 1984). These factors, which were introduced into the modeling procedures, were:

-plot boundaries
-plot size
-plot shape
-access to the plot
-residential plan
-road system
-utility and service

In order to test the perceptions of villagers about the above factors, two basic techniques of modeling were used in the research. The first was a series of prepared three dimensional models demonstrating a variety of combinations of the physical planning factors. An open ended, self directed approach comprised the second technique, allowing residents the opportunity to make up their own models. Both of these techniques were presented in the kgotla meetings, defined earlier as council meetings among tribal members or, in the case of Mahalapye, members of the same ward, held to discuss and decide neighborhood and ward matters.

3. The procedure for the prepared models

The prepared models were used to generate discussion among ward members in the eleven Mahalapye wards, to obtain planning information and to help prepare them for ultimately generating their own models. As a prelude to the modeling exercise, one kgotla meeting was held in each of the eleven wards to discuss general village growth issues with the residents. A second series of kgotla meetings were held to obtain data about plot layout, infrastructure and services. Considerable time was spent describing to ward members in the Setswana language various features of the prepared models. Each of the eleven kgotla meetings was attended by approximately 50 members from each of the eleven wards.

The models designed for the research were made to scale and used natural and manufactured materials to obtain the most accurate representation of actual plots, plot boundaries and the houses themselves. House models replicated a traditional round or rectangular, one bedroom mudbrick house, known as <u>ntlo</u>. They also depicted the spacious compound with its open courtyard, called the <u>lolwapa</u>.

Because of the large number of residents attending the <u>kgotla</u> meetings, not all were able to examine and discuss the models in detail. But, since the meetings continued for several hours, many residents were able to voice their opinions about the models. Cultural norms of the Tswana prohibit the domination of any one individual or small group, which for this purpose ensured a certain degree of representation of the larger ward.

The three prepared models presented at the <u>kgotla</u> meetings, depicted in Figures 2-4, include four distinct residential plans. The first two, represented on one model board (see Figure 2), are described as:

1. traditional allocation plan and

2. land board allocation plan (the present system).

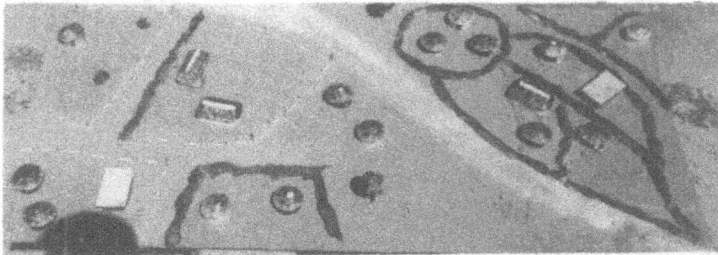

Figure 2 Model of Land Board Allocation Plan (1. of road) and Traditional Allocation Plan

These models are similar in their plan to the layouts presented in Figure 1, B and D, reflecting the infilled traditional pattern and the present, unplanned allocation mode of the land board, respectively.

The third and fourth models, presented separately (see Figures 3 and 4), are described as:

3. modified traditional plan and

4. urban-like, grid plan.

The third or modified traditional plan purposely introduces several new factors to test. While it has a somewhat traditional look in the sense that it has an open space similar to that found in the Bwamangato tribal pattern (Figure 1 A),several new elements make it quite different. These new elements are: varied plot size, planned plot access, and a designated public space. In the fourth, the urban-like grid plan, slightly similar to the 1960's settlement pattern (Figure 1 C), rationalized, rectangular plot boundaries with some access to plots were introduced as variables.

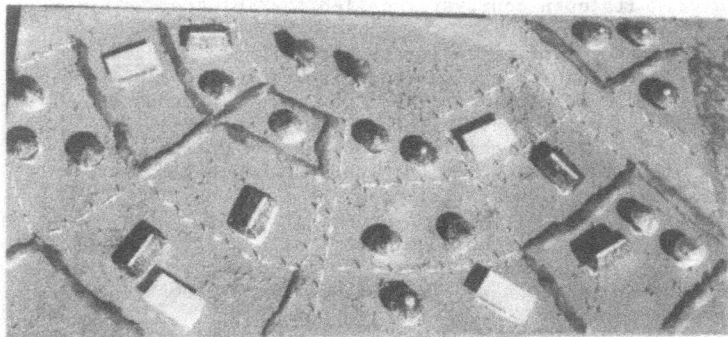

Figure 3 Modified Traditional Plan

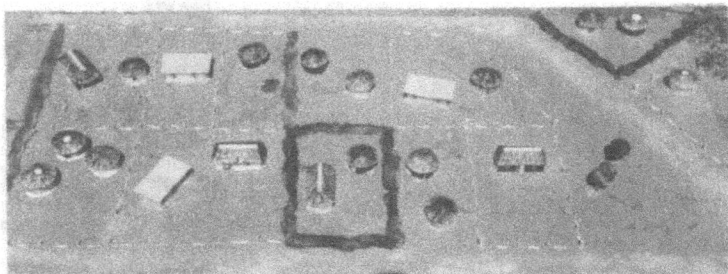

Figure 4 Urban-like Grid Plan

4. Findings from the prepared models experiment

The findings from the prepared models experiment are presented in the order in which they appear above: 1) traditional allocation plan, 2) land board allocation plan, 3) modified traditional plan and 4) urban-like grid plan. Each model will be presented first in terms of its perceived advantages, followed by its disadvantages.

a. Traditional allocation plan Because of residents' familiarity with the traditional plan, it was immediately recognizable to them in its model form (see Figure 2). While some residents saw advantages in the traditional plan, the large majority did not. The perceived advantages of that model are stated first, followed by its disadvantages. (Team Consultants 1984, pp.98-102)

(1) Advantages of Traditional Plan

-Families which live physically close to each other are likely to share with each other

108

(ii) Disadvantages of Traditional Plan

   -Limited vehicular and pedestrian access to the plot

   -water connection to the compound difficult because of
   clustered character of plots

   -common boundaries not easily maintained given that refuse and
   dirt can infiltrate the next plot

   -pit latrines on a neighboring plot could end up very close to
   one's house

   -narrow and winding roadways resulting from this pattern
   present a danger to children playing

   -the clustering effect makes it difficult for lorries to enter
   a plot

   -access to a compound often requires crossing one or more
   neighboring compounds

Many of the above perceived disadvantages result from the "moder-
nizing" influences which have reached the village on an increasingly
greater scale, namely automobiles and lorries and water and sanitation
facilities. Furthermore, these disadvantages are related to attitudes
towards kinsmen and neighbors which have altered as a result of the
increased scale of social relations. While social linkages among
villagers have broadened considerably, a greater feeling of exclusivity concerning one's plot has evolved, resulting in less cooperation between kinsmen and neighbors where property is involved.

b. Land board allocation plan Residents attending the kgotla meetings
recognized the land board model (see Figure 2) as the allocation
procedure presently being followed in Mahalapye.

   (i) Advantages of the land board allocation plan

   -a better pattern than the traditional because it offers
   access to the compound on all sides

   -the lines of the plot are straight

   -access from one plot to another can be accomplished using
   paths or lanes

   -since fences or boundaries are not shared, each plotholder is
   responsible for its maintenance

   (ii) Disadvantages of the land board allocation plan

   -since the plots are not always squared off, it is difficult
   to plan where to place one's house

   -the pathway between compounds is sometimes used for the
   disposal of waste, with no agreement between neighbors as to
   whom will clean it

109

-since roadways cannot always be placed perpendicularly, they often result in sharp curves which are dangerous to children

-the plots allocated now are not as large as those offered prior to the time of the land board

-too much space between plots is wasted, it being too small to be used for separate plots

Further discussion by ward members following the presentation of the land board allocation model indicated a concern for the additional cost of roads and water lines, given the erratic location of plots. Despite its disadvantages, based on their close familiarity with it, residents generally favoured the land board plan.

c. Modified traditional plan This model (see Figure 3) immediately elicited negative responses on the part of residents, but for two very different reasons. On the one hand, the model brought back memories to some of the old kgotla pattern, with its kraal, accompanied by the tight spacing of plots. On the other, it reminded others of the urban plan of low income municipal council housing.

(i) Advantages of the Modified Traditional Plan

-central area, if planned, might be useful for location of services, such as a clinic, store, or water standpipe

While the above advantage was stated, it was only elicited after some discussion and from a minority of respondents; in other words it was not an immediate response based on residents' first observations or reactions to the model. On the other hand, several disadvantages surfaced immediately.

(ii) Disadvantages of the Modified Traditional Plan

-no access to plots by road or pathway (except for those plots at the periphery)

-because of the spokewheel residential pattern, some plots are larger than others

-the lack of separate boundaries caused many of the same problems as the traditional plan, including ownership, waste and maintenance

-since plot boundaries are curved, it conveys an unplanned appearance

The critical test for this model was the size of plot and proximity to services, namely the larger the plot the greater the distance from services and, conversely, the smaller the plot the closer to services. Residents rejected this almost out of hand, even stating that they would much prefer the larger plot and the necessity of walking further to the services, such as a school, clinic, water standpipe, store. Possible improvements on this model were only offered with great reluctance and after some prompting. Road or pathways introduced

along the common boundaries were suggested as possible improvements
to a basically unacceptable plan.

d. Urban-like grid plan   Ward members' response to this model was
generally positive, with certain reservations. It was perceived as
having elements of both an urban plan (such as in the low income, self
help housing schemes in the capital city of Gaborone and other urban
centres) and the present land board system of allocations.

(i) Advantages of Urban-like Grid Plan

-lines of the plot are straight and the corners squared, for
the most part

-the roads do not have curves dangerous to pedestrians,
especially children

This plan represents a compromise with the land board plan, in that
plot size is more or less consistently the same size for each. But
the urban-like grid plan has some disadvantages not possessed by the
land board practice.

(ii) Disadvantages of the Urban-like Grid Plan

-the presence of common boundaries poses the same problems
seen in the other models

-slightly varied plot size was of continued concern

A solution recommended by respondents concerning the common boundary
issue was to place a roadway along the back sides of the plots,
parallel to the frontside roadway bordering each plot. Furthermore,
they expressed a desire to have a connecting road or pathway at the
side of every fourth or fifth plot.

5. Conclusions from the prepared models experiment

The prepared models experiment worked effectively in eliciting useful
responses from the villagers of Mahalapye concerning the development
and planning of the future design of their village. Use of this
technique enabled residents to easily sort out their likes and dis-
likes and discuss them in a meaningful way. Based on use of the
fixed or prepared modeling technique, villagers were able to demonstrate that they clearly understood the planning issues, in terms of
both the physical planning as well as the socioeconomic side. In
other words, they were able to conclude decisively on such factors
as: (a) the physical parameters of the most desirable plot; (b) the
underlying social or human rationale for their physical choice; and
(c) the economic element which is determining of cost. What is more,
the modeling approach allowed the researchers to systematically
prioritize residents' responses on these points.

The following is a summary of the findings from the prepared models
experiment, presented in terms of the original physical planning
elements introduced into the models:

-Plot boundaries   It is clear from the models experiment that the residents desire clearcut boundaries between their plots, representing a clear distinction from the traditional pattern of shared boundaries.

-Plot size The expressed desire is for large plots, approximately no less than 1,400 metres and as large as 2,000 metres, a preference which has evolved somewhat recently in relation to the increased use of the village plot for economic purposes.

-Access to plot While in the past access to the plot by way of other, neighbors' plots was desirable, presently it is considered undesirable, due in part to the need for vehicular access resulting from new ways of living and doing business.

-Residential plan The preference here is for a combination of physical planning factors including the plot, roads and services (see below), which can best be characterized as a rationalization of the land board model, i.e., spacious, squared, bounded plots with maximum access by way of straight roads and paths and with "reasonable" access to services.

-Road system With the presence of vehicles and their everpresent danger to children, residents express a desire for straight roads, in addition to which they want access to their plots via paths and roads.

-Utility and service While residents express a preference for "comfortable" distances between their plots and water standpipes, clinics, schools, stores, etc., they are willing to trade off the size of their plot against the distance to services.

The above summary of findings suggests that the modeling technique used in this experiment effectively elicited the salient factors required for the socioculturally and physically adaptable design and planning of Mahalapye. It now remains for the presentation of the open ended modeling experiment to corroborate the prepared models research.

F. RESIDENTS' PREPARATION OF THE SELF DIRECTED MODELS

Using the same avenue of the kgotla meetings employed in the prepared models experiment, open ended, self directed model building was carried out as the final step in the Mahalapye physical planning exercise. These meetings were only held after the prepared models research was performed. The purpose of the open ended experiment was twofold: (1) to test the factors utilized in designing the prepared models experiment and (2) more importantly, to provide villagers the opportunity to map out their own preferences for future plot and residential planning purposes.

The methodology used was to have ward members at the second series of kgotla meetings first discuss their preferences for plot and residential patterns. This was followed by a request by the consultants that the group recommend several ward members to build the actual models based on the discussions. Upon constructing the models with materials supplied by the consultants, (see Figure 5) discussions of

112

other possible options were held, which on several occasions resulted
in changes in the original design.

In every single kgotla meetings carried in the eleven wards to test
the self directed physical planning process, certain shared principles
of planning and design emerged. As Figure 5 suggests, clear spatial
dimensions and attributes of the plots were designated by villagers.
The common elements in the self directed models are as follows:

1. Common planning factors in the self directed models

   —one, unvaried plot size

Figure 5 Residents Constructing Self Directed Models

   —basically squared plots

   —boundaries on all sides of the plot such that no border touches a
   neighboring plot

   —access from at least two sides of the plot

It became clear from this modeling exercise that access to their
plots was defined by residents in a rather specific manner. That is,
access was specified broadly to include an informal pathway in contrast to a constructed road or path. Furthermore, existing standards
for roads, whose physical condition is packed dirt and gravel, were
described as adequate for future planning purposes. Of some concern
to residents was the width and degree of curve of the roadways.
These, in turn, are linked to villagers' perceptions of the safety of
their children and, secondarily, vehicular convenience. For main

113

roads it was deemed that two oncoming vehicles should be able to pass one another without slowing. On lesser roads or lanes, it was preferred that two oncoming vehicles should simply be able to pass one another.

As a result of changing social relations in Mahalapye, a greater feeling of exclusivity about individual plots has developed. This in turn has resulted in altered perceptions about proprietorship and the boundedness of land. Also involved is the increased importance of the plot as an economic entity, perhaps requiring more exclusive rights.

Concerning access to the plot, as described earlier, two sided access was deemed essential by the self designers. For the other two sides of the plot it was felt that foot paths would be adequate, so long as they were designed to prevent human elimination and the dumping of garbage.

2. Summary of self directed models

The use of self directed models confirmed the planning factors elicited through the prepared models. Questions of plot shape, boundaries, and access were confirmed in the self directed experiment. Also, broader planning issues such as the residential plan, road system and utility lines were corroborated in discussion of the villagers' own designs. Furthermore, the self directed modeling exercise and the ensuing discussions elicited common agreement among residents concerning a utility corridor or right of way. Residents agreed that the placement of a water pipeline or aboveground electrical line on their plots was an acceptable solution to provision of services so long as the land board apprised them of that at the time the plot was allocated. Given the foreknowledge about where a particular line would be placed in the future, residents would not build a structure where it would block access or, in the case of a pit latrine, contaminate a water line.

G. SUMMARY OF PREPARED AND SELF DIRECTED MODELS

The approach using the four prepared models employed planning principles based on earlier studies and preceding discussions with villagers. The self directed approach was based on a limited number of residents' own conceptions of appropriate planning. Both approaches were effective in deriving new information for planners and verifying existing understandings about residents' satisfactions and dissatisfactions with the present residential system and infrastructure. The combined exercise also underscored the present difficulties in administering land allocation and in the planning and provision of services. The present allocation mode is, on the one hand, satisfactory to villagers because it is a) generous in terms of plot size and b) somewhat laissez-faire concerning plot alignments. It is not totally satisfactory, on the other hand, in that it is uncoordinated, lacking both internal consistency and a set of administrative linkages with agencies of government providing facilities and services. For these reasons it is also not cost effective.

The above constraints are due in part to the unavailability of trained planning and administrative personnel at the district and village levels. This lack of trained personnel is a condition of Botswana's presently improving state of development and, of course, the reason for the presence of donor agency technical advisers such as the Canadian Team Consultants who carried out the study and the architect and social anthropologist who advised on the modeling exercises described in this chapter.

H. APPLICATION OF THE RESEARCH TO BOTSWANA'S MAJOR VILLAGE PLANNING

Since the typical developing country and donor agency planning effort usually requires more time than has elapsed since the completion of the study reported here (1984), little information is available concerning the study's impact on Mahalapye's planning. Because of existing priorities, neither the sponsor of the study, the Canadian International Development Agency, nor the Ministry of Local Government and Lands has reached the point where it is able or ready to act on the planning study. In any case, a preliminary or draft plan must be drawn up which reflects the study's findings, so that a consensus can be derived on the part of village, district and national planners and politicians. Nevertheless, the author has recently been informed that, despite the usual bureaucratic delays in the development process, interest in utilizing the study's findings is strong among central government officials. More especially, it has been enthusiastically received by Mahalapye officials and villagers generally and by councils in other villages which have received copies of the consultant's report. Given the politics of Botswana, in which rural populations are energetically represented in Parliament by their elected officials, it is presumed by the author that the proposals contained in the report will obtain a widespread hearing at critical levels of representation.

I. CONCLUSIONS

The modeling approaches used in the Mahalapye village planning study were successful for several reasons. First, the researchers had an excellent rapport with the villagers. Second, the villagers seemed to realize that the consultants were there to assist them. Third, villagers understood and appreciated the benefits of the research. Fourth, open discussions were held in which present and future planning needs were openly and frankly discussed with villagers. Fifth, existing planning conditions could be concretely and systematically represented in the prepared models. Sixth, the self directed approach permitted villagers to alter or retain those planning factors on which they had reached a consensus in the prepared models exercise. Seventh, the consultants were able to obtain continuous feedback from villagers on the findings. And, eighth, based on the author's earlier experience in Botswana (Mason 1979; 1980), it is quite probable that the conclusions from the modeling experiment will see the light of day in their ultimate application to the village planning process.

The participatory approach to village research and planning in Botswana, as seen from the modeling exercise described here, has application to the social and physical planning of human settlements generally. In a developing country setting such as Botswana, the approach described requires the integration of sociocultural, economic and technical disciplines. In other words, this research and planning activity could not have taken place in the absence of knowledge of the society, language and culture in which it was carried out.

Finally, it is self evident that the bottom up approach to planning has a strong potential in Botswana. The fact that participation is already a desirable end in Tswana society and, furthermore, that voicing opinions about the people and conditions surrounding them is deeply embedded in Tswana values, made the research not only plausible, but that much easier to carry out. In many societies, including some of those in the so-called developed category, east and west alike, this modeling experiment would have been simply implausible. In Botswana, the research described in this chapter not only elicited the richness of the participatory tradition, it provided definitive information to be used in the village planning process.

NOTES

[1]   An earlier, abridged version of this paper was presented in a symposium on Current Perspectives in Housing, Culture and Design at the Society for Applied Anthropology Annual Meeting, March 13-17, 1985, Washington, D.C. The author is grateful to Team Consultants, Calgary, Alberta, Canada for the use of their data, diagrams, and photographs and to architect planner John van Nostrand for his collaboration in the field research in Mahalapye. Support for his consultancy was provided by the U.S. Agency for International Development. (Mason 1984) The author assumes responsibility for the interpretation and any resultant errors.

Bibliography

Bryant, Coralie, and White, Louise C., Managing Rural Development: Peasant Participation in Rural Development, Kumarian Press, West Hartford, Conn., 1980.

Cohen, John, et al., Rural Development Participation: Concepts for Measuring Participation for Project Design, Implementation and Evaluation, Cornell University, Rural Development Committee, Ithaca, N.Y., 1977.

[DTRP] Department of Town and Regional Planning, Ministry of Local Government and Lands, Government of Botswana, Primary Centres in Botswana (Draft), Gaborone, 1979.

_____, Mahalapye Village Development Plan (Draft), Francistown, 1980.

Hardie, Graeme, Tswana Design of House and Settlement: Continuity and Change in Expressive Space, Dissertation, Boston University, Boston, 1980.

Mason, John P., "Social Research of Resident Preference, Need and Ability to Pay: Towards a Framework for Physical Planning Standards in Botswana's Self Help Housing in Site and Service Areas", Cooperative Housing Foundation, Washington, D.C., 1979.

_____, Mansion in the Sky: A Lesson in Self Help Housing from Gaborone, Botswana, Cooperative Housing Foundation, Washington, D.C., 1980.

_____, and Jesse Jones, Jr., "Priorities for Paced Growth in Mahalapye, Botswana: A Survey of Residents' Perceptions of Change and Its Affordability", Cooperative Housing Foundation, Washington, D.C., 1981.

_____, "Report on Sociologist's Consultancy to the Mahalapye Village Upgrading Project", Cooperative Housing Foundation, Washington, D.C., 1984.

Schapera, I., Native Land Tenure in the Bechuanaland Protectorate, The Lovedale Press, Lovedale, 1943.

TEAM Consultants, Mahalapye Upgrading Feasibility Study (Draft), Calgary, Alberta, Canada, 1984.

United Nations, Department of Social and Economic Affairs, A Manual and Resource Book for Popular Participation Training, 1978.

8. Environmental modelling: the view from Ecuador

SUSANA JACOME

INTRODUCTION

A wide variety of alternatives to housing have been studied and
implemented in third world countries, alternatives ranging from
finished "standard" housing to self-help housing. Nevertheless, among
this variety of solutions there are very few that are satisfactory or
adequate for "poor" users. Poor users are seldom taken into
consideration when proposing solutions to their housing problems; their
needs are great but their economic resources are scarce or nonexistent.
Some solutions propose user participation in the process and innovative
uses of resources. This paper explores some of these alternative
solutions which consider user participation through environmental
modelling, and analyses their applicability when technicians have to be
involved in third world, low-income, housing design situations.

Irregular or Squatter Settlements have been widely studied and
defined. Lerner (1979) refers to them as "a human flotsam and jetsam
that has been displaced from traditional agricultural life without
being incorporated into modern industrial life". Urquidi, (1975) sees
squatter settlements as "reception centers":

"These centers are or have been reception centers, by and
large, for the poor and unskilled migrants from rural areas
and the lesser urban zones. The expansion of these
communities has been so rapid and unexpected that it has been
impossible to supply them with essential services ... water,
sewerage, light and the other usual municipal services ...
They lack schools, health units, protection and amentities
... The land on which they are settled is frequently subject

118

to flooding and erosion, their housing consists largely of hovels ingeniously contrived from waste metal, wood, stone or board."

A very high percentage of the population living in third world countries do not use architects to "solve their housing problems". They do not need and luckily they can not afford one, since those having to live in government-provided housing live in architect designed houses which do not relate at all to their basic requirements. Evidence of this statement is vast; ranging from the Pruitt-Igoe public housing program in Saint Louis in the United States which was demolished; to a government housing program in Colta, a small country in the Ecuadorian Andes, which was never used by the indians. Doxiades (1963) affirms that existing architects do not design more than five per cent of all buildings created all over the world, and that in qualitative terms, a very large part of even this limited activity is of very low quality either because of the forces of inertia or because of a misunderstanding of the architect's role.

The question that comes to mind is that of the role of the architect in relation to this housing issue. Bruce Bentz (1981) points out that alternatives to traditional housing should be a major concern of the occupant, designer, architect, industry and government. Doxiades (1963) sees the only justification for architecture in the developing world as its connection with the overall evolution of society:

"The architect must adapt himself not only to the changing world, but also to the changing requirements of his profession and even to the notion that he may be on the wrong course altogether and may have to alter it ... architecture is no longer a matter to be decided solely by an architect, but must be thought out in conjunction with many other people and co-ordinated with many other views. Nor is it any longer sufficient to say that we can indeed create the best architecture but that government can not finance it, so that it all remains stillborn, a vague cipher on paper. This is not architecture but merely designing. Architecture exists only if it is implemented with actual building ..."

A new role for architecture in relation to this housing issue is required, one of understanding the new dimensions of the problem and the complexity of the forces which cause the present situation. Only this will lead to a study of new alternative techniques for finding solutions.

DEFINITION OF THE PROBLEM:

Before analyzing alternative solutions to housing problems, it becomes important to somehow define the housing problem in the third world. Housing is a right of all individuals. Nevertheless enormous deficits of housing exist not only in third world countries, but also in other areas. These deficits are not only quantitative, but also and principally qualitative, relative to what constitutes a basic way of living and satisfying human needs.

Housing shortages result from a rapid population increase basically caused by the shift of population from rural to urban areas. Unequal income distribution causes the majority of the population to create an "insolvent demand" in relation to the housing market. Finally, rampant real estate speculation pushes up costs of building sites and serves further to concentrate income. As an approach to the problem it will be important to explore several factors that influence or are part of the problem: economic factors, land tenure and government action.

Economic Factors:

Third world countries face severe economic problems which daily serve to enlarge the gap between rich and poor. Urban areas are growing rapidly; A World Bank study done in 1972 says that by 1980, 1/4 of the population in developing countries, some 550 million will live in cities. This number will grow to 1200 million by the year 2000 when 1/3 of the total population of the developing world is likely to be urban.

Urban growth in many Latin American Cities is not solely a result of industrial development and job opportunities in the urban areas. This growth is also a consequence of the deterioration of rural areas and the inability of peasants to survive in their own native environment.

The Third World today represents the setting of the most rapid movement of people from countryside to city. The socio-economic conditions of the cities are preferred by peasants who migrate to urban areas in the hope of finding improved living conditions.

Cities in developing nations are unprepared to absorb this gigantic growth and squatter settlements appear as a consequence. Although admittedly jobs are more plentiful in urban areas, they are insufficient. Also inadequate infrastructure and scarcity of urban land created by the speculation process, helps to bring about squatter settlements. The poorest groups, who initially migrate to the inner city slum areas in search of improved job opportunities, are pushed into the fringes of the cities, the only place with available land.

Housing (housing quality) is a major issue. Squatter settlements appear to be the only possible alternative to housing the poor and they are growing at incredibly high rates in urban areas. Examples of this extraordinary urban growth in Latin America are, for example:

Rio de Janeiro had 1/5 of the population living in _favelas_ by 1965. Lima by 1970 had 1/3 of the population living in _barriadas_. Mexico City has currently over 40 per cent of its population in Managua living in irregular settlements.

Analyzing housing phenomena in relation to supply and demand factors, we would find that this composition represents shortage of housing and basic human services predominantly affecting the poor population. There is a high demand for housing in the lower income groups but little or no supply from private or public sectors. Low income housing does not represent a profitable investment in traditional market terms.

Public investment directed towards the poor is, in Third World countries, necessarily limited and requires fiscalization and direct sudsidies in order to meet urban standards. Poor populations cannot afford housing under these conditions. Housing in these terms, could then be defined as an expensive commodity beyond the economic reach of the poor whose salaries, if existing, often barely meet their basic needs for food. The economic inaccessibility of low income families to standard urban housing gives them none but the following alternatives:

a) To over-utilize existing built spaces following a filtering down pattern whereby single family central city houses are transformed into multifamily slums

b) To move to illegal land subdivisions with low or non-existent service levels and land use standards. It is here, in these spontaneous and often illegal settlements that creative use of a wide variety of construction materials, owner participation and that of friends and relatives as well as skilled carpenters and masons make it possible for a poor population to afford housing.

Land Tenure:

Uncontrollable growth in Latin American Cities is coupled with a land speculation process which aggravates an already bad situation. As previously stated the peripheral zones of major cities are largely divided or invaded by new settlers. As a result of this process, prices of land experience sudden increases, and inflation of land prices make it profitable to leave undeveloped inner-city lots. Great amounts of land in the fringes of the cities are parcelled and sold in small plots. Although no infrastructures or utility services are provided, the land is invariably sold at profitable urban land prices. Owners foresee substantial profits in anticipation of their properties becoming urban land. A recent World Bank study reports that only 40 per cent of the urban land in Bangkok and Buenos Aires is unoccupied. This finding is important as these two cities are cities which have substantial squatter settlements.

Various types of transactions can take place under these conditions. In the city of Quito some have been detected:

1. Legal transactions: A gradual subdivision of land close to a consolidated area on the periphery of the city where land is sold by the owner. The fragmentation of big farms located near the urban perimeter (agricultural land converted into urban land) is legal when permitted under the Agricultural Land Reform. Some infrastructure is provided and the land is sold by the owner.

2. Illegal transactions: They are the most common form of fragmentation that occur when farms outside the urban perimeter are subdivided and sold without legal permits for subdivisions, thus they are sold without any land ownership document. (deeds) Land is sold by speculators at profitable prices; no infrastructure whatsoever is provided.

121

3. Invasions of land: Organized groups seeking solutions to their housing problems invade land in an effort to settle at least somewhere. Government policies are now accommodating the laws and legalizing the ownership of invaded lands.

The implications of these processes are:

- more rapid city growth
- The encouragement of land speculation and social marginalization caused by the constant push of the poorest into the fringes of the cities.
- Increase of urban land values.
- A process of an unbalanced increase in population density within the city occasioned by the leapfrogging of land use patterns.
- Accumlation of capital in few hands

There is a lack of effective regulatory control of land speculation by the government; moreover, governmental policies sometimes encourage these processes.

Government Action:

The housing problem is a reflection of the intense sociopolitical structure of a country and shows the degree of development or underdevelopment of Third World countries. Low income housing is not a profitable investment, therefore it is not produced by the market. The incomes perceived by the urban poor are too low for investing in standard housing. The incapability of the private sector to "solve" housing needs demands government intervention. Government policies in relation to housing tend to reinforce private capital investment.

Through different public organizations, governments in the different countries have been proposing and building "solutions" to housing. Nevertheless, Government actions are mainly directed to finance housing programs in order to make them accessible to larger middle-income groups; they are not directed towards the poor. A World Bank study in six cities (Bogota, Ahmedabad, Hong Kong, Mexico, Madras, Nairobi) concluded that the cheapest housing units currently produced by the public sector were unaffordable by 35 per cent to 68 per cent of the urban residents.

When housing is viewed as an expensive commodity, government policies are often directed to amplify the demand of the lower sectors of the population through credit mechanisms and different types of subsidies which permit increased buyer solvency. In reality the poorest people have no access to this type of credit mechanism, cannot obtain adequate housing and have to make their own provisions as best they can.

Turner's (1976) comments in relation to government actions are:

"To treat housing as a commodity is silly enough, but to assume that it must or should be supplied by ever larger pyramidal structures and centralized technologies is suicidal. Yet this is the basis of all modern housing policies - a quick-sand in which all sink - ... The modern tendency of central government and even international agencies to involve themselves in the detailed planning, building and

management of people's dwellings is complemented by another common
and wasteful absurdity: the private determination of land prices by
aggregated decisions and actions.¨

He does not feel that government has no role, but that there should
be a radical change of relations between people and government, a
relation in which government ceases to persist in doing what it does
¨badly and uneconomically¨ - building and managing houses - and
concentrates on what it has the authority to do, ¨ensure equitable
access to resources which local communities could not provide for
themselves¨.

Government is an important financing source in Third World countries
(may be the only source) so the role of government in relation to
housing should be defined precisely ... ¨the attitudes adopted by
governments vis-a-vis their squatter population will be crucial in this
respect¨ (Peter Ward 1977)

Government actions have been ineffective. They were not intended to
really solve the problem of housing when perceived as an expensive
commodity for the poor. These programs have been primarily directed as
groups in society that could have access to credit systems. Government
bureaucracies, as financing sources, have had all the power. The user
who has access to credit, on the other side, had no voice or choice.
The products of such a relationship have been housing programs in which
user's needs are rarely considered. They are the product of
authoritarian decisions taken by those with the financing resources and
the decision-making power.

¨Against the recurrent discovery of the insoluable problems of a
conventional housing strategy for the poor, came the discovery of the
squatter settlement not as a problem but as a solution. Fieldwork by
people such as John Turner, William Mangin, and Elizabeth and Anthony
Leeds depicted the ¨squatter settlement¨, rising in cities not as
¨rings of misery¨, ¨creeping cancers¨ and ¨slums of despair¨, but as
evolving communities, active, organized, self mobilizing; and the
housing stock therein as substandard only if looked at at one point in
time, a stock in progress, on the way to becoming adequate through
piecemeal investment over time by the individual household¨ (Lissa
Pettie 1976).

This different point of view brings about a whole range of
alternative solutions to housing. Housing is seen as a process where
time is a factor and the squatter settlement a self evolving community.
In place of static situations involving slow change, we are now caught
in a dynamic situation bringing the most rapid changes in the way.
What is really different in these situations is the tempo of change, a
squatter settlement might appear from night to day, and the
consolidation process takes a very short time.

If architects are to be involved in the process, new attitudes are
required. Doxiades (1963) says: ¨The basic problem of architecture
today is the addition of the dimension of time to the three dimensional
synthesis we have had to handle up to now.¨ Housing cannot be a final
product anymore. Housing should be an evolving structure, flexible

enough to change over time and more important, it should be the product
of its users.

Participation appears in the process as a magic world:

"Interests in users needs or user participation is not rooted in
romanticism about human involvement, but rather in the recognition
that users have a particular expertise different than but equally
important to that of the designer. This expertise then needs to be
integrated to the process that concerns itself with environmental
change" (Sanoff 1978).

It is important to look for a participation process that deals with
the problem as a whole. A participation process that permits users and
technicians to know about their needs and possibilities (economic,
technical) as well as to know about his neighbors needs and
possibilities. Turner (1976) sees participation occurring only if
participants are free to choose:

"If citizen participation is necessary, it is essential that the
participants, enterprises and institutions they employ should be free
to use the resources available ... Not only must resources such as
building materials and equipment, manual and managerial skills,
building land and financial credit be accessible, but their users
should also be free to employ them in ways compatible with their own
requirements without inhibiting the freedom of other".

The importance of participation when dealing with Third World poor
squatters might be that we are dealing with people whose values and
life styles are not the same as those of "westerns", a category into
which almost all technicians fall. Stea (1982) mentions different
values among Third and Fourth World people such as:

- Maintenance of a sense of community may be more significant than
  individual achievement.
- Decision might be made in a community fashion rather than
  individually.
- Egalitarian rather than hierarchical relations might prevail.
- Ideas in relation to land and land tenure may be decidely
  different.
- Roles and aspects of architecture may be differently conceived
  (e.g. Rapoport, 1969).
- The significant elements of house and settlements may be
  categorized in ways other than ours.
- Ideas of what goes with what are unlikely to be the same.
- In summary, the architectural patterns indicative of environment-
  culture/behavior relations are likely to be different.

Low income housing research was done in Esmeraldas, a tropical city
in the Ecuadorian Coast (Jacome, Rios 1981). This study was part of a
housing design project thesis for 400 workers of an Oil Refinery who
were members of a Cooperative. They were given a piece of land some 2
kilometers away from the city, close to the Oil Refinery. The
objective of the project was, among others, to propose users
participation in the design of their habitat in order to diminish the
authoritarian impositions of technicians; participation will also

facilitate the detection of community needs and their compatibility with individual needs.

The sample was 12 per cent of the total population. The idea was to detect, through personal interviews and visits to their houses, needs and requirements that were in accordance with their living style which could facilitate design. It was of great importance to see the way space was organized in their houses as well as their attitudes and behavior in the different spaces.

Most of the workers, about 69 per cent of the total, were young migrants from small towns or the countryside who had moved to Esmeraldas and were living in the city slums. 52 per cent of the total population sampled were younger than 19 years old and 41 per cent ranged from 20 to 39 years old. They are indeed a young population that can tolerate and easily adapt in their transition to urban life. 86 per cent of the total members of the Cooperative did not own a house.

The number of people living in a house fluctuates with time. Family composition is very large and usually more than one relative lives together with the family, specially when they have moved to the city. In 41 per cent of the families sampled, the number of members ranged from 5 to 10, 32 per cent of the families sampled lived with more than one relative; and in 8 per cent of the houses, there were two families living together. Not only relatives but also friends would come over and live in the house and users adapted spaces very well to these constant changes.

The public-private domains of street and housing were difuse. The street was the continuation of the house, a place for sitting in, not only passing through, the place to gather and communicate with friends. The house is a shelter with most of the living done outdoors, there is a high social interdependence which allows for mutual help and the support of familiar social networks. Their concerns for private land ownership were not very high, indeed, their physical territoriality was not well defined.

Varieties of space use is very common in all houses. Use and perception of space is different. They do not always value as highly the importance of specialized spaces for different activities that take place in a house. Most of the areas were areas of multiple use, only kitchens and bathrooms were specialized areas.

Mainly local materials, such as wood and cane were utilized for building. In spite of living in a tropical area their houses were cool, only 20 per cent used fans or other instruments for ventilation while the majority developed a very good natural system by leaving open spaces at critical points and creating air currents. Nevertheless, when the potential users were asked about their preferences, the major determinants of house form were the prestige of new materials and the value of private zones. They express the importance of security as a determinant of spatial organization and the need for green recreational areas.

These findings have their importance because the way in which space and people in space are organized affect evaluation and the design of the environment. The results of this research led us to the definition of their need for housing as "something" that should be flexible, that could evolve and change overtime in relation to their needs and requirements. An effective space where the best use of local materials and resources occur, a human scale integrated to the ecological cycle. There was a need for integrating public and private spaces, their perceptions of privacy were not the same as ours; in fact, the street was their living room and their bathrooms were in areas outside the house.

If architects had to provide their input in a situation like this, participation in the process could be vital, a participation process that permitted the architect to "work with" and learn from the user, not to "work for" and try to teach him new values.

There has been a considerable movement towards involvement of users in the definition of their environment. Participation appears as a communication process through which users supply behavioural information to planners or architects, and they then supply the users with information about possible alternative innovations. (Lawrence 1979).

But participation has been used for different purposes (Arnstein 1969):

- It has been used for manipulation where people were placed on "rubber stamp" advisory committees as a way to get their support, (to pretend that the poor and ethnic minorities are involved in planning programs).

- Participation as an informing mechansim; information is commonly utilized too late in the processes, usually too late for users to have any impact on the final product. This is a one way flow of information.

- For consultation; it should take place early in the process and be used.

"If information that has been got is not connected with other genuine models of participation, there is no way of guaranting that the citizens concerns will be actually acted on.. (Arnestein 1969) "The public hearing with experts seated on a raised platform, presenting design and planning solutions, and the community seated as an audience prepared to ask the right questions seems a rational form of participation of most use" (Stea 1982)

- For placation: There are instances where some true representation is allowed by the "power elite" while it makes sure that it is never enough representation to challenge their traditional power.

- For partnership or redistribution of power if there is a power base in the community.

- For delegated power: To acquire decision making power through negotiation with public officials.

- For citizen control: sometimes, people have power and govern their own program or institution.

The concept of participation has faced problems since its introduction in the 60's, and the falure of some of its methods have caused in many instances the abandonment of participation in the design process, but the results are the production of less effective satisfactory architecture.

"If participatory design methods have shortcomings this should not be levelled at the tenents of public participation, but primarily at the means currently employed to involve users in the design process ... in conclusion, a redefinition and a diversification of participatory architectural design methods is suggested" (Lawrence 1982).

New ways of applying an old form of simulation, environmental modelling, have been developed and experimented upon by Stea (1980), Bentz (1981), Lawrence (1982), among others. Bentz and Stea use small scale models which have been tested and found to be useful tools for participation. These alternatives deal with the use of modelling kits whose elements can be be manipulated, and which allow decisions to be revoked, as much as users want. Playing games could permit the users to define their own spaces in accordance with their spatial needs and values.

"The technique enables the conversion of most of the user designer interaction into visual, graphic and most important manipulative forms bypassing the translation of visual linking into verbal form and back again, so characteristic of traditional participation" (Stea 1980).

Modelling appears as an alternative way of communication that can be understood, manipulated, utilized, and is financially feasible, in a Third World situation. "Rural folks in particular are often further intimidated when confronted by urban researchers who they assume will evaluate what they produce as being or urban standards" (Stea 1980). Modelling reduces the number of misunderstandings in the two-way user designer communication process.

This is especially important where cognitive and other cultural differences exist between participants and professionals, since much of the population in squatter settlements come from rural areas. Experimenting with the modelling kit with a Navajo community, Stea (1978) discovered that while Navajo Indian children were afraid to be verbally communicative, the building models were non-threatening objects to which they could easily relate. Through the childrens relations to the toys, then we lean something new about the fluidity of the traditional Navajo extended family homestead. What is needed for Third World design participation, therefore, is both a method of communication and a technique for representation (Stea 1981) and modelling appears to fill these requirements.

Bentz proposes an approach to the improvement of housing that includes users involvement in the design process by the use of a modelling kit that permits them to design their own houses. He points out that a building system comprised of factory produced components can provide a substantial repertoire of desirable designs, can relationalize production and can provide opportunities for users involvement ... "A shell or envelope design provides opportunities for flexibility, adaptability, add-ins and the use of versatile furniture and equipment." (Bentz 1981)

A self housing program, directed for middle income people, was implemented satisfactorily in Canada. Users participation in the design process through modelling their own houses permitted users satisfaction. Besides, 2/5 of the total costs were saved in comparison with conventional housing.

"Despite the programs financial advantages over conventional housing, rising costs have had the effects of making the program unaffordable for many deserving citizens. CHAP (Cooperative Housing Action Program) has to reassess its one family - one house - one lot policy. Multiple family dwellings and shared land are an inevitable next step. This new posture, when it is assumed, will necessitate a new approach to users involvement in the housing process. The modelling kit and a building system could play an important role in this necessary transition." (Bentz 1981)

In the Esmeraldas housing project we proposed housing cells whereby land was shared by a group of 8 families. Houses were self-built by the utilization of a system of wooden components. Users' participation in the design process was non-existent, but their evaluation was refreshing. They liked the idea of sharing spaces in which their children could play and be safe; they liked the idea of having a house that could grow over time, with interiors that were flexible.

The validity of this evaluation is nevertheless questionable because it was done showing the potential users nice graphics and drawings of how their houses would look. It could be that their "I like it" refers only to the graphics, not to the context. It could also refer to the interest we demonstrated in trying to interpret their needs, or our perception of what we thought their needs were.

Having a modelling kit in that process, would have allowed users participation in the resolution of the design of their own houses. The only thing we did was to give them a variety of possible housing arrangements with the use of the designed components, and that is somehow restricting their own choice.

Questions such as their acceptance of shared land, that were very much discussed among us, could have been solved or at least discussed with them. We saw them living in areas where land was common to many people, and we assumed they could easily accept that. The advantage we saw in our proposal was that users' share of land provided them with open areas that could be more efficiently used by themselves. High costs of land would not have allowed them to acquire open spaces that could be big enough for their own use.

It appears that the "what do you want?", "What have you got?"
communication problem appeared in this evaluation, where we thought we
knew what they needed and just presented to them in nice graphics that
they might not have understood. Participation through modelling would
have reduced all these steps.

CONCLUSION

In situations of scarcety of economic resources, the costs of mistakes
are too high to be afforded. Public housing programs have usually gone
from one failure to another not only in Third World countries but
elsewhere and there are many examples that speak for themselves. One
of the most dramatic cases is the Pruitt-Igoe architectural awarded
public housing project, built in Saint Louis, which was partly
demolished 20 years later as a result of its unpopularity and
vandalization.

When architects are involved in designing low income housing,
efficiency and the best use of resources is of extreme importance.
User participation in this process appears to be fundamental. Housing
has to be seen not as a final product, but as something that can evolve
over time as economic resources become available; the users are the
only ones who are capable enough to define their needs and priorities.
Communication through modelling could permit interaction between users
and builders and the use of modelling kits can be an efficient way of
getting users involvement in the design process. The elements should be
simple enough to be understood and manipulated by the users. "What is
required is the use of a visual spatial form that be composed of
elements familiar to the user and that permits an "as if" stance".
(Kaplan 1977)

Consensus for policy implementation could be experienced and obtained
through environmental modelling. "As a participatory
dynamic/perceptual technique for simulation, environmental modelling
could facilitate transduction, communication and interaction between
users and policy makers" (Stea 1982). A modelling kit could serve as a
useful tool to test hypotheses in relation to potential users reactions
to policy changes and standard variations. It could be interesting for
example to test users reactions to the sharing of land with other
neighbours. Concerns in relation to the rise of expectations among the
population where these programs were carried out could be a restriction
for the use of modelling kits.

Bibliography

Arnstein, S. (1969) 'A ladder of Citizen Participation', in Journal of the American Institute of Planners.

Bentz, B. (1981) 'Transition: User Participation in the Design of Housing', Open House International, 6(2).

Doxiades, K. (1963) Architecture in Transition, Oxford University Press, New York.

Jacome, S and Rios, C. (1981) 'Unidad Vacinal de 400 Viviendas para los Obreros de CEPE en Emeraldas", Tesis de Grado, Facultad de Arquitectura y Urbanismo, Universidad Central, Quito.

Kaplan, R. (1977) 'Participation in the Design Process: A Cognitive Approach' in Stokols, D. Perspectives on Environment and Behavior, Peldnum, New York.

Lawrence, R. (1982) 'Designers Dilema: Participatory Design Methods', in Francescato, G. ed. Knowledge for Design (EDRA 13), College Park, Md, EDRA.

Sanoff, H. (1978) Designing with Community Participation, Dowden, Hutchinson and Ross, Stroudsberg, Penn.

Stea, D. (1980) 'Environmental Modelling as Participatory Planning', Fourth World Studies in Planning //5, UCLA School of Architecture and Urban Planning, Los Angeles.

Stea, D. (1982) 'Cross Cultural Environmental Modelling', in Blaird. D. and Lutkus, A.D. eds., Mind Child Architecture, University Press of New England, Hanover, NH.

Turner, J. (1976) Housing by People: Toward Autonomy in Building Environments, Marion Boyars, London.

Urquidi, V. (1975) 'The underdeveloped city', in Hardoy, J. ed. Urbanization in Latin America: Approaches and Issues, Garden City, New York.

9. Environmental deterioration: a historical (and futurological) perspective

JOHAN GALTUNG

1. WHY DOES THE ENVIRONMENT DETERIORATE?

Apart from some partial victories the degradation of the environment continues. Why this is so is not so difficult to understand. The reason lies partly in our economic systems and partly in our ability, through the scientific-technical revolution (STR), to bend nature, to process her more than ever before so as to yield goods and services - that sometimes may prove to be "bad" and "disservices", in disguise. It does not seem, incidentally, to be a question of whether that social system is "capitalist" or "socialist" - almost regardless of how those terms are defined. The decisive causal factors are much simpler, actually so simple that for that very reason they are often overlooked in what passes as "sophisticated" analysis. They are: (1) the transition from limited, small economic cycles to extended and expanding economic cycles and (2) transition from cyclical to linear ecological processes.

Let us start with the expansion of economic cycles. By an "economic cycle" is simply meant the way in which Nature, Production and Consumption are linked together:

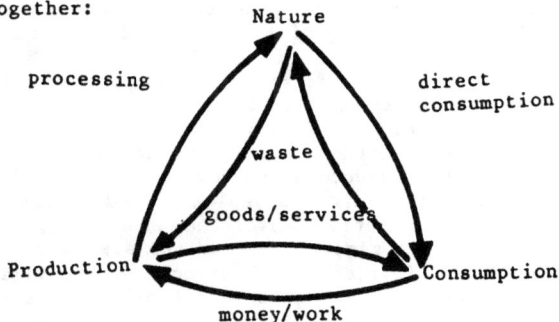

Nature

processing   direct consumption

waste

goods/services

Production   Consumption

money/work

131

Matter is taken from nature for direct consumption (water, air; harvesting) or indirect consumption via production, meaning **processing**. Agriculture is one way of processing nature, and no longer a soft one. Matter also comes back to nature, viz., as waste - as agricultural industrial waste from production, and household waste from consumption. Thus, **nature is the big loser**, exchanging her natural/raw/primary materials for waste products. The winners are (hopefully) human beings who benefit from the end consumption, and (certainly) those who make a living/profit from the various links in the chain between nature and end consumption. Clearly, had Nature been an economic actor in her own right this would not have worked. Nature would have put up at least as much a struggle as human beings do over the terms of exchange between the goods/services demanded and the money or work supplied to buy them; the struggle of consumers and workers for cheaper goods and higher salaries. But Nature is patient so she needs good spokesmen before Nature hits back with more than degradation: with total disruption - desertification.

Then there is the second factor: the transition from cyclical to linear ecological processes. The scientific-technical revolution has had two clear consequences:

- to make it possible to process much more raw material from nature than ever before, and particulary more non-renewable resources, from the mineral "kingdom", including water and air. Inorganic resources played relatively speaking, a less important role earlier. The plant/animal "kingdom", the biosphere, that through quicker bioligical processes is more renewable, is also threatened with the extinction of species - however - organic raw materials are also processed more than before.

- to send back to nature waste products in qualities and quantities nature cannot handle, meaning cannot absorb (CO_3), cannot break down (plastic), some of them toxic to human beings and/or other parts of nature (SO_2). Efforts to hide them, or to dilute the contamination prove largely unsuccesful: they show up, sooner or later.

In short, the twin problems of depletion and pollution. At deeper levels of analysis these processes also threaten the very resilience or maturity of eco-systems. Through these processes diversity is reduced and equilibria based on symbiosis break down, among other reasons because of changes in the composition of the systems. The ultimate possible consequence of all of this is **desertification**, today threatening one fifth of the earth's land surface.

However, as indicated above, this apparent triumph of the natural sciences in helping processing nature to a hitherto unknown extent is not operating alone. We would have only a minor fraction of the problems today **if the economic cycles had remained so limited in extension that producers and consumers would themselves have faced the consequences of their own depletion and pollution.** The key production/consumption unit in human history, the family farm, has survived through generations for the simple reason that the consequences of irrational householding are visited upon the perpetrators or at least their offspring - a strong argument, incidentally, in favour of hereditary farms so that one cannot run away from the consequences through good salesmanship. Soil depleted renders poor harvests. Products that are polluted cannot sustain healthy human bodies. And this applies not only to agricultural production but to any type of production: the negative consequences that come home to oneself have a great impact on the conscience.

This does not mean that "enlightened self-interest" has been in the past, a sufficient condition for sound ecological behaviour, and it is not necessary as a condition either. All that is being said is that it helps tremendously. Consider some important implications:

- **nomadism was based on this insight,** but with the conclusion that when the environment was sufficiently depleted (pollution being less important, only "scientfic man" has been capable of making waste products nature cannot handle) the time had come to select another place for depletion/littering. The places could be on a cycle, ultimately coming back to the point of origin when nature had repaired the damage and the renewal had taken place, thereby negating the predation - as do Mongolian shepherds, with their **yurts,** today.

- **"enlightenment" may have been insufficient":** people may not have been sufficiently aware of the harmful consequences of their action; the negative increments per year may have been almost imperceptible, and when cumulative and/or synergistic effects show up as a catastrophe other explanations (e.g. supernatural) may have been found.

- **"self" may have a class character:** the economic cycles may have been very limited spatially, but the pollution/depletion consequences may have been pushed onto the lower classes in society, in the form of dwindling food resources and a life close to garbage dumps literally speaking;

- **priority may have been given to more immediate interests:** even the family farm will deplete their own soil mercilessly and eat the grain set aside as seeds when the only alternative seen is starvation.

In the European Middle Ages all these factors were at work. The economic, particulary agricultural, cycles were limited in extension. But the consequences of very irrational ecological behaviour were pushed onto the serfs and peasants, who then were faced with starvation, their soil being depleted futher. Ultimately this led to the "nomadism" of the lower layers into cities and to places far away, and of the higher layers into piracy, brigandry, crusades and other efforts to get away. What happened was interpreted in religious terms consistent with medieval mentality. The cataclysm known as the Black Death related to all of this, as the final **coup de grace.**

And yet, in spite of this, it is undeniable that the opportunity given after the Middle Ages - and increasingly so - to build economic cycles so that the harmful consequences in terms of depletion and pollution are not visited upon oneself, has increased tremendously. Commercial capitalism has been followed (perhaps also preceded) by commercial socialism. Cars and car factories can pollute, and nature can be depleted, thousand of miles away from corporate offices, located in beautiful parks where birds still sing and decisions of ecological significance for places far away - for instance by exporting polluting

industries as "development aid" - are taken. Exhaust in the air-
conditioning shafts of these offices, industrial effluents in their
drinking water, and a gradual transformation of their parks into
wasteland might have been a powerful heuristic if it were seen as
linked to corporate action, and not as the pranks of wicked ecological
action groups. In the car factory itself it might even be easy to do
this: the drinking water could come from the river, downstream of
course; the air from the smoke-stack. The class character of the
mechanisms that prevent this from happening is rather crucial to the
understanding of the whole issue, yet left untouched in typical (inter)
government analyses. One reason for this is related to international
class structure: "expanding, even unlimited" economic cycles is another
way of saying "free trade", meaning the free flow of raw materials, of
capital, of labor and of the finished products, whether under
private/corporate or public/bureaucratic auspices. But the ecological
consequences of that is obvious; to displace the depletion and the
pollution to the corner of the world where people are so weak that they
cannot protest, and/or to the corners of the geography so far away that
nature's protests are not felt - by diluting pollutants in the
atmosphere, and oceans, or hiding them in caves, until they make
themselves felt, again.

How, then, can we nevertheless feel the consequences? Through
exactly the above mechanism of "enlightenned self-interest", since
there is "only one earth", said to have essentially a space-ship
economy. **But this type of consciousness is mediated.** It is not
immediate, as for the farmer destroying his own soil, or the manager
drinker his own polluted water. Hence, for consciousness to be strong,
when the economic cycles are expanding, one has to be

> **very enlightened** - through scientific or other knowledge
> **have an extended self** - empathy with other regions, other classes,
> and with nature located on that expanding cycle (and elsewhere)
> **have a long-term perpective** - solidarity with coming generations.

If people had all of this, then much would have been different. But
we know perfectly well that only a few people can be said to rank high
on all three characteristics. And it is not enough to rank high on
only two of them. The last two - **synchronic and diachronic solidarity**
- are excellent human qualities but not helpful alone if not backed up
by knowledge. Knowledge with only one of these moral qualities very
easily leads to refined forms of exploitation into the other corner
where the moral light is not shining. A government may well practise
socialism at home and exploit other countries ecologically; or there
may be intergovernmental cooperation in avoiding the type of ecologcial
harm that hits the higher classes, pushing it onto the lower classes
all around the world, e.g. in the form of very high food prices because
of soil depletion. In addition, although one can readily recognize the
presence of these three traits, in the many ecological action groups
(and among artists, the most sensitive part of humankind, in general),
one can just as easily recognize the **absence** of one, two or three of
them in those who decide, in the public or private sector, over the
construction of economic cycles. The result is environmental rhetoric,
some recycling and cleaning-up exercies. But the environmental
deterioration continues as the cycles expand and penetrate more deeply,
economically and administratively. And the worst consequences are for

future generations.

Thus, our general moves, now slow, now fast, toward local ecocatastrophes (the global ones are still far away) are based on the interplay between the unlimited expansion of economc cycles, and the linear impact of the scientific-technical revolution, or between industrialism and capitalism, private and state, and industrialism, to put it in words that convey almost the same if one thinks of the international character of these two phenomena. One may argue back and forth over the tremendous benefits of these two institutions relative to the tremendous costs involved; exploited people everywhere. Clearly, today very few people, and only in very few places, are willing to contract economic cycles and soften industrialism to the point that rational ecological behaviour becomes a must and almost automatic, and not only an ideology. Tomorrow this may change, but the benefits seem to outweigh the costs for most people, and not only for elites. Given that, the prospects for the successful turning of the many negative environmental trends are negative indeed. Major ecocatastrophes are considerably more when there is depletion on one end and pollution on the other end of these linear processes - and maturity reduction all over.

To explore this further, let us look at the four different situations that derive from the two key dimensions:

Table 1. Four different contexts for ecological action

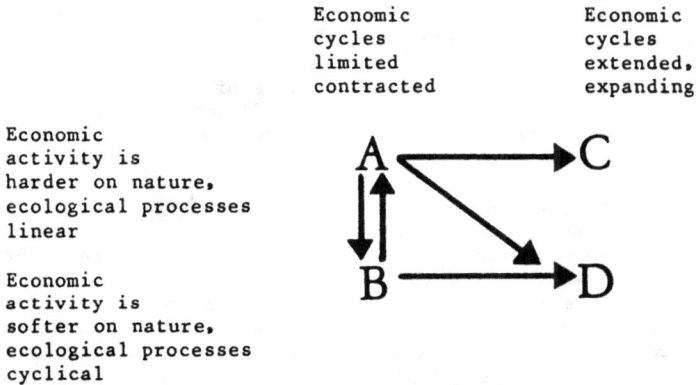

	Economic cycles limited contracted	Economic cycles extended, expanding
Economic activity is harder on nature, ecological processes linear	A	C
Economic activity is softer on nature, ecological processes cyclical	B	D

From what has been said above it follows that in general we shall have either case A or case D. When economic activities get harder, meaning linear processes with depletion on one end and pollution on the other, the local consequences become so unbearable that the system will collapse. One alternative is back to A. Another is to have the consequences removed, and one way of doing this is to have the cycles expand so that the more unplatable consequences can be accommodated, simply because they happen far away (The A -> B -> D sequence in Table 1). However, even with soft activities consequences can be felt far away, for to the man-made economic cycles must be added the non-manmade long-range ecological cycles brought about by the movement of air (winds) and water (rivers, currents), (the A -> C sequence in Table 1). So, it is essentially case B that is of less interest:that combination is not viable, at least not in the longer run, leading to A or D depending on what is modified. Today that would mean to D - contraction and softness are exceptions. Moreover the transition to D may also be direct from A - indicated in the figure, as when trade and industrialism go hand in hand.

Case A has, today, a touch of the utopian, but is by and large what the green movement in the first world stands for. It is probably much more realistic than people commonly believe. It presupposes not less but more, but then also much better science and technology, capable of making do with limited resources, scratching nature gently, using sun, wind and running water and biomass, three-dimensional agriculture, electronic processing, miniaturized industrial processes, recycling and cleaning-up nodes in the cycles. And yet the major asset is not to have to rely on abstractions for ecological action: **the consequences, good and bad, come home literally speaking.** For this to be true, however some conditions have to obtain. There has to be **understanding** of ecological cycles and how they intermesh with economic cycles. There has to be **solidarity within that community, meaning that there must be limits to inequity and inequality, limits to how much the community can be a class or even caste society with the bad consequences displaced downwards. And extreme poverty, and greed** may ruin this, too, giving low priority to ecological considerations. In societies with steep class gradients the gains from the limited economic cycle may easily wash out as the European Middle Ages have shown: there are limits to predation.

Case C is an extention of case A, either because of nature's own action, or because it is found necessary (by whom?) to expand the economic cycles, to trade and exchange with far away places. Essentially this calls at the very least for solidarity with those places, located as they are on the same ecological and/or economic cycles. The consequences at least have to be made understood, and vividly. Yellow rain, dark or red snow, poisoned waters, have to be felt both by sender and receiver as a link between sender and receiver, a harmful one, so much so that something has to be done about it. Something like a tracer element in an organism, or the tricks geologists make use of to trace undergroud currents would be useful. Economic/ecological cycles must be seen to be understood; the abstract has to be made concrete. And yet it is clear that from understanding there is no immediate link to positive action, except in a context of empathy. For man-made economic cycles this is not so important: the import of a polluted product may be stopped, likewise the export of a product based on depletion of non-renewable resources. For the non-manmade ecological cycles brought about by wind and water in motion it is worse; intergovernmental action is needed, based on any mixture of the usual three forms of power: persuasion, bargaining and force. With internationalization of cycles environmental action also has to internationalize, even when the economic activity is relatively soft on nature. Hence the care for international action in this field - it follows from the movements in atmosphere and hydrosphere. But case C is solft, hence easier.

Case D is the tough one, and the typical one. It is doubtful that much can be done to improve this case. There is so much to be gained; in terms of power, profit and privilege from being on top of this type of cycle, specializing in secondary, and more recently in tertiary sectors of economic activities, as is well known. Whether there is much to be gained for those not at the top from this type of activity over which they have very little control is another matter. Hence, the best contribution to environmental protection would probably come about if people could be convinced that systems of types A and C can be at least as effective, particulary in the longer run, in overcoming extreme poverty as in societies of type D. To show that, however, other types of expertise is needed than that provided by economists whose narrow thinking is typically geared to hard industrialism (with linear ecological processes) and long distance trade (expanding cycles); processing case D systems would belong to the key ingredients of a package of environmental action, as would constructive activity to promote systems of case A and C; case B being ruled out by its own logic, but nevertheless empirically frequent.

Today, however, that activity is an uphill fight except in some countries that are more enlightened, less inegalitarian and exploitative of other parts of the world, and far from misery, particulary the Northern European welfare states. And even in these countries environmental action is needed, for they do engage both in hard industrialism and in extended cycles. The methods typically used to put some constraints on case D are:

- **to counteract hard industrialism:**
  pollution aspect: criminalization, with detection, fines and other punishment
  depletion aspect: price mechanisms (oil and soil being good examples)

- **to counteract transmission to other countries:**
  national pollution law extended to international law
  international price mechanisms for the depletion aspect.

The contention here is that this will hardly work, for some very simple reasons. Thus, for the polluter what is bad about pollution becomes no longer the toxic impact, but the possibility of being punished, which ultimately is a question of being detected. And that, in turn, easily becomes similar to the relatively parallel field of arms production and control: it is so much easier to conceal and cheat than to control and detect. To get out at night with a truck with an open valve, letting the toxic flow out slowly while the truck is driving fast; or the same for a ship - particularly in international waters - is so much easier than detecting such things. The detected dumps for toxic waste products are of course only a small fraction of those really existing. Thus, it is the industrial process itself that has to be changed through softer, more cyclical technologies, and the economic cycle itself that has to be limited enough to be understood, and controlled by those directly concerned.

Similar arguments apply to the price mechanism: from being a question of preserving the basis of sustenance for life on earth it becomes a question of guaranteeing that there will be people able to pay. And that, in turn, becomes a question of creating a society so that the

demand becomes inelastic within a range of prices: people simply **have**
to have even an increasingly expensive commodity, regardless of price -
one key example being oil - if it has been made sufficiently
indispensable, with no easily available alternative. And soil is an
equally good example: prices for the use of cultivable soil to build
dwellings or factories may be increased to discourage people from using
the ground that way. The net result is likely to be more expensive
housing, and more expensive industrial products; with obvious class
implications. In short, efforts to let the consequences come **home to**
the polluter and depleter by creating an artificial micro-environment
around that person with its rewards and punishments are not likely to
yield environmentally beneficial consequences, except in particulary
law-abiding and economically rational societies. The burdens will
simply be pushed onto the consumer - as is usually the case. It is the
social construction of case D itself that is problematic, even **wrong.**
And case D is typical.

So far the exploration of why the environment deteriorates has been
linked to the ever-expanding **economic** cycles, engendering production
and consumption processes that not only deplete and pollute nature but
also are so complicated and far apart socially and spatially that they
become exceedingly difficult both to understand and to control.
Obviously there are also many benefits from these expanding economic
cycles: more than compensating for the costs at least for those on top
of the cycles. But the cost in terms of direct destruction of nature,
and thereby reduction of the basis of sustenance for human beings today
and tomorrow, are tremendous. However, all of this becomes much worse
when to "economic cycle" is added a special case: the cycles of
military activity. There are two of them: one dealing with the
production of the means of destruction (arms, in a broad sense), and
the other dealing with their **use,** with the production of destruction
itself (war). Consumers of the first cycle of arms production and arms
trade are above all governments but also all kinds of anti-governments;
the "consumer" of the second cycle are, ultimately, everything and
everybody, the environment and the human-made environment, people here
and everywhere, now and in the future. Military cycles today also show
unlimited expansion, not only for the production and consumption of the
means of destruction - very similar to other modern economic cycles,
only growing faster - but also for the production and consumption of
destruction itself. Conventional weapons are more like limited
economic cycles: they hit here and now. But nuclear weapons and the
other weapons of mass destruction recognize no such limitations: winds
and currents may carry the fallout very far, and destructive radiation
is long lasting. In general terms the biosphere is more vulnerable
than the lithosphere, and in the biosphere animals (and humans) are
more vulnerable than plants, and higher plants more than lower plants.
The possible survivors would be lower plants and animals and micro-
organisms. But atmosphere and hydrosphere are also vulnerable, meaning
that a nuclear war makes large parts of the world devoid of human
beings, uninhabitable and lifeless, with only very long term recovery
prospects. And this is only counting the effects on the environment.
Social and cultural effects are at least equally devastating.

If modern war leads to environmental deterioration it can probably
also be stated that environmental deterioration may lead to war, as
resources for the sustenance of human life become increasingly scarce.

The capacity of most people, in power or not to tolerate this when it
"only" hits people much lower down and far away is, as mentioned,
impressive. But the environmental deteriorationn brought about by what
today is "normal" economic activity, including arms production, will
sharpen the struggle for scarce resources, oil being one example, water
probably soon becoming another. If military destruction is added to
this the wars become self-reinforcing, vicious circles. Destruction of
resources makes resources more scarce; scarcity leads to more conflict,
and easily to more destruction. This, then comes on top of the general
degradation.

2. AND WHAT CAN BE DONE ABOUT IT?

The question, then, is what to do about all of this. This is a
question of strategy, and the question of strategy is always a problem
of why to do it, what to do, who shall do it, how, when and where, at
whose costs/benefits.

The question of why is not difficult to answer. There is a very high
level of verbal consensus in the world about this already, not the
least due to UNEP's excellent work in articulating the problem, in
describing it perhaps rather than analyzing it - the latter being
difficult given UNEP's closeness to governments and theirs' to
corporations, and direct and indirect dependence on funds from the
biggest depleters and polluters. The world is simply going down-hill
environmentally speaking, with some exceptions in terms of reversals of
trends such as the pollution of rivers and lakes. Such national and
international, governmental and nongovernmental work of information
certainly has to continue and to be stepped up; like in the excellent
educational center Los Molinos in the province of Alicante, Spain. But
it should also undergo a qualitiative change. Data on levels of
depletion and pollution are indispensable. But more analysis is needed
that could lead to a deeper understanding of why there is so much
environmental deterioration. One form of presentation here would be in
terms of economic cycles, showing very clearly who processes nature
from where into products for the consumption by whom, and with what
environmental effects for producers, consumers and others. Extremely
useful at this point would be law to the effect that products should
carry environmental impact statements, possibly with a warning, like
the warning on cigarette packs and advertising in many countries. For
both purposes training in seeing environmental deterioration in terms
of cycles and processes, and not only as states of affairs is
indispensable. The language of discourse should be not only ppm and
rates but flows on social and spatial maps, indicating clearly who are
the producers and who the consumers of the deterioration. Yearbooks
ranking identified and named countries and corporations in terms of
their contribution to environmental deterioration and what they do to
improve the situation could also be very useful.

The question of what to do is more problematic. It has been stated
above that the best situation is probably when the economic cycles are
limited, and the economic activity is soft on nature so that the
ecological processes are cyclical (case A). At the same time there has
to be understanding, solidarity, and neither extreme poverty, nor
disaster, nor greed. Pure (Theravada) Buddhist societies may be

examples of this; green wave communities in the West likewise - and
there are many others. Hence work for as much social transformation as
possible in that direction will not only lead to the abatement of the
deterioration, but to removal of causes. But the general trend in the
world, except for some small areas, is as mentioned in the opposite
direction - ever expanding economic cycles and economic activities that
are hard on nature, and through that, and also directly, on people.
Hence, **what** to do becomes a question of designing double track goals
and strategies. **Small is beautiful,** among other things because
smallness mobilizes the enlightened self-interest in environmental
matters of everybody, like it does inside a house, in a family.

But **some big is necessary,** not only because of the prevalence of case
D economic systems, but also because of Nature's own ecological cycles,
leading to case C even when activities are soft. Consequently a good
world, environmentally speaking, would probably be one where a much
higher percentage than today of the total economic activity is run on a
case A basis, and that which is run on a case D basis is done in such a
way that the polluters/depleters themselves have to pay for
environmental restoration, repairing the damage, **and do so in
competition with products from case A economies.** This last point is
absolutely essential to prevent increased costs being pushed onto the
consumers. Such a policy could at the same time serve as a stimulus to
that type of economy, leading to much more work on environmentally
sound technologies. And to this should then be added the necessity not
only of a good structure, but also of an enlightened population:
understanding and solidarity, with nature and humans, today and
tomorrow. One without the other, education without structure or vice
versa, never works well.

The question of who shall do it obviously calls for many answers. It
calls for actors at all levels - local, national, international. And
of all types: public as well as private, and among the latter
associations as well as corporations (indeed). It is actually more
complex than the usual division into governmental and nongovernmental
actors, among other reasons because the local level is so important and
so are the corporate (business) actors. However, there is another
distinction that also has to be kept in mind: between those who produce
environmental deterioration, public or private, and those who are the
consumers or victims of it. Most people are in the grey zone in-
between, neither direct producers nor explicit, direct victims. It is
true that when producers and consumers of toxic pollutants are brought
close to each other (as in the Minimata, Seveso and thalidomide cases)
the situation gets tense and confrontational. But from the idea,
generally agreed, that the perpetrators of environmental crimes should
be brought to court (rather than into positions of power where
environmental control is concerned) it does not follow that the victims
could not be made more positive use of. They have suffered the
consequences on their own bodies and hence developed a level of
consciousness different from that which comes from reading and
watching. Personal experience leads to experienced persons - for
action.

It is important that actors working for a safe and sound environment
can coordinate. Excellent work has been done to achieve this: UNEP at
the governmental level, and **the Environmental Liaison Centre (ELS,** also

in Nairobi) at the nongovernmental level. Conferences scheduled so
that the two can interact can be very significant. It may well be,
however, that the NGO's should see themselves less as pressure groups
on the governments, and more as actors in their own right. They are
often closer than governments to the local level where truly sound
evironmental practices can best be realized, for the reasons given;
this is where case A systems have to be built. They are engaged in
countless small and big experiences and experiments, sometimes behind,
very often ahead of governments that are big and move slowly, if at all
- spending much of their time simply trying to catch up conceptually,
and with data. Most important among the NGOs are probably trade
unions, political parties and churches since they constitute links
between the local and the national, the individual and the public. All
the NGOs should of course use conferences to bring pressure on
governments, but equally just try to inspire each other, exchange
experiences and experiments, mobilizing more people, doing things, not
only admonishing governments to do this and that, which governments may
be unwilling/incapable of doing. Governmental conferences have their
own logic, chaining resolutions and reports to each other in time. The
strength of the NGO level is that it is less formal, often in a
position to carry out some action, at least at the local level,
immediately. NGOs should build on this potential, thus compensating
for some of its lack of formal power. Hence, more important than the
parallel coupling to governmental conferences is the coupling - in
series - of NGO conferences to each other, over time.

The question of **how, when and where** to engage in environmental action
can best be answered in the same way as the question of **who**: in the
spirit of **diveristy** and **symbiosis**, the two key characterisitics of
mature (resilient) eco-systems. Ecologically concerned people should
be learning from ecology, in other words. In concrete terms this means
in as many ways as possible, at all times and all places but
symbiotically; meaning that there should be some interaction and even
synergistic effect, something more gotten out of it than what one puts
in. One group is interested in appropriate/intermediate/soft
technology, another in local self-reliance, a third is concerned with
the position of women. If brought together the work in the same
concrete setting could produce a technology that would make a higher
level of local self-reliance and of equality between the sexes
possible. And here the government enters. The government prepares
legislation: could that legislation also systematically encourage the
type of economic cycles that would generate more direct action against
deterioration, out of enlightened self-interest as argued above? Much
coordination and a good overview are needed to have actors at all
levels and kinds work so that some synergy is produced, not being
irrelevant to each other, or worse: working at cross-purposes even when
not wanting to do so. On the other hand, there are many interest,
values and perspectives in the field of environment, and conflict among
the actors is not only inevitable and natural, but also needed. To
leave it to the biggest polluters, public and private, to preside over
pollution control alone is much like having narcotics dealers preside
over narcotics control - it usually does not work. Hence the need for
very diverse, and very symbiotic action.

The question **at whose cost/benefits** is a rather important one: there
is no social control, and particularly no social transformation with

the purpose of somebody gaining without somebody losing something. The costs should ideally be minimized and pushed upwards in society where they can better be borne, not downwards where the costs are more than high enough already. Which means that there is a problem of conversion. How can one get most of the same goods and serices, so that the consumers do not suffer, and at least not fewer jobs, so that the workers do not suffer if there is to be a conversion to environmentally more healthy, or at least less destructive, economic cycles? Many would argue that case A economics, or green(er) economies would solve both problems, among other reasons because it also might include more artisan and less industrial modes of production - with lower productivity, but higher quality, including environmental quality. But experience seems to show that only coutries that have already been very far into the problems of case D economics will start producing population groups arguing for reversals of the trends or at least for new structures that preserve some of the advantages of case D but with a heigher level of case A systems mixed into it. Consequently it may be that such countries (especially the Northwestern European welfare states) will have to be counted upon to make some experiments "on behalf of humanity" here - together with Third world countries that have sufficient amounts of traditional structures intact to build constructively on them.

The question **to what extent** is more easily answered: until our indicators inform us that the environmental deterioration has been stopped, reversed and an acceptable **and suitable** level of humans/environment symbiosis have been attained. But there is a problem here. It is not enough to slow down, stop and reverse the process of deterioration; an acceptable stage should also be attained. Do we have good images of what that stage is, or have we been so concerned with the negative processes that we have forgotten to think of what is the goal beyond stemming the negative slide down-hill? This is important, and environmental actors of all kinds would do well to devote more time and energy to goal-formulations. This means that there should be indicators not only of negative development (pollution and depletion, for instance), but also of positive development (level of maturity of eco-systems, for instance, in the sense of neither undermaturity, nor overmaturity). At this point indicators of humans/environment symbiosis should be included, of good symbiotic relations whereby nature gives to humans and humans give back to nature so as to build a stronger nature - as in the proverbial sayings of some American Indians. Spiritual dimensions of this symbiosis should also be included.

In conclusion, and given the seriousness of our predicament today, one might also go one step further where strategy is concerned. Modelled on the excellent work done by NGOs in the field of human rights, particularly the Amnesty International, why not have an **Environment International** organisation whose task it would be, at the nongovernmental level, to monitor environmentally relevant trends and action. The organization would publish reports on the activities of governments and corporations, the key actors in this regard - public and private. The reports would go to the roots of the phenomena, giving information not only on the extent of the destruction, but also on why, and who-did-it, with names. There could then be international committees concerned with victims and perpetrators adopted by them,

helping the former, putting pressure on the latter. Above all these
committees would, with the help of the central organization, make both
parties aware of alternative modes of production and consumption so
that it does not only become an organisation for the dissemination of
moral norms and sanctions. The world also has the right to know who
the key polluters and depleters are - and the right to act accordingly.

10. A better world not Utopia

ROBERT SOMMER

ABSTRACT

Incremental improvement within a larger conception of social change is
a better strategy for environmental psychology than utopianism or the
search for perfection. Action research connects theory development and
experimentation to implementation and dissemination of findings. Two
applications of an action research model are described in the
development of institutions designed to strengthen user participation
and control.

The year commemorated by George Orwell in his novel **1984** is
appropriate for discussing utopia. The term, meaning a "not place"
was used by Sir Thomas More in 1516 to describe an imaginary island
with a perfect political and social system, and presently means any
place or state of ideal perfection. Orwell was distrustful of those
who sought perfection in human affairs and considered the search for
utopia to be incompatible with humane values. Still, throughout his
life, Orwell remained dedicated to the improvement of society. The
apparent paradox of a consistent search for social betterment without
an image of utopia can be explained with reference to Orwell's view
about democratic socialism. Orwell (1984) commented that democratic
socialism doesn't claim to make the world perfect; it just tries to
make the world better. Paul Goodman (1971) suggested that behavioural
scientists should put aside any pretentions about the total
reconstruction of society and concentrate upon tinkering and minor
repairs. When they see something broken or gone haywire, they should
try to fix it.

Incrementalism is a strategy of successive refinements and improvements. It does not seek perfection, an absolute concept, but betterment, which is a comparative concept. From an operational standpoint, the comparative and absolute are not wholly divergent. To be effective, incremental changes should be made in the light of larger conceptions of social good, conceptions which resemble the ideas in Plato's allegory of the cave. They are intangible and ineffable; they should not be reified.

I will begin by describing an incrementalist strategy in which minor improvements are made within a larger conception of social change. This can best be accomplished by an action research model which applies theory and research directly in the change process. Two applications of an action research approach from my own research will then be described. These will involve the development of two institutions, the farmer's market and the consumer cooperatives, intended to strengthen user participation and control.

Incrementalism is a good strategy for those interested in environmental change. Rather than attempting to create a perfect building, neighborhood, or city, we strive for tangible improvements in what already exists within the context of larger ethical values. Furtherance of any single value is likely to come at the cost of other values. Improved roads may attract more cars and worsen air quality. Growth controls in the city may raise land costs and rents for apartment dwellers. The standards used in evaluating social improvement will depend upon individual and societal values which will often be in conflict. This is a primary reason why a state of perfection cannot be reached in environmental design. There can be no perfect park of perfect office building in the sense that all values of all people are completely satisfied or that no further improvements are possible. There are only objects and systems that work better or worse than other objects or systems from the standpoint of other participants. This is not a rejection of value, critical judgement, and standards, or a cry of helplessness and hopelessness. It is a recognition that value does not inhere in the outside world but is a product of human action and judgement.

As environmental psychologists, our efforts at social improvement must be accompanied by systematic documentation and refinement of theory and method to establish the conections between the particular and the general. Like other academics, we regard knowledge as universally shared rather than proprietary. We consider it unethical for an environmental psychologists to generate knowledge about defects within a particular type of building and not share this information with colleagues. Unlike monks and holy people whose good works are often limited to silent meditation and dedication to God's will, our deeds are accompanied by scribbling and babbling. If the implications of the social scientist's contributions to a single project can be developed and made available to those involved in similar projects, the impact can be magnified.

Incrementalism does not reject the development of new prototypes which become experiments to be evaluated and tested against what already exists. Innovation coupled with evaluation are the basis of Campbell's (1969) experimenting society, Hutchins' (1986) learning society, and Goodman's (1971) world of tinkerers. While engaged in minor tinkering in airports to make the waiting areas more comfortable for passengers (Sommer, 1969), I was also aware of the need for alternatives modes of public transportation. I spent years doing research on bikeways (Kroll and Sommer, 1976) and helped to created a bikeway system that became a prototype used throughout North America. While the bicycle is a very humane and energy-efficient means or intracity transportation, it is not practical for intercity and international travel. There is nothing inconsistent in doing research to improve passenger waiting areas in air terminals and at the same time developing standards and policies for alternative modes of transportation.

Anasocial and Catasocial Institutions

My first studies in environmental psychology focused on settings which diminished contact between people. Osmond (1957) called these **sociofugal** and contrasted them to **sociopetal** places which increased human contact. Like other researchers, I soon became aware that the problems were more fundamental than furniture arrangement, corridor length, or wall colour. These environmental factors influenced behaviour and needed attention but they were connected to larger institutional problems.

The early sociofugal settings studied by environmental psychologists were connected to larger **catasocial** institutions designed architecturally and organizationally to minimize user participation and control. Significant change in the settings required not only change in proximate situational variables but institutional reform to increase level of user participation and power sharing to make catasocial institutions more **anasocial**. Anasocial institutions possess the following characteristics: local control, facilitation of contact in a supportive environment (not like an elevator), comprehensibility (human scale), support for local economy and the local culture. While the early work of environmental psychology concentrated on catasocial institutions which minimized user participation and control, there has been a shift of interest recently in the direction of anasocial institutions, exemplied in the work of Whyte (1980) on city plazas, Moles (1970) on posters and public space, Francis (1981) on neighborhood parks, Seamon (1980) on markets, and Korosec-Serfaty (1978) on public squares.

Action Research

Action research (Lewin, 1946) provides a useful model for bridging the gulf between research and application on the traditional academic research model. Studies are generated from theory and then tested or applied in the outside world. Action research requires the involvement of potential user of the information in problem formulation, selection of methods, data collection, dissemination. Since the research is intended to contribute simultaneously to theory and to practice, there should be dual dissemination of findings to academics through the technical journals and to practitioners through direct and prompt feedback. Action research also involves technical assistance to local organisations to conduct their own research.

I have been using an action research in work with two institutions dedicated to increased user participation and control, the **farmers' market** and the **consumer cooperative**. These anasocial institutions can be contrasted with their catasocial counterpart in the food marketing system, the national chain supermarket.

Supermarket chains aim for an international image and name recognition, and therefore repeat the same physical forms and symbols throughout their branches. Little attempt is made to express the values of artifacts of local culture. Employees are treated as interchangeable and required to wear company uniforms. Managers are transferred between branches minimizing their connection to place and neighborhood. Products are standard and possess little connection to the local economy. Money flows to central headquaters and does not remain in the community. Store branches are sut irrespective of the needs ot local residents if the branch becomes unprofitable. Supermarkets turn their backs on neighbourhoods, placing a buffer of parking space between themselves and nearby streets.

The interior layout is extremely sociofugal. Two visitors form Japan commented on the sterility and standardization ot the American supermarket which "takes away the social pleasures of shopping" and removes the vitality, excitement, and exchange of opinion and gossip of the traditional marketplace (Isogai and Matsusnima, 1972). A French visitor observed that American supermarkets "all look alike and you could do your entire shopping without exchanging a word with anybody" (Griswold-Minors, 1980). The low level of interaction is a product ot the physical layout and the social organization. Orbits of employees and customers are separated, reducing contact between them. On those rare occasions when a customer sees an employee in the aisles putting goods on the shelves or adjusting prices, the shopper is reluctant to bother this busy person wose chief responsibiltiy is to service the merchandise rather than the customers. Employees possess no special knowledge of the products; they will not know where an item was grown or how it was processed or its freshness. They will only know the location of the product in the store. The manager's office is hidden in the back for security reasons. Stocking and loading areas are off-limits to customers. Shopping areas are sociofugal due to the narrowness of the aisles and the absence of designated interaction spaces. Customers who want to converse can do it side-by-side at the risk ot blocking the aisles or front-to-back with their snopping wagons between them. Shelves are too high for conversation across aisles. Checkout lines visite propinquity but not in an arrangement conductive to interaction. The parking area is too dangerous and unappealing for extended conversation.

Farmers' Markets

Farmers' markets are local institutions in which small farmers sell their own fruits and vegetables directly to customers. Tne markets are held outdoors in good weather and, in the United States, the selling is done adjacent to the rear of pickup trucks, thus minimizing the amount ot loading and unloading. There is great freedom of action for shoppers who travel back and forth among the vendors checking varieties, prices, and quality. Behavioural mapping showed more informational and social encounters at farmers' markets than at nearby commercial supermarkets (Sommer, Herrick, and Sommer, 1981). The only type of interaction more frequent at the supermarket was perfunctory conversaton with an employee, which was typically a remark such as "Have a nice day" from the checkout clerk. Semantic differential ratings show that the farmers' market was perceived as a more friendly, intimate, and social space than was the supermarket by its customers.

Viewing the farmers' market as a type of anasocial institution rather than focusing strictly on its physical characteristics, directs attention to organizational, political, and economic issues which might otherwise be neglected. We documented that prices at farmers' markets averaged 34 percent less than prices for the same items at nearby supermarkets. Doubleblind flavour trials showed that several farmers' markets produce items were preferred over similar items from supermarkets. There was a trend for supermarket items to excel in appearance because of the more intense cullage which results in higher prices to the consumer. Farmers' market customers adjust their food consumption to seasonal products to a significantly greater degree than do supermarket customers. The markets assist small farmers and thereby help preserve family farms. In addition, farmers' markets brought people downtown which had a positive impact on their image of the central city. City planners regard the farmers' market as a useful tool for revitalizing the downtown.

This information was shared with the academic research community through the technical journals and with small farmers, agricultural officials, and the public through trade periodicals and general interest publications (Sommer, 1980). The findings of the research were disseminated in the national media, mentioned in testimony at legislative hearing, and included in programs to assist farmers' markets. The number of farmers' markets operating in the state has risen steadily and sales volume has increased. The research on price savings was instrumental in obtaining government funds to establish farmers' markets in inner-city neighbourhoods.

Consumer Cooperatives

Co-op stores follow principles developed in 1844 by a group of 28 unemployed British flannel weavers calling themselves the Rochdale Society of Equitable Pioneers. Their model of consumer cooperation spread throughout the world to strengthen the role of consumers in the marketplace. Consumer control increases the anasocial qualities of consumer cooperatives. Unlike the traditional cooperatives in Sweden, Denmark, or Great Britain, which are highly centralized in their operations, the co-ops I have studied tend to be small, local, and participatory organizations whose members exchange volunteer labour for price savings. Co-op stores provide a means by which consumers can exercise control over food distribution at the local level.

The cooperative movement lacks a research tradition. Even in Scandinavia, which is regarded as most advanced in consumer cooperation, there is relative absence of good social science research (Pestoff, 1983). The absence of systematic information results in each organisation repeating the errors made by its predecessors. Using an action research model, we hoped to demonstrate the value of research and how co-ops could do it themselves.

The higher rate of social contact found in co-op stores (Sommer and Horner, 1981) is a product of both organisational and architectural factors that minimize social and physicl distance among workers, management, and shoppers. Volunteer workers identify with shoppers who are fellow co-op members and with other staff. Few areas of the store are off-limits to anyone. The manager is readily accessible and is found alongside the volunteer workers. Members elect a board of directors to set policy and periodic meetings bring together all segments of the organization.

The physical layout of the co-op store differs radically from the stark linearity of the commercial supermarket. The store is probably in a recycled building and reflects the life of the neighborhood. The interior is jumbled, without long empty aisles, and there is emphasis on whole and unprocessed foods for ecological reasons and price savings. Customers are encouraged to recycle containers. The stores attempt to serve as a hub for progressive organizations and activies in the community and political information is found on bulletin boards. The stores practice a form of "food politics" in attempting to teach people to live lower on the food chain and support regional agriculture.

We undertook behavioural mapping of co-op stores to determine levels of social interaction. We prepared design guidelines for the bulk food containers which many of the stores used. I wrote an article on the architecture and layout of an ideal co-op store that could encourage consumer participation and convey a maximum of product information rather than adopting the commercial strategy of increasing impulse purchases and desocialising the shopping experience. We also looked at some the structural problems faced by cooperatives who occupy a marginal niche in the food distribution system.

Dissemination of the findings took place through the technical journals as well as direct feedback to local groups and in periodicals directed specifically to the co-op movement. We found that the local organisations needed assistance in interpreting research findings and developing their implications for action. Such standard social science practices as sampling technique, statistical significance, and variability were unfamiliar. Local dissemination is more than mailing clients a tabulation of the data. It must involve continued assistance in interpreting and applying the findings.

The next step in the research program was evaluation of impact. To improve research practice, it is necessary to evaluate research impact. Did the findings reach the people who could use them and did the research influence their actions? The last stage of our program involved teaching the cooperatives to conduct their own research. We have provided examples of questionnaires, interview schedules, and price comparison methods that they can adapt to their own needs, thus minimizing the need for re-inventing the wheel. Several self-help pamphlets were written to introduce the organizations to the ideas of sampling, questionnaire construction, and interview methods. The pamphlets are currently distributed by book services associated with the cooperative movement. We have been gratified to find that many of the organizations for whom research was a remote activity at the start of our collaboration, are now conducting their own surveys and price comparisons on a routine basis. The quality of a survey, in terms of professional standards, is often less important than the questions asked and the timeliness of the findings.

Conclusion

The research model of academic social science involving studies generated from theory and tested in the laboratory does not seem useful for solving real-world problems. The separation of problem formulation, method, and dissemination from practice represents a major flow in this approach. Researchers trained in this model tend to ignore critical problems facing society. In a world faced with the threat of nuclear war, unchecked population growth, and degradation of air and water quality, one is reminded of Freud's (1932) comment about "the unpleasant picture that comes to mind of mills that grind so slowly that people may starve to death before they get thier flour". The mills of academic psychology don't produce the kinds of flour that make nourishing bread. The flour is so refined and this that it can only be used by an elite among bakers to make expensive cakes for wealthy clients. While I personally like desserts, they are often of little nutritional value and most people in the world cannot afford them.

The research on farmers' markets and consumer cooperatives illustrates how an incrementalist strategy fits into a larger agenda of social change. When I mentioned incrementalism, I know that some of you wondered if this might produce only minor cosmetic changes and leave the major problems untouched. The explanation is that small tangible improvements are undertaken in a larger theoretical framework. The research on farmers' markets was at one level setting-specific, but at another level addressed institutions which increase consumer control, strengthen local culture, and improve the situation of small farmers. Individual studies are joined within a larger agenda of social change. It is not utopian in the sense of aiming for a perfect institution or society, but one that is marginally and incrementally better than what has gone before. This is a model for environmental psychology that George Orwell could endorse. It is not the traditional research paradigm applied outdoors but a very different type of paradigm. How the problems are generated is different, the selection of methods is different, and what is done with the information is different. George Orwell provides a strategy of social change through incremental improvement and Kurt Lewin provides an approach by which environmental psychologists can link their research to theory and to action.

Bibliography

Campbell, D. T. Reforms as experiments. American Psychologist. 24, 402-429. 1969.

Francis, M., Cashdan, L., and Paxson, L. The making of neighbourhood open space. New York: Center of Human Environments, 1981.

Freud, S. Letter to Albert Einstein written in 1932. Republished in Taking off. 1, p 19. 1983.

Goodman, P. Conversations. Psychology Today, p. 96 November 1971.

Griswold-Minois, R. A French view of Sacramento. Sacramento Bee Scene, p. 4.July 27, 1980.

Hutchins, R. M. The learning society New York: Praeger, 1968.

Korosec-Serfaty, P. The appropriation of space. Proceedings of the 3rd International Architectural Psychology Conference. University of Strasbourg Press, 1978.

Kroll, B. and Sommer, R. Bicyclists' response to urban bikeways. AIP Journal. January 1976, 42-51.

Isogai, H. and Matsushima, S. Market places of the world. Palo Alto, California: Kodansha International Limited, 1972.

Lewin, K. Action research and minority problems. Journal of Social Issues. 1946, 2, 34-46.

Moles, A. L'affiche dans las societe urbaine Paris: Dunod, 1970.

More, T. Utopia. New York: Norton, 1975.

Orwell, G. 1984. New York: Harcourt, Brace, 1949.

Orwell, G. A radio biography. Program produced by the Canadian Broadcasting Corporation and broadcast an PBS on January 24, 1984.

Osmond, H. Function as the basis of psychiatric ward design. Mental Hospitals. April 1957, 23-29. (2).

Pestoff, V. Dilemma facing Swedish consumer cooperatives: Can members, markets, authorities and employees all be optimised? Chapter in C. Crouch and F. Heller, Eds), Organisational democracy and political processes. Chichester, UK: John Wiley, 1983, p. 433-453.

Seamon, D. and Nordin, C. Marketplace as place ballet: a Swedish example. Landscape. 1980, 24, 35-41.

Sommer, R. The lonely airport crowd. Air Travel, April 1969, p. 16-22.

Sommer, R. Farmers' markets of America. Santa Barbara, CA: Capra, 1980.

Sommer, R. Cooperation by design. Communities. 1983, 51, 4-9.

Sommer, R., Herrick, J. and Sommer, T. R. The behaviour ecology of supermarket and farmers' markets. Journal of Environmental Psychology. 1981, 1, 13-19.

Sommer, R. and Horner, M. Social interaction in co-ops and supermarkets. Communities. 1981, 49, 15-18.

Whyte, W. H. The social life of small urban spaces. New York: The Conservation Foundation, 1980.

11. New life styles and new architecture

MARTIN KRAMPEN

INTRODUCTION

The Problem

Undoubtedly, architecture has changed in the past two decades. The
"old" functionalism of "modern" architecture no longer commands the
universal support amongst the architectural profession that it once
did. But the visions of the modern movement for an architecture in
keeping with the life-styles of an enfranchised working class,
responsive to the needs of a broad range of the population, have been
lost in the return to a dominantly visual, stylistically formal
approach to many current buildings. Yet since the pioneering work of
Buckminister Fuller and the many other experiments in new building
forms there have been architectural traditions that recognise the
inexptricable links between approaches to architecture and ways of
living. The reticence of architects to examine closely the
possibilities provided by these traditions has usually been based on a
fear that the new life styles required by a different architecture
would not find any supporters amongst the citizens for whom they see
themselves working.

A study was therefore designed to find out how a new and unusual type
of life in a new kind of architecture, Green Solar Architecture (GSA)
promoted by the planning team LOG ID in Tuebingen (FRG), would be
accepted by the population. The name of the team is an abbreviation of
"Logical Ideas" and the buildings of GSA have been called "Green Arks"
(LOG ID 1983a).

This architecture enables people in temperate latitudes to live together with plants the whole year around in a glass-house facing south or south-west. Only if it gets too cold in the glass-house do the inhabitants retire to an attached, conventionally walled core-house. The dwelling surface of the core-house should be of the same size as that of the glass-house, where predominantly evergreen Mediterranean species are planted in the ground. Advantages of the GSA are healthy living in an atmosphere enriched by oxygen, energy saving by the passive use of solar energy, enhanced quality of life by the colours and smells of the plants and reasonable building costs (since the glass-house components are constructed from pre-fabricated materials).

Even with all these apparent advantages a new life style is demanded of the inhabitants of the Green Arks. They must dwell among the plants and take care of them (although the watering is done by a sprinkler system layed in the ground). Who are the people wanting to have such a building? Who would be ready to share their living space with plants?

Changes in environmental cognition

The first model building according to the principles of GSA was exhibited at a gardening fair in Baden-Baden from April to October 1981, (LOG ID 1983b). Five years later 25 new GSA constructions had been finished and 20 existing houses had been equipped with an attached glass-house. Some families passed their third or fourth winter in their Green Arks and reported heating fuel savings of up to 50%. Also, in 1985 forty clerical workers moved from their old air-conditioned office landscape into a large GSA glass-house. This unusual list of successes by the young LOG ID team (founded in 1976) can only be explained by reference to a larger context. This context might best be described as a drastic change in people's environmental attitudes and cognitions.

According to representative surveys (Bunz 1973), in September 1970 only 40% of the citizens of the FRG had heard about Environmental Protection. By November of the same year there were already more than 50%, and one year later 90% had heard about it. In the Autumn of 1970 17% of the population still thought that Environmental Protection meant ¨protection from theft and crime¨, 13% ¨civil defence¨ or ¨youth protection¨ and 11% ¨guaranty of national security¨. One year later the concept had attained a clear contour. These data indicate that at the beginning of the seventies, apparently, there had been in the FRG the start of a change in cognitions about the environment. That change was a part of what Inglehart (1977) has called a ¨silent revolution¨ which began to develop within all Western industrialized nations at that time (Fietkau et al 1982). This hypothesis gains support from the results of the ¨Environmental Survey¨ which was carried out by the Berlin International Institute for Environment and Society¨ in the USA, in England and in the FRG (Fietkau et al 1982; Fietkau, Kessel and Tischler, 1982).

One result of this survey is that the "silent revolution" can be pinpointed by three variables which clearly discriminated between respondents

1. The condition of the environment was held to be either a small or a large problem by the respondents.

2. Science and technology - either respondents believed in more science and technology to solve environmental problems, or they postulated that only changes in society would help.

3. Growth - either respondents believed there were no limits to growth or they thought that there were such limits.

If these three variables are dichotomized the following eight response types result (Table 1)

Table 1.

Eight Response Types Concerning Environmental Problems (Fietkau et al 1982).

Environmental problems	Can be solved by	Limits to growth	Types
are small	technology	no	1 (rearguard)
		yes	2 (establishment)
	social change	no	3 (weakly active, establishment followers)
		yes	4 (undecided middle)
are large	technology	no	5 (nature conservationist establishment followers)
		yes	6 (nature conservationist)
	social change	no	7 (young, lower class, environmental sympathizers)
		yes	8 (vanguard)

These eight response types may be considered a scale by which cognitions concerning environmental problems and social change can be measured. They correspond to certain groups which have different roles in society. Fietkau et al (1982) have presented the distribution of these eight response types in the USA, in England and in the FRG.

Their results show that the distributions of the eight cognitive types are rather similar in the three industrialized nations. Since this study is concerned with the question of how people in the FRG

Table 2.

Indicators of different types of socio-political groups, after Fietkau et al. 1982.

Environmental problems	Can be solved by	Limits to growth	Types	population	male	mean age	education	income	service sector	business leaders	members of parliament	mean support peace movement	mean need for nuclear power
large problem	change in society	yes	8. vanguard	29	62	38	hi	lo	56	5	22	6.01	2.81
		no	7. young, lower class, environmental sympathizers	2	72	36	med	lo	58	0	1	5.52	3.31
	better technology	yes	6. nature conservationist	20	56	46	lo	lo	44	9	9	4.89	4.67
		no	5. nature conservationist establishment followers	3	76	36	med	med	33	1	5	4.15	5.47
small problem	change in society	yes	4. undecided middle	15	53	41	lo	med	51	8	18	4.05	4.98
		no	3. weakly active establishment followers	1	59	46	med	hi	33	3	1	3.75	5.47
	better technology	yes	2. establishment	24	71	47	med	hi	33	52	27	3.14	5.90
		no	1. rearguard	5	81	42	hi	hi	22	23	16	2.44	6.39

would accept the GSA, indications of the eight types given by Fietkau et al (1982) for the population of the FRG are given in Table 2.

As shown in Table 2, on the scale between vanguard and rearguard, attitudes toward the peace movement and nuclear power are distributed among the eight response types as one would expect. Fietkau et al (1982) also show links as might be expected to the backing of an unrestrained market enconomy, exploitation of natural resources, environmental risk and economic growth.

To explain the phenomenon of this "silent revolution" Inglehart (1977) has postulated a change in values. Referring to Maslow's (1954) hierarchy of needs, he argues that new values will arise when the basic material needs of people are taken care of.

The new values arising after the basic materials needs have been satisfied are defined as "post-material" values. Postmaterial values give priority to the equilibrium between people and nature over growth. This requires control of technical scientific and economic processes. As a consequence small (or medium) technology, economy and politics (decentralization) are necessary. The "old" values of proficiency and consumer society as well as "old" politics are therefore severely criticized.

Experiencing the nonhuman environment.

It is to be expected that a change in the experience of the nonhuman environment goes with this change of values and the attendant demand for societal change. The nonhuman environment includes on the one hand the world of manmade objects. Thus together with the new values a new type of functionalism arises in design and architecture. The design of an object is only acceptable if the extraction of the materials for its fabrication is compatible with ecological principles and if its recycling is guaranteed. Not objects but entire production/destruction cycles are to be planned. In addition a new "carefulness" with respect to old, existing objects arises.

On the other hand, there is also a change in the experience of the nonhuman "natural" environment (Searles 1960).

In classical psychology the description of a person's relation to the Self and to the Other has been the main concern. Now there are also the beginnings of considerations of an individual's or a group's relationship to the nonhuman environment - at least as a necessary complement.

In order to explore this new trend a questionnaire has been constructed tapping various dimensions of environmental experience (Krampen, Espe and Seiwert 1984). The dimensions which have been found so far are:

- Life in big cities

- Modernist life style
  (from housing developments to holidays out of catalogues)

- Stimulus seeking
  (speed, adventure)

- Hobby/craft
  (and repairing)

- Being alone
  (in one's four walls)

- (Apprehension of) environmental pollution

- (Interest in) nature

- (Interest in) plants

- Animals

- (Sensibility to) weather changes

- Tobacco smoking

Some of these dimensions correlate significantly with demographic and other data which had been collected in a panel study together with the data on environmental experience. Among those correlations were some of interest for the present discussion: e.g. Materialists (as apposed to post materialists) preferred a modernist life style, had little apprehension of environmental pollution, showed little interest in nature and in plants.

Hypothesis

In the context of value change and the changing experience of the nonhuman environement the answer to the problem of how people will accept a new form of life and architecture becomes easier to predict. It is proposed that changes in values and in environmental perceptions might moderate a positive response to new living projects and new types of architecture such as GSA.

METHOD: QUESTIONNAIRE FOR POTENTIAL USERS OF GSA

Direct Questions

All subejcts in this study received, together with a questionnaire, one picture of the outside and one of the inside of an existing building constructed according to the principles of GSA. The text of the first question referred to the outside picture, introduced briefly the concept of GSA and went on:

"Have you heard or read about a house such as this?"

The text of the second question referred to the picture of the inside as follows:

Have a look at the inside of the house. Could you imagine living in this house?"

Table 3.

Twenty statements on GSA with percentage of positive endorsement

%

01. + One develops quite a new feeling of domestic life. 70

02. + One saves energy. 64

03. + The higher oxygen content in the air is good for your health. 63

04. + Through the plants' growth colours and smells, light and shade change; that brings variety into dwelling. 62

05. + You are one with nature - inside and outside merge into each other. 48

06. + You live all year around as in a summer garden or during holidays. 45

07. + House work is more interesting: to care for plants is more fun than vacuum-cleaning. 44

08. + The changing temperatures stabilize health. 31

09. - You have too much work in continuously caring for the plants. 31

10. + The house can be produced at a reasonable price in a series. 22

11. + Since the plants bind dust the house remains cleaner. 21

12. - Since the greenhouse is too hot during the summer and too cold during the winter you live most of the time in the core-house; that has too small a dwelling surface. 18

13. - You sit in the house like on a salver. 16

14. - Since the house does not wear well and you must constantly reckon with glass fracture costs are too high in the long run. 16

15. - One has too much dirt in the house. 12

16. - You are tied to the house in an inconvenient manner. 11

17. - The constant fluctuations of temperature are unhealthy. 11

18. - Such a tight life together with plants is depressing. 7

19. - This holiday atmosphere diverts too much from daily duties. 5

20. - A life together with plants is unhealthy. 3

Statements about GSA

In addition to the two direct questions the questionnaire contained 20 statements about GSA prefaced by the sentence:

"Which of the following statements apply to this house?"

The 20 statements are given in Table 3. Their ranking corresponds to the percentage of positive endorsements obtained in this study. There were some more questions asked in the questionnaire. These concerned demographic information (sex, age, schooling, income) and whether the subjects owned a home or planned to build one.

The Sample

A total of 374 subjects, members of a panel organised by the Institute of Societal and Economical Communication of the Hochschule der Kuenste Berlin, filled out the questionnaire. 164 were female, 210 male. In this panel younger persons, subjects with higher education and residents of Berlin are slightly over-represented with respect to the total population of the FRG. Nevertheless, the sample may be considered quasi-representative. The 374 panel members who filled out the questionnaire on GSA in this study had all filled out the questionnaires on materialism/postmaterialism (from Fietkau et al 1982) and on experiencing the nonhuman environment about a year earlier. The data of both studies could thus be connected subject by subject.

Analysis of the data

Construction of an acceptancy index.

Of the total of 20 statements about GSA only 8 were significantly correlated with the second direct question ("Could you imagine living in this house?"). These eight items could be distributed with one positive and one negative statement each into the four dimensions "cost" (items 10 and 14, Table 3), "cleanliness" (items 11 and 15, Table 3), "home-feeling" (items 06 and 13, Table 3) and "health" (items 08 and 17, Table 3). Since in each of the four dimensions a subject could either make a positive or a negative statement or both, three scores were possible: 1 point for endorsing the positive statement, 2 points for scoring both the positive and negative items, 3 points for answering the negative statement only. The scores from each of the four dimensions can be combined to produce a global index, which may vary between 4 points (1 point on each of the four dimensions) and 12 points (3 points on each of the four dimensions).

From the global index five groups of subjects may be differentiated with respect to their readiness to accept GSA:

    4-5 points = very positive
      6 points = rather positive
      7 points = only moderately positive
      8 points = neutral
 9-12 points = negative

Note that the lower the scores are the higher is the subjects' readiness to accept GSA.

RESULTS

Direct questions and statements

The question: "Could you imagine living in the house" was answered with the highest score ("Yes, I can well imagine that") by 40% of the sample (N = 374). The rank order of the 20 statements according to the percentage of endorsement is given in Table 3. From Table 3 one can see that the positive statements about GSA are endorsed by a higher percentage of the subjects than the negative statements.

Values and readiness to accept GSA

Since the panel subjects participating in this study had on a previous occasion filled out a set of scales on materialism/postmaterialism, and ideology of proficiency/new left (two dimensions which had emerged from a factor analysis) each subject's readiness to accept GSA as measured in the present study could be compared with her/his position on materialism and proficiency taken in the previous study. The results of this comparison are given in Table 4.

Table 4.

Values and readiness to accept GSA, postmaterialists as ambivalents and materialists.

	Cost	Cleanliness	Home feeling	Health	Global index	N
All Subjects	1.94	1.91	1.70	1.79	7.35	(374)
Postmaterialists	1.78	1.81	1.59	1.65	6.85	(142)
Ambivalents and Materalists	2.01	1.97	1.76	1.84	7.59	(202)
Significance level of the difference,	p= .00	.01	.01	.00	.00	

162

From Table 4 it can be seen that subjects with postmaterial values accept GSA on the whole and in the different dimensions (cost, cleanliness, home-feeling and health) significantly more than subjects with ambivalent or materialist values.

In Table 5 a comparison between the postmaterialism/materialism or the proficiency ideology/new left scores and the readiness to accept GSA is made.

Table 5.

Values and readiness to accept GSA, distribution of materialists and backers of proficiency ideology in five groups of attitudes toward GSA.

| | | Groups differentiated by the global index of readiness to accept GSA | | | | | |
		all subjects	very + tive	rather + tive	little + tive	neutral	negative
Materialists (6-30 scale points)		12.03	10.08	12.61	11.61	11.86	13.44
	N	(305)	(46)	(47)	(51)	(91)	(70)
Proficiency ideology (3-15 scale points)		7.58	8.78	8.15	7.75	7.05	6.96
	N	(298)	(42)	(51)	(49)	(92)	(64)

On the postmaterialism/materialism scale subjects could potentially score from 6 to 30 points. If the scores on that scale are compared with the five different degrees of readiness to accept GSA the lowest scores on materialism (the highest scores on postmaterialism) are found, in Table 5, in the group which accepts GSA most and vice versa. On the scale measuring the ideology of proficiency/new left subjects could potentially score 3 to 15 points. Likewise according to Table 5 the highest new-left-scorers (and the most critical of the proficiency ideology) are also the ones who accept GSA most and vice versa.

Experiencing the nonhuman environment and readiness to accept GSA

If the data on experiencing the nonhuman environment from the previous study are compared with the data of the present study on readiness to accept GSA, some significant differences appear as shown in Table 6.

As can be seen from Table 6 people who score lowest on "modernistic life style" accept GSA most and vice versa (p = .00). Subjects high on stimulus seeking accept GSA most and vice versa (p = .02). Those who are most apprehensive of environmental pollution would like to live most in a house of GSA and vice versa (p = .01). People with the highest interest in nature accept GSA most and vice versa (p = .00). There is also a tendency for people who are interested in plants to accept GSA most (p = .07).

163

Table 6.

Experiencing the nonhuman environment and readiness to accept GSA

High values = High scores on a dimension

		Group differentiated by the global index of readiness to accept GSA					
		all subjects	very + tive	rather + tive	little + tive	neutral	- tive
Life in big cities		18.35	17.66	18.75	18.73	17.90	18.75
6-30 scale pts	N	(334)	(51)	(56)	(56)	(95)	(76)
Modernist life style		17.93	15.62	16.49	17.78	18.36	20.13
7-35 scale pts	N*	(335)	(51)	(57)	(55)	(96)	(76)
Stimulus seeking		18.30	19.64	19.68	18.32	17.67	17.13
7-35 scale pts	N	(328)	(51)	(54)	(56)	(94)	(73)
Hobby craft		17.89	19.23	17.60	17.30	17.50	18.13
6-30 scale pts	N	(329)	(51)	(55)	(56)	(93)	(74)
Being alone		13.68	13.68	13.69	13.03	13.76	13.89
4-20 scale pts	N	(327)	(47)	(54)	(56)	(96)	(74)
Environmental pollution		29.64	31.17	30.68	29.77	29.00	28.52
8-40 scale pts	N*	(338)	(52)	(57)	(57)	(96)	(76)
Interest in nature		23.26	24.98	23.87	23.64	22.66	22.11
6-30 scale pts	N*	(338)	(52)	(57)	(57)	(96)	(76)
Interest in plants		39.89	41.59	40.19	39.92	39.94	38.39
11-55 scale pts	N	(338)	(52)	(57)	(57)	(96)	(76)
Animals		6.25	6.41	6.51	5.86	6.27	6.20
2-10 scale pts	N	(302)	(46)	(52)	(53)	(84)	(67)
Weather		9.18	9.04	8.84	9.62	8.98	9.46
3-15 scale pts	N	(293)	(47)	(50)	(50)	(81)	(65)
Tabacco smoke		5.11	4.97	5.39	5.02	5.12	5.04
2-10 scale pts	N	(307)	(47)	(51)	(49)	(89)	(71)

Note: * = $p < .01$

Table 7.

Demographic data and readiness to accept GSA

	Cost	Clean-liness	Home feeling	Health	Global index	N
All subjects	1.94	1.91	1.70	1.79	7.35	(374)
Sex						
Male	1.91	1.90	1.72	1.84	7.39	(210)
Female	1.97	1.92	1.68	1.73	7.31	(164)
Significance level of the difference p =	.32	.70	.49	.07	.67	
Age						
- 34	1.73	1.86	1.51	1.65	6.78	(129)
35 - 49	1.92	1.87	1.76	1.90	7.46	(94)
50 -	2.12	1.98	1.84	1.84	7.78	(151)
Significance level of the difference p =	.00	.17	.00	.00	.00	
Education						
Elementary school	2.05	1.91	1.82	1.93	7.73	(123)
Further schooling	1.86	1.92	1.60	1.77	7.17	(128)
Junior college degree	1.89	1.89	1.68	1.67	7.14	(122)
Significance level of the difference p =	.02	.90	.02	.00	.00	
Income (Subjective ratings: Level 1 = very high, Level 6 = very low)						
Level 1, 2	1.89	2.17	1.72	1.89	7.68	(29)
Level 3	1.89	1.86	1.70	1.74	7.20	(160)
Level 4	2.02	1.91	1.71	1.84	7.50	(110)
Level 5, 6	1.94	1.88	1.68	1.60	7.11	(35)
Significance level of the difference p =	.30	.05	.99	.10	.23	
Planning to build own home	1.70	1.81	1.58	1.62	6.72	(48)
Not planning	1.97	1.92	1.72	1.81	7.45	(326)
Significance level of the difference p =	.00	.17	.14	.03	.00	
Renting an appartment	1.85	1.87	1.65	1.73	7.11	(225)
Owning a home	2.09	1.97	1.75	1.87	7.69	(137)
Significance level of the difference p =	.00	.09	.16	.02	.00	

Demographic data and readiness to accept GSA

Concerning the demographic data and readiness to accept GSA some significant results are given in Table 7.

As can be seen in Table 7 there are significant differences in the readiness to accept GSA between younger and older people (p = .00), between people with higher and elementary school education (p = .02), between people living in rented appartments and house owners (p = .00) and between people planning to build a house of their own and those who had no such plans. Comparing Table 7 with Table 4 it can be seen that subjects planning to build a house and postmaterialists are the ones who are most ready to accept GSA. This and other combinations of values and demographic data are shown in Table 8.

Table 8.

Planning to build, home ownership and values as predictors of readiness to accept GSA.

	Cost	Clean- liness	home feeling	health	global index	N
Planning to build own home	1.70	1.81	1.58	1.62	6.72	(48)
Not planning but postmaterialist	1.82	1.85	1.62	1.69	7.00	(121)
Not planning, ambivalent or materialist, renting apartment	1.98	1.92	1.76	1.882	7.50	(96)
Not planning, ambivalent or materialistic and home owner	2.15	2.03	1.78	1.91	7.88	(79)
Significance level of the difference p =	.00	.07	.13	.01	.00	

DISCUSSION

Summing up the results the profile of those ready to accept GSA can be described as follows: these people tend to be young, with, in general, less than 34 years of age. Their education is rather high but their income low. They live in a rented appartment but are planning to build a home of their own. They are against a modernistic life style (e.g. housing developments). They are stimulus seekers (i.e. they like speed and adventure) and this confirms that they belong to the younger age groups. They are apprehensive of environmental pollution and have a clear interest in nature and plants. Their values are postmaterialist and they are critical of proficiency ideology and consumer society.

166

A look back to Table 2 suggests that those ready to accept GSA might be found mainly among the socio-political vanguard, the young sympathisers of the ecological movement and perhaps, in addition, among the preservationists who are more optimistic with respect to science and technology. This spectrum covers 30-50% of the population in the FRG. This must then be those 40% of the subjects participating in this study on the readiness to accept GSA who said that they "can imagine living in this house".

A reasonable assumption can be made that this 40% of the population is not served at present by ecologically functional and responsible designs of messages, objects and buildings. Instead of being engaged in postmaterialist values designers tend to flirt with postmodernist styling or prefer to do business in concrete with the society's establishment or the rearguard. They waste their time - just as when the "old" functionalism emerged - with formalist games and historical eclecticism. But the time is now ripe for the birth of a "new", of an ecological functionalism.

Bibliography

Bunz, A. R. Umweltpolitisches Bewusstsein 1972: Beitrage zur Umweltgestaltung. Heft B 5 Untersuchung des Instituts fur angewandte Sozialwissenschaft (INFAS) Berlin, Erich Schmidt Verlag.

Fietkau, H. J., Kessel, H., Coopersmith, J., Milbrath, L. W. (1982) Restructuring cognitions and values in revolutionary social change Berlin, International Institute for Environment and Society Prepublication 82 - 16.

Fietkau, H. J., Kessel, H., Tischler, W. (1982) Umwelt im Spiegel der oeffentlichen Meinung. Frankfurt/New York, Campus Verlag.

Inglehart, R. (1977) The silent revolution: Changing values and political styles in western publics. Princeton: Princeton University Press, 1977.

Krampen, M., Espe, H. and Seiwert, M. (1986) Entwicklung und Erprobung einiger Skalen zur Erfassung des Erlebens der nichtmenschlichen Umwelt. Vortrag auf der 26. Tagung experimentell arbeitender Psychologen 15. - 19. April 1984 an der Universitat Erlangen/Nuernberg Berlin, Hochschule der Kunste, (mimeographed).

LOG ID, (1983a) Gruene Archen. In Harmonie mit Pflanzen leben. Frankfurt, Fricke Verlag, 1983.

LOG ID, (1983b) Das Haus in Baden-Baden. Frankfurt, Fricke Verlag.

Maslow, A. H. (1954) Motivation und personality. New York, Harper.

Searles, H. F. (1960) The nonhuman environment in normal development and in schizophrenia. New York, International Universities Press.

12. Ambience or environment: or, what is the correct view of nature?

THURE VON UEXKULL

1. Nature and Environment

"We treat the world as if we had a second one in the boot of the car,"
wrote a 17-year-old (Jugend, 1984), summarily evoking what our
industrial culture understands under the title "Environment and Human
Action." This neat quote raises the question, though, of whether the
word "environment", of "Umgebung" captures what the 17-year-old means
by "our world", and what lies behind the cogent accusation that we
treat our world like some tent manufactured by the leisure industry
which can be replaced by a new one whenever it wears out.

One used to say instead of "our world" nature. But this term seems
to have come into disrepute. For some it seems too romantic, for some
others too scientific, for yet other too vague in the age of space
travel. When in 1860 the baltic biologist and discoverer of the mammal-
egg, Karl Ernst von Baer (1860) held his famous lecture on the theme
"Which is the correct perspective on nature?" in St. Petersburg (now
Leningrad), things were different again. In those days one could still
use the word freely and would be understood. One understood something
other than "physical environment" or "physische Umgebung".

But what was understood, and what has so changed about our
relationship with nature that we are afraid to call it by name? Our
relationship to nature has changed radically and obviously, because a
dream of humanity has been fulfilled, which the politician, philosopher
and physicist Francis Bacon as early as 1620 in his "New Canon of the
Sciences" identified as the highest goal for human striving for power:
"the power and rule of humanity over Nature (die Gesamtnatur)." This
dream has largely been realized, thanks to the advances in natural

sciences and technology in the 20th century.

Meyer-Abich (1979) points out that history has proved Bacon right in his judgement of the priority of power over nature above other goals of human striving for power; for history has shown that power over nature better guarantees power of one man over another and one state over another than all efforts of a more narrowly political kind.

But the euphoria over this victory was short-lived. Since the 1970s the mood has changed. The report of the Club of Rome on the Limits to Growth was a catalyst. What Huxley's vision of the future in 1932 - "Brave New World" - had failed to achieve, now happened: We are beginning to look around in our environment, and we find, as Peter Glotz has formulated: "a mass death of nature which is taking place all over the world. "Hundreds of thousands of plant and animal species," he writes, "die in the space of a few decades, and no-one will be able ever again to give them a name. It is estimated that in 20 years between 1/7 and 1/5 of all species now living will be extinct. In the Federal Republic, to cite a current examle, only 10-30% of the plant and animal species can survive in a milieu that is as acidic as the rain which now falls from the sky." (Glotz, 1984).

Admittedly, the hardbitten core of the immovable apostles of economic growth would not challange this. They announce, still unmoved, the venerable news of technical progress which will solve all problems. Complaints of dying plants and animals are treated as sentimental chatter; for this has been happening throughout the Earth's history, and if humankind were to live in future without birdsong, blossoming meadows and rustling forests, between concrete bunkers, drawing their energy from nuclear power stations and their food from retort kitchens and battery farms - so what? A new balance will be attained which, thanks to the potential of science and technology, will bring humans new advantages.

But this optimistic prognosis makes one mistake: to forget that man is part of nature, and that change in nature will also change man and the form of his life with other men. - Glotz draws our attention to the political and social consequences which can already be identified from this change in nature, and which have led to a situation in which economic and ecological crises are played off against one another. He reminds us of the arguments of the industrial associations which announce in response to every environmental protection measure the destruction of their competitiveness and the danger to jobs of every measure to save energy. He prophesies a hysterical confrontation of new popular movements and the productivist core of society. He concludes that, with a simple continuation of trends to date, liberal democracy cannot be upheld as a form of political organization for human society and is incompatible with the simultaneous pressure of economic and ecological problems.

A perspective on nature which has such consequences is obviously not the right one! But where does the fault lie, and what does an alternative look like, which is not reduced to a shortsighted "back to nature" and the slogans of the iconoclasts calling for an end to science and technology?

If, in search of an answer, we seek to find the common denominator of things without oversimplifying them, then we can say that there are two **perspectives** on nature, but each of these has different criteria for the correctness of their view. Both are equally scientific in the sense of empirically provable hypotheses, and both have a positive relationship to technology in the sense of the application of their research results. But the criteria for what they understand by value and use are different. We can grasp this difference by using two concepts, if we say that for one perspective nature view means "Umgebung," or environment for the other "Umwelt" or ambient. This brings me to my main theme: what do these two concepts express, and where do they differ?

For Karl Ernst von Baer, the criterion for the correct perspective was the ability to see this difference, i.e. to inform us in what relationship "nature as Umgebung" or environment stands to "nature as Umwelt" or ambient. Only he didn't use the concept "Umwelt" or ambient. It is a pity that we have not learnt to see this difference, to the great disadvantage of movements which have "environmental protection" nailed to their banner, and don't really know if they should be active for protection of nature as "Umgebung" or environment or as "Umwelt" or ambient.

2. Difficulties of Terminology: View and Concept

This incapacity has also to do with or disturbed relationship to language. Gipper (1971) quotes the great Swiss linguistic researcher Ferdinand de Saussure, who said that the idea most philosophers - and we may add most natural scientists and, as their willing pupils contemporaries too - have of language is reminiscent of our forefather Adam, who called the animals to him to give each a name. We thought we had only to place a name label on things and processes in nature, as in a zoo or botanical garden, and the vocabulary of every language would contain a catalogue of the things we meet in nature.

Gipper points out that things are not so simple, because rather than a pre-existing thing being named, something with which we interact would be ascribed human meaning and thus put into language. Thus the word "Baum" is a sound (which, like the words tree or arbre can be almost random in different languages) which does not identify **an object** in an objectively given world, but **a concept**. It is the **concepts** which create the objects with which we interact. - The concepts label the programmes of our interactions, i.e. the schemata of our actions in interaction with appropriate excerpts from nature. Environment and human action cannot be viewed and defined independently of one another. Both exist only within the confines whose pattern is retained in our language.

·Here, we have the theme of our conference with all its background and open problems in a nutshell: 'Nature as Umgebung" environment and "Nature as Umwelt" ambient derive from human actions for which we carry the responsibility (in our own interest, too). Each action begins with a perception which interprets its object (Gegenuber) in the light of the action **goal**, or as Karl Ernst von Baer says, creates a perspective on the object (Gegenuber). This perspective produces, from among the

totality of impression we receive, the necessary orientation for
action.

Environment and human action are thus conflated, make up, as we say
today, a system. But human action in itself is made up of two
components: of perception and movement as interdependent activities,
or, as Jakob von Uexkull (1920) formulated it, of "perceiving" and
"effecting" or "operating". Whoever takes only one of these into
account distorts things. Bertalanffy (1968), the founder of modern
systems theory, accuses the philosophers of having paid insufficient
attention to this relationship and having seen themselves only as
perceiving observers and not as operating actors:

"It seems to be the most serious shortcoming of classic accidental
philosophy from Plato to Descartes and Kant, to consider man primarily
as a spectator, as an 'ens cogitans' while for biological reasons, he
has essentially to be a performer, an 'ens agens' in the world he is
thrown in."

But spectator and performer cannot be separated: for action, human
action, begins with what Karl Ernst von Baer called "perspective on
nature", and this perspective interprets things in our environment -
for the goals of our intervention and thereby brings them into line
with concepts which find their way into our language. Language can
therefore both reveal and conceal our relationship with things. With
the concept "Umgebung" or environment she reveals our relationship with
a nature to which we have put ourself on an opposite bank. Observe
"objectively" as not participating outsiders. Hereby language conceals
the fact that we thus interpret nature as the object of our action.
With the concept "Umwelt" or ambient she reveals the metaposition in
which we take into account both ourselves and our relationship to
nature.

This relation between nature, perception and action was analysed more
exactly by Jakob von Uexkull at the beginning of the century and he
coined the concept "Umwelt" for it. What does this concept "Umwelt"
which means the world as perceived by the subject portend and which
Bertalanffy translates with the word "ambient".

3. Nature as "Umwelt"

Jakob v. Uexkull developed a model which represents the relationship
between a subject and the objects of his perception and action in the
framework of a unitary event processs; as a functional circle. In this
model, the inderdependence of perceptions of noticing and acting or
effecting or operating is made clear.

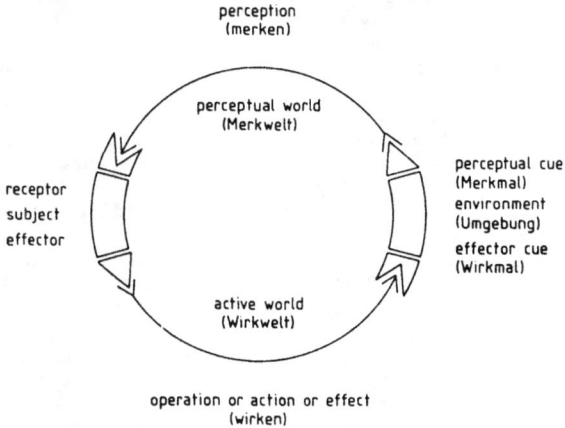

perception
(merken)

perceptual world
(Merkwelt)

perceptual cue
(Merkmal)
environment
(Umgebung)
effector cue
(Wirkmal)

receptor
subject
effector

active world
(Wirkwelt)

operation or action or effect
(wirken)

Note: The function circle. The perceiving and acting subject and the
received and acted upon object (the Umgebung) are parts of a
cyclical process (eines kreisformigen Geschehens), of a system.
In this system, the Umgebung or environment only becomes
available to the subject in the forms of his sensory and motor
organs (Sinnes- und Aktionsorgane). Perception or ¨noticing¨ and
action or ¨effecting¨ or ¨operating¨ are therefore predetermined
by biological structures (the perceptive and motor organs). In
that way, the Umgebung (environment) is transformed into the
¨Umwelt¨ (ambient), which reflects the biological possibilities
of the subject, and which can be devided into a perceptual world
(Merkwelt) and an active or operational world (Wirkwelt).

The advantage of this model for our problem lies in the opportunity
of confronting the one-sidedness of which Bertalanffy accuses the
philosophers, who only admit of the ¨res cogitans¨, with that of the
behaviouristic natural scientists, who only take the ¨res agens¨ into
account. J. v. Uexkull finds the tendency to these ¨one-sidedness¨
with many people, and speaks of ¨perceivers¨ ¨Merklinge¨ and ¨actors¨
¨Wirklinge¨, both of whom would experience and judge nature in a very
different, but to the same extent onesidedly distorted ways.

In his ¨General Systems Theory¨ L. v. Bertalanffy presented the
perception of nature, which J. v. Uexkull's ¨Umwelt¨ introduced into
modern biology with this concept, more exactly. He describes how,
according to Uexkull's ¨Umwelt¨ theory every living being cuts a slice
out of reality appropriate to his (its) own perceptual and effective
organs. He elaborates this by the example of a single-cell organism,
like Paramecium, which only has one answer, the ¨flight¨ reaction, to
all possible stimuli of chemical, thermal or tactile kind. For
Paramecium the world consists of two things - the hostile, from which
it flees, and the friendly, with which it stays and finds its
nourishment. This primitive world is quite sufficient to lead the
being, which has no specific sensory organs.

As this example shows, the organizational and functional plan of a
living being determines what can become ¨stimulus¨ and ¨characteristic¨

to which the organism responds with a certain reaction. According to
J. von Uexkull's expression, any organism, so to speak, cuts out from
the multiplicity of surrounding objects a small number of
characteristics to which it reacts and whose ensemble forms its
"ambient" (Umwelt). All the rest is nonexistent for that particular
organism. Every animal is surrounded, as by a soapbubble, by its
specific ambient, replenished by those characteristics which are
amenable to it. If, reconstructing an animal's ambient, we enter this
soapbubble, the world is profoundly changed: many characteristics
disappear, others arise, and a completely new world is found.

J. von Uexkull has given innumerable examples delineating the
ambients of various animals. Take, for instance, a tick lurking in the
bushes for a passing mammal in whose skin it settles and drinks itself
full of blood. The signal is the odor of butyric acid, flowing from
the dermal glands of all mammals. Following this stimulus, it plunges
down; if it fell on a warm body - as monitored by its sensitive thermal
sense - it has reached its prey, a warmblooded animal, and only needs
to find, aided by tactile sense, a hair-free place to pierce in. Thus
the rich environment of the tick shrinks to metamorphize into a scanty
configuration out of which only three signals, beaconlike, are gleaming
which, however, suffice to lead the animal surely to its goal. Or
again, some sea urchins respond to any darkening by striking together
their spines. This reaction invariably is applied against a passing
cloud or boat, or the real enemy, an approaching fish. Thus, while the
environment of the sea urchin contains many different objects, its
ambient only contains one characteristic, namely, dimming of light.

So much for Bertalanffy's description. Two points must be added:

1) What holds for simple creatures holds in principle equally for
more complex ones. Only their ambients are richer and more
differentiated than those of Paramecium, tick or sea urchin. Most
important, they frequently exhibit characteristics absent from our
human ambients. The bat orients itself according to echoes from
soundwaves not audible to us. Von Frisch discovered in 1914 that the
ambient of bees contained no red, but ultraviolet, a colour to which
our eye is blind. Here too the general principle obtains, that all
behaviour, be it the search for food, defence from enemies, the finding
of the sexual partner or raising of young is coupled with a perception
which guarantees the being a correct orientation. Every question as to
how the behaviour of a creature functions is therefore in large part a
question of its orientation, and therefore of its perceptual world
(Merkwelt). (Dyer and Gould 1983).

2) Almost more fascinating than the countless ambients closed to our
direct observation, whose unexplored exciting contents form a challenge
for every natural scientist, is the evidence of how subtly the
creatures of the most varied type are attuned to the things in their
ambient and to one another. J. von Uexkull draws on concepts from
music and speaks of "point" and "counterpoint" to describe the pairing
of male and female, hunter and prey, plant and animal, which we
encounter throughout nature. The mutually attuned interdependence of
bee and flower is one example of this among countless others.

Plessner (1976) has spoken of a "rule of complementarity"

(Entsprechungsregel) which would say, for example: where there is a
mouth, there, is also food, where there is a weapon, there is also an
enemy, etc. This rule describes a general principle, according to
which nature ties (integrates) elements into a system in which every
effort (Leistung) finds its complementary effort (Gegenleistung); every
role its complementary role (Gegenrolle), without which the original
effort and role would not have come about. So any part complemented by
the other, brings about the performance of the system as a whole.
Examples of this are fin and water, wing and air or hoof and ground.
They show how complementary efforts result in the complete achievement,
in these cases: swimming, flying or running.

The doctor knows this contrapunctal structure of relationships as the
interplay of nucleus and cyclo-plasma in the cell, of parenchym cells
and supportive tissue in organs, of organs with different functions in
the organism and of organisms and ambients in social forms, families,
groups or peoples. He knows - or should know - that disturbances in
the contrapunctal interplay on every level will mean illness.

Here we find a fundamental and in its fundamental character a simple
rule, according to which the environment of life-forms enter in the
ambient of living beings into a "partnership" the violation of which
sooner or later, in this or that form, rebounds on the partner who
violates the partnership.

In this perspective on nature as ambient environment is not, as it is
for our industrial society, a resource basis, which can be exploited
regardless. She is rather in countless thousands of ambients, in the
greatest variety of ways, partner of the most different living beings.

All these ambients are attuned to one another like the tones of a
powerful symphony. The task of natural science in searching for the
basis of an effective environmental protection (Umweltschutz) is
therefore the discovery of the rules of composition of this symphony.

But, how shall we answer the hardbitten pragmatists, who tell us with
a shrug of the shoulder that such programmes are mere sentimental
luxury in the brutal competition between industrial nations?

4. Man and his Ambient

We shall reply that the erroneous interchange of environment and
ambient leads not only to the ignoring of ecological problems with
their political dangers, but that above and beyond this directly to
dangers to the physical and mental health of each and every one of us.
We are not just users in the cycle of nature, the disturbance of which
threatens our material basis of life; each of us is a part of nature,
surrounded with that soapbubble, which allows us an orientation for our
activity. Jakob von Uexkull speaks of a "firm, but for the external
observer invisible, shell" and emphasizes its essential functions.
Ambient is demonstrably an indispensable organ, the "anatomical"
stuctures of which can be described as follows:

"Every man who looks around in nature finds himself in the middle of
a round island, covered by the round dome of the sky. This is his

visual world which contains all that is visible to him. And this visible material is ordered according to the meaning it has for his life: All that is close, and can have an immediate effect on man, is full size; the distant and thus less dangerous is small. The movements of distant things can remain invisible to him whereas the movements of nearby things frighten him... Things which approach the human being invisibly, because they are concealed by other objects, reveal themselves to his ear through noises or his nose as smell and, where they have got very close, by touch. Proximity is characterized by an ever denser protective wall of the senses. Taste, smell, hearing and sight surround man like four layers of a veil which gets thinner and thinner on the way out." (Uexkull, 1936).

Our ambient therefore has the function of a second skin which cuts us off from our environment and simultaneously connects us to it. Injuries to this second skin damage our health. The blind, deaf, or people who have lost feeling and pain in parts of their body are continually under threat of doing themselves harm. They can no longer transform environment into ambient because the organ which regulates the partnership between the impeded and their environment, fails.

But blows of fate, which are experienced as loss of an object, also lead to injuries to the second skin. A scarcely surmountable literature on illnesses which arise after the loss of close persons, after exile, among guest-workers, after unemployment, etc. documents the significance of the subjective ambient for our health.

If we try to follow the pathology of human ambients, we arrive at a paradox: the objects of the human world are - admittedly - objects of our subjective ambients. The sun, which traces its line across the sky, is the property of the person in whose world it shines. In this respect there are as many suns as there are people whose eyes allow a visible world to arise. But the sun is - also - the object of a world of knowledge, in which only one and the same sun exists for everyone, which each perceives according to his position at the time of observation.

We cannot perceive the objects of the world of knowledge because we cannot simultaneously occupy the position of all observers. We call this world "physical environment", which incorporates the same "objective" reality for all creatures. Our knowledge of this reality sets man apart from his animal co-creatures. It has given him, finally, that power over nature of which Francis Bacon dreamed.

If we pose the question, from where do we get this knowledge of a world which is not available to our perception, then we get an answer which is important for our examination of the pathology of human ambients. It is: Our knowledge of this world beyond our perception derives from the damage we suffer when we are not able to transform environment into ambient in which partnership relations become visible.

Piaget (1975) with his investigations of development of child intelligence has brought light to the puzzling process, which one could call the transformation of the natural ambient of man.

He speaks of a "Copernican shift" and understnads by this a change in

behaviour related to nature which is only found in the slightest form
in the primates most closely related to us: At the age of two, the
child begins to organize his ambient according to a near principle. Up
to this time it has built up as all higher living beings according to
programmes of schemata of its sensory perceptions - its perceptual
world - to its movements - its effective or operational world. This
new principle is the child's power of imagination which can reproduce
in memory events which have disappeared from the scope of perception.

Now, injuries which the child has suffered in his ambinet can be held
fast transformed to objects from which one must protect oneself, or
which one learns to deal with. The long process begins, of building up
a world of knowledge in which, a I described above, speech and with it
the society into which the child was born play an increasing role.
Thus a "reality" emerges from the subjective ambient, in which the
possibilties of new forms of action on the basis of common programmes
become the ruling principle.

True, also this reality remains the personal possession of each
individual, and remains for his lifetime his own firm, for the external
observer invisible shell or his second skin.   But this skin is no
longer formed by the biological programmes of his living needs, but by
linguistic concepts which contain the ideas for intercourse with nature
which have been developed by the language community of a given culture.

Berger and Luckmann (1969) speak of the "social construction of
reality," which the individual encounters as his "everyday reality" or
the scientist as the abstract reality of his profession.

In our industrial culture all these realities are characterized by an
excess predomnance of the action of the operational side and an atrophy
of the perception side.   Our technical achievement society produces
"actors" (Wirklinge) who are of the persuasion that, alone or in a
team, they cannot only change nature at will but also create nature as
the need arises. For them, nature is a serial product of the leisure
industry which can be replaced anytime when worn out.   Children
(already) learn to build up or destroy artificial ambient with a press
on a lever or button, and are reinforced in their early phantasies of
omnipotence.

"Observers," ("Merkinge") in whose world there are still plants and
animals whose own life one can observe and whose contrapunctal
interplay one can experience with awe, are neither required nor
supported. At best, in order not to disturb our reality, they are kept
in separate spheres, as artists, so long as there is not danger that
their view of the world should take on a guiding function for others.

In this way, the pathology of our reality is pre-programmed: the
socially induced and supported crippling of our perceptive world is
congruent with our blindness to the injury to our partnership with our
environment, i.e. for the damage our hypertropic operational world or
world of action does to nature. It is also congruent with the loss of
feeling for damage we do to nature in ourselves. Reality is losing its
protective and orienting function for the individual, which it used to
have, as ambient for his physical and mental well-being. The rapid
increase of sicknesses which are based on direct of indirect self-

abuse, alcoholism and drug addiction, traffic accidents, wrong or excessive eating, to name just a few illnesses of the welfare and achievement-society, and the inability of a purely technical medicine to counter them, put our health systems out of balance.

There is one ray of light in this sad panorama: The nature sciences, which in their attempt to construct an objective world of knowledge, saw nature as environment of non-participant observers, noticed that they had overlooked a central factor: the natural scientist himself. His role as observer i.e. his perceiving and doing and the socially formed patterns of his knowledge cannot be eliminated from his own observations. The great discovery of physics in the 20th century was the insight that the nature which confronts them in their experiments is influenced by their own action, that the physical environment is congruent with the operational world (of action) of the physicist.

The English physicist and astronomer Sir Arthur Eddington formulated this discovery as follows: Man had discovered a puzzling footprint at the gates to the unknown and as he followed it he found out after long detour: it was his own.

Walt Disney has captured in a picture the predicament of the researhcer who, in an environment bereft of all subjective characterisitics, discovers his own footprint as a melancholy adventure of his hero Donald Duck.

Bibliography

Baer, K. E. v. "Welche Auffassung der Natur ist die richtige, und wie ist diese Auffassung auf die Entomologie anwendbar?" In: Grundlagen aus Kybernetik und Geisteswissenschaft, Bd. 3, 1962, Beiheft. 1860.

Berger, P. and Luckmann, Th., Die gesellschaftliche Konstrucktion der Wirklichkeit, S. Fischer, Frankfurt, 1969.

Bertalanffy, L. v., General System Theory, George Braziller, New York, 1968.

Dyer, F. C. and Gould, J. L. 1983. "Honey Bee Navigation", American Scientist, 71, 587, 1983.

Gipper, H., Denken ohne Sprache? Padagogischer Verlag, Dusseldorf 1971.

Glotz, P. "Keine Angst vor Wunschen", Der Spiegel, 12, 129 f, 1984.

Jugend vom Umtausch ausgeschossen. Eine Generation stellt sich vor. Rowohlt, Hamburg, 1984.

Meier-Abich, K. M. "Die gesellschaftliche Wirklichkeit der Natur." In: Eisenhard, C. (Hrsg.), Humanokologie und Frieden, Klett-Cotta, Struttgart, 1979.

Piaget, J., Der Aufbau der Wirklichkeit beim Kinde, Ges. Werke Bd.2. Klett, Stuttgart, 1975.

Plessner, H., Die Frage nach der Conditio Humana, Suhrkamp Tascnenbuch, Frankfurt, 1976.

Uexkull, J. v., Theoretische Biologie. 1. Auflage, Springer Verlag, Berlin 1920.

Uexkull, J. v. Nie geschaute Welten. Die Umwelten meiner Freunde, S. Fisher, Berlin. 1936.

Brief biographies of
contributors

BRUCE BENTZ, industrial designer, was born in 1939 in the USA. He received undergraduate and graduate degrees from the University of Wisconsin and a Master of Design degree from the Royal College of Art in London, England. He teaches at the University of Alberta in Edmonton, Canada.

Full time research activity was carried out during 1978-80 in the Department of Design Research, Royal College of Art resulting in a modelling kit that was tested in the context of the Cooperative Housing Action Program in Alberta.

For the last seven years this research has involved the design and testing of four modelling kits. The kits are used by nonprofessionals to assure more user control and user satisfaction with the end product through their involvement in the housing process.

Bentz's research in user participation has included a major project with Alberta Housing and Public Works and has resulted in numerous reports, published articles, exhibitions and presentations at environmental design, design research and housing conferences in New Zealand, the United States, the Netherlands and Australia.

KAREN CRONICK from Case Western Reserve University in the United States with a B.A. degree in 1963 did graduate work at the Simon Bolivar University in Venezuela. At present she conducts seminars on research methodology at the Central University of Venezuela and does research on causal attribution, both in relation to academic and social experiences and citizen participation.

JOHAN GALTUNG: Born 1930 in Oslo (Norway), he received one Ph.D. in Mathematics (1956) and one in Sociology (1957). He held too many academic positions to cite them all here. As Assistant Professor he started at Columbia University, New York, Department of Sociology, in 1957-1960. In the 60's he was UNESCO Professor at FLASCO, Santiago, Chile. At the University of Oslo he was Professor for Peace Research (1969-1977). He was Director of the Inter-University Center at Dubrovnik from 1973-1977. 1981 he was Special UNEP Consultant for the Second Special Session on Disarmanment (UN), 1982 he was Fellow at the Wissenschaftskolleg zu Berlin. Among the places where he has held Visiting Professorships are: New Dehli, Copenhagen, Paris, Kampala, Essex, Trinidad, Bonn, Berlin, Geneva, Havanna, Bukarest and Princeton. He is consultant to UNESCO, WHO, UNEP, Council of Europe and 5 other international institutions. The most prominent topic of his more than 700 publications is peace research, but also social science methodology. He is Professor honorario at the Universidad de Alicante and the Freie Universitat Berlin.

MARTIN KRAMPEN received his Ph.D. in Psychology of Communication at Michigan State University after studies of Theology, Psychology and Visual Communication at the Universities of Tubingen, Heidelberg and at the Hochschule fur Gestaltung in Ulm. He has taught at Carnegie Institute of Technology, the Universities of Waterloo and Toronto (Canada), the Hochschule fur Gestaltung (Ulm) the Universities of Stuttgart (FRG), Bolonga (Italy) and Geneva (Switzerland), and was professor of Social Psychology and Semiology at the University of Gottingen. He is now professor for Theory of Visual Communication at the Hochschule der Kunste, Berlin. He wrote Meaning in the Urban Environment (1979), and co-edited Classics of Semiotics (1986). His main research area is the Semiotics and the Ecology of Visually Perceived Information.

RODERICK J LAWRENCE graduated in architecture from the University of Adelaide, South Australia, in 1972 with first class honours. After two years work in professional practice, in Sydney, he took up a post-graduate research fellowship at St John's College, Cambridge. He has a Masters Degree and a Doctorate. From 1978 until 1984 he worked at the Ecole Polytechnique Federale de Lausanne in Switzerland. Since then he has been a consultant to the Committee for Housing Building and Planning of the Economic Commission for Europe and a visiting lecturer and researcher at the School of Architecture at the University of Geneva. In 1985 he was a Visiting Research Fellow at the School of Social Sciences at the Flinders University of South Australia and a guest lecturer at the Faculty of Architecture at the University of Adelaide. He is now appointed to the Centre for Human Ecology at the University of Geneva. He has published numerous articles in English and French concerning behavioural parameters in house planning from cross-cultural social and psychological perspectives that address historical processes.

JOHN P MASON - Director of the U.S. Agency for International Development "Development Studies Program" and Adjunct Professor of Public Administration at the University of Southern California, Washington D.C., trained as a social anthropologist. He has done fieldwork in Libya, taught at the American University of Cairo, served as a social planner for the United Nations in North Africa and a consultant in shelter and squatter upgrading in Africa, the Middle East and Caribbean. Prior to his present position, he was a vice president with research and evaluation functions for a Washington D.C. - based international consulting organisation. The modelling exercise described here was a result of longterm technical assistance to the Government of Botswana.

EUCLUDES SANCHEZ, graduate from the Central University of Venezuela in psychology, did graduate work at the London School of Economics and Political Science, University of London. At present he is head of the Department of Applied Research of the Psychology Institute, member of staff of the School of Psychology of the Central University of Venezuela and teaches social psychology in the same university both at the graduate and undergraduate levels. He has done research in environmental psychology, social technology and social participation.

JOAN SIMON is Associate Professor at the University of Guelph, responsible for housing courses in the Department of Consumer Studies and a partner in Simon Architects and Planners in Toronto, Canada. Her practice, publications, research and teaching interests focus on the social and cultural aspects of residential design. Recently she has participated in a major study of housing projects in Canada for women and she is currently working on a book on post-indusrial neighbourhoods to be published in 1987. She has been a member of the Board of the Canadian Housing Design Council and chairman of the National Advisory Council on Aging Taskforce on Senior Citizen housing.

ROBERT SOMMER. After receiving a Ph.D. in Psychology in 1956 from Kansas University, he was a research psychologist at several mental hospitals before going to the University of Alberta in 1961, and the University of California in 1963 where he has remained. He has been a visiting professor in the Architecture Departments at Berkeley and the University of Washington, and consulted on various design projects. His most recent books are Social Design (1983) and A Practical Guide to Behavioral Research, 2nd Ed with Barbara A Sommer (1986).

DAVID STEA was educated as an aeronautical engineer and experimental psychologist. Following in his father's footsteps, he later studied architecture at Stanford University and, informally, at Rhode Island School of Design, USA. As one of the founders of environmental psychology, he expanded Kevin Lynch's studies of urban imagery into the field of environmental cognition, the subject of several books he authored individually and together with Roger Downs. More than 20 years ago, he began to expand the base of his work cross-culturally, and he has since taught, practiced, and done research in human-environment relations in many countries spanning all inhabited continents. While working with Maori communities in New Zealand in 1978, he devised a now widely-used variant of "environmental modeling" which treats design participation as a communication process.

In 1984, David Stea initiated a training program in intercultural communications for environmental design at the International/Intercultural Centre for Built Environment in Santa Fe, New Mexico, USA. He is now Director of the Centre, which is supported by the Fund for the Improvement of Post-Secondary Education of the U.S. Department of Education, as well as Adjunct Distinguished Professor of Architecture at the University of Wisconsin and Adjunct Professor of Planning at the University of New Mexico. He has published more than 75 articles in architecture, planning, geography, and environmental psychology, and is currently working, together with Mete Turan on a book narrating a comparative study of early settlements in Anatolian Turkey and Anasazi settlements in the South western USA.

MARTIN SYMES took his first degree and professional diploma in architecture at Cambridge with Sir Leslie Martin. His final year (1965) thesis proposed an Airport plan which eliminated passengers walking to and from the approach to aircraft. His first years of employment were with leading architects in the United States and in the United Kingdom. Besides teaching architectural design, Martin Symes worked as a consultant with D.E.G.W. and, in 1978-79 joint-edited the "Architects Journal" "Handbook on the Use of Redundant Buildings for Small Businessnes". In 1979 the URBED Research Trust produced his "Accommodation for Entrepreneurs" and in 1981 he circulated a report on "The Image of the Science Park". A sabbatical at the University of California Berkeley and at Princeton University in 1980 led to papers at meetings of PAPER, EDRA, and IAPS (of which he is currently Secretary). His interests in environmental policy were further developed in a joint paper read at the 1983 PTRC meeting in Brighton on "Urban Development grants - Lessons from American Experience". His teaching now concentrates on urban design and he has written extensively on this problem

He is now tutor to the postgraduate degrees and diploma in architecture at London University. He is consultant on professional development to the Government of New Zealand.

THURE VON UEXKULL, born 1908 as the son of Jakob von Uexkull (1864-1944) whose work on "Umwelt"-research influenced his scientific interests. As professor of internal medicine at the University of Ulm he tried to integrate psychotherapy into medicine on the basis of an ecological approach. In 1976 he retired and moved to Freiburg (southern Germany). His interest is now focused on Semiotics, its importance for medicine, and the possibility of describing the relationship between human beings and their environment as sign processes.

ESTHER WIESENFELD graduated from York University, Canada, in 1973 where she earned her basic undergraduate degree. She did graduate work in Israel and Venezuela. She is a researcher at the Psychology Institute of the Central University of Venezuela and is on the teaching staff at the same university in both the graduate and undergraduate levels of the psychology department. She has done research on crowding, in problems related to public housing projects and has also been working in problems related to environmental psychology, citizen participation and social technology.

Index

191

For Product Safety Concerns and Information please contact our EU
representative GPSR@taylorandfrancis.com
Taylor & Francis Verlag GmbH, Kaufingerstraße 24, 80331 München, Germany

* 9 7 8 1 0 3 2 8 1 6 5 3 1 *